To Colin,

a Toast to your
leadership &
vision!
Oct 2014
Joaquin

Korean Political and Economic Development

Crisis, Security, and Institutional Rebalancing

This volume is part of the multivolume study
Rising to the Challenge of Democratization and Globalization in Korea,
1987–2007

Harvard East Asian Monographs 362

Korean Political and Economic Development

Crisis, Security, and Institutional Rebalancing

Jongryn Mo and Barry R. Weingast

Published by the Harvard University Asia Center
Distributed by Harvard University Press
Cambridge (Massachusetts) and London 2013

Printed in the United States of America

The Harvard University Asia Center publishes a monograph series and, in coordination with the Fairbank Center for Chinese Studies, the Korea Institute, the Reischauer Institute of Japanese Studies, and other facilities and institutes, administers research projects designed to further scholarly understanding of China, Japan, Vietnam, Korea, and other Asian countries. The Center also sponsors projects addressing multidisciplinary and regional issues in Asia.

Library of Congress Cataloging-in-Publication Data
Mo, Jongryn, 1961–
    Korean political and economic development : crisis, security, and institutional rebalancing / Jongryn Mo and Barry R. Weingast.
        pages cm. — (Harvard east asian monographs ; 362)
    Includes bibliographical references and index.
    Summary: "Mo and Weingast study three critical turning points in South Korea's remarkable transformation and offer a new view of how Korea was able to maintain pro-development policies with sustained growth by resolving repeated crises in favor of rebalancing and greater political and economic openness"—Provided by publisher.
    ISBN 978-0-674-72674-1 (hardcover : alk. paper)   1. Korea (South)—Economic policy—1988–
2. Korea (South)—Political and government—2002–   I. Weignast, Barry R.   II. Title.
    HC467.96.M62 2013
    338.9515—dc23

                                                                                    2013007737

Index by Mina Park

♾ Printed on acid-free paper

Last figure below indicates year of this printing

23   22   21   20   19   18   17   16   15   14   13

To Youngkee and Dongrye Moe

To Sue and Tom

Acknowledgments

Over the half dozen years during which we have worked on this book, we have benefited enormously from the support, encouragement, and intellectual engagement and comments of many people and several institutions. It is a pleasure to acknowledge their help.

The Korea Development Institute and the Harvard University Asia Center both provided institutional support, including a series of meetings at which we received valuable feedback and suggestions. The book is far better for that feedback. This volume is part of the multivolume study *Rising to the Challenges of Democratization and Globalization in Korea, 1987–2007*. Throughout the project, KDI president Oh-Seok Hyun has shown remarkable patience as well as support, and we thank him for his commitment.

We also thank the organizers of the project, Barry Eichengreen, Dwight Perkins, Yung Chul Park, and Wonhyuk Lim. Their efforts have been central to all stages of our volume, from inception to final draft, from fostering greater focus to ensuring that we met the various deadlines associated with the overall project.

A wide range of scholars provided helpful comments, challenges, suggestions, and direction. We here include Alice Amsden, Robert Bates, Jose Edgardo Campos, Paul Chang, Stephen Haber, Ron Harris, Paul Hutchcroft, Margaret Levi, Michael McFaul, Gabriella Montinola, Katharine Moon, Randall Morck, Ramon Myers, Nahni Nellis, Douglass North, Josiah Ober, Myunglim Park, Sangyoung Rhyu, James Robinson, Shinji Takagi, John Wallis, Steven Webb, Yishay Yafeh, Jong

Sung You. Perhaps our largest intellectual debt is to Stephan Haggard, who at several points made critical suggestions that improved the organization, focus, and content of this book. We also thank Sam Weingast for helpful research assistance.

The Hoover Institution at Stanford University has been an important institutional base for both of us. It is a pleasure to acknowledge the support of the director, John Raisian, and deputy director, David Brady.

Finally, we thank our families: Kyungsook, Gunn, and Sunna, and Susie and Sam.

Contents

Tables and Figures

Figures

Korean Political and Economic Development

Crisis, Security, and Institutional Rebalancing

CHAPTER I

The Phenomena to Be Explained: Three Turning Points in South Korea's Modern History

Having been ravaged in both World War II and the Korean War, South Korea in the 1950s was a poor nation threatened by hostile forces. Seen by the American occupiers as a buffer between the free Japan they sought to promote and the communist threat in Asia (Cumings 2005, 310), few at the time expected South Korea to become an economic powerhouse. Yet today Korea is one of the few sustained success stories in the developing world. Although Brazil and Mexico had their "miracle" decades, they could not sustain their high growth. South Korea has faced its share of problems, but in each case it has surmounted them. Today, it is well along in the process of becoming a rich industrialized and democratic nation (Hahm 2008). How do we explain this transformation, and what role in it did democracy play?

The outline of the story we tell is not new. In the years of Syngman Rhee's presidency following the Korean War, the regime was relatively corrupt and insular, successful at procuring huge resources from the United States while deflecting U.S. goals of economic integration with Japan (Woo 1991, Cumings 2005). South Korea during this period failed to begin working toward long-term economic development. Following the 1961 military coup, Korea under President Park Chung Hee started on its path toward the development state, especially in the 1970s. Korea remained an authoritarian regime until 1987, when it experienced an abrupt transition to democracy. Plagued by money problems in politics generally (Haggard and Mo 2000) and especially during the 1997 financial crisis, Korea has nevertheless continued on its path of reform and economic growth.

Economists have long dominated the study of economic development. For several decades they have had by far the best tools with which to study development, and their approach has revealed the types of policies necessary to produce economic growth. Their techniques have helped explain South Korea's economic success. Moreover, the East Asian experience in general—Korea's in particular—has provided many new economic lessons about development (World Bank 1993).

Missing from the economists' approach, however, is an understanding of the incentives facing political officials. Economists studying development have just begun to consider why officials in most developing countries fail to choose policies that economists identify as fostering economic growth (see, e.g., Acemoglu and Robinson 2006a, Bates 2001). The form an economy takes—and hence a nation's economic development—is endogenous to the political system. Therefore, a complete explanation of economic development must not only address the policies that lead to growth, but also the political institutions and incentives that lead political officials to choose and sustain those policies (North 1981). The purpose of this book is to provide a deeper explanation for South Korea's success in pursuing its transition from a poor and threatened developing country to one of the richest economies in the world. Such a successful transition is rare. Outside of Europe and the Anglo-American countries, since World War II only a small number of countries—including Japan, South Korea, and Taiwan—have completed or nearly completed the transition. We seek a new explanation for Korea's success, but one in which the general argument fits other cases as well.

Our work rests on recent advances and new approaches in the study of political economy. And because we see the politics and economics of policymaking and development as intimately related, we focus on the role of institutions, particularly political institutions and credible commitments in development. Studies in these and related areas point the way toward a new integration of politics and economics in the development context.[1]

A New Logic of the Development Problem

In the chapters that follow, we draw on the new perspective developed in North, Wallis, and Weingast (2009), which we refer to as NWW.[2] Building on the political economy works just mentioned, NWW provides an integrated political economy approach to understanding both the persistent problems of underdevelopment and how a small number of states have made the transition to developed economies. In this chapter, we provide a brief summary of the framework's logic. In the next chapter, we present a more in-depth examination of the framework.

The logic of the NWW approach rests on the idea that developing and developed countries fall into different *social orders*, or ways of organizing the polity, economy, and society. The principal difference arises from the concept of access: Does a society restrict access to valuable rights and privileges to a small group of elites, or does it sustain widespread access in the form of rights and rule of law for a large group of citizens? A specific type of access is of central importance to the difference between the two social orders: who can form an organization and rely on the state for enforcement of the organization's contracts.

Following this distinction between two types of access—limited versus open—we define two different social orders. *Limited-access orders* explicitly limit access to organizations, privileges, and rights in all component systems: politics, economics, and society. Citizens typically cannot on their own form formal organizations but instead must gain the

---

1. For recent advances in political economics, see Acemoglu and Robinson (2006a, 2006b); Bates (1983, 2001); Besley (2006); Grossman and Helpman (2001); Persson and Tabellini (2000); Rodrik (1999); Rodrik, Subramanian, and Trebbi (2004); Stein et al. (2005); and Tilly (1992). On the role of institutions see, e.g., Easterly (2003); Greif (2006); Haber et al. (2007); North (1981, 1990); NWW (2009); Rodrik, Subramanian, and Trebbi (2004); Roland (2000); Spiller and Tommasi (2007).

2. Two works develop further the NWW approach. North et al. (2012) applies the NWW approach to problems of economic development, including eight integrated case studies. Cox, North, and Weingast (2012) provide a more in-depth investigation of political development and, especially, the incentives that allow some developing countries to achieve it.

permission of the state. Limited access to organizations implies that the degree of competition is restricted in both politics and economics. In contrast, *open-access orders* foster widespread access to organizations of all types. Citizens have the right to form organizations for a wide range of economic, political, and social purposes without requiring political permission.[3] Open-access orders therefore foster competition in each system.

Another difference between the two social orders concerns personal versus impersonal exchange. Nearly all relationships in limited-access orders are personal: how an individual is treated depends on who they are, especially their position in the social hierarchy and with the dominant coalition. Economic exchange is also personal, requiring face-to-face interaction for the vast bulk of transactions. Rule-of-law institutions are necessarily impersonal (Weingast 2010); they involve rules, regulations, and laws that treat large classes of people and organizations the same way. Natural states, because they are personal, cannot support rule-of-law institutions. The personal basis for political decisions therefore hinders impersonal exchange through contracts. As historians of the transformation from personal to impersonal exchange explain, the reliance on personal exchange limits the ability of people to capture the gains from specialization and exchange (North 1981, Greif 2006). Indeed, the personal basis of policymaking combines with limited access to limit investment, specialization and exchange, and the division of labor, all standard elements of economic growth.

Open-access orders, in contrast, foster impersonal exchange. Rule-of-law institutions support extensive impersonal contractual relationships. These institutions also enforce the rights of all citizens, not just those of a narrow elite, allowing them to capture gains from exchange in a wider range of circumstances than limited-access orders characterized by personal exchange. The transformation to impersonal exchange and relationships based on explicit and enforceable contracts greatly expands the ability to capture gains from specialization and exchange.

----

3. Open-access orders typically employ an administrative process for creating new formal organizations whereby anyone who meets a well-established set of impersonal criteria can automatically form an organization. This administrative process is typically nonpolitical (and based on rule of law), and stands in contrast to the limited access orders personalistic system of forming formal organizations.

To gain a better understanding of the logic, stability, and behavior of limited- and open-access orders, we begin with the relationship of violence to society. All societies must solve the problem of violence. This is a first-order problem and has significant implications for how societies are organized and the policies they pursue. Many scholars in the development field believe that violence is an important problem but one limited to the so-called failed states. As such, they consider it a special problem in development, not one central to all developing countries.

Cox, North, and Weingast (2012) show that this view is wrong. They studied regime duration since 1840 in a sample of 162 countries. The data show that 50 percent of all regimes last only eight years, and that 75 percent last only a generation, twenty-four years. Violent succession is a prominent and regular, if episodic, feature of the developing-country environment. In contrast, violent succession is relatively infrequent in the top decile of countries by income, with the median regime lasting sixty years. Turning to the richest developing countries, Cox, North, and Weingast show that these countries look more like the poor ones than they do like rich ones. A regime in the median among the group of richest developing countries lasts twelve and half years, whereas the median regime in the poorest half of developing countries lasts but seven years.

For most developing countries, the problem of violence is endemic, and violence potential is distributed rather than concentrated in the government. Because violence is so costly for a state, developing countries organize themselves in ways that limit it. Violence therefore directly affects the policymaking process, including policies affecting the economy.

Standard economic approaches to development fail to attend to the problem of violence; they therefore miss central features of the development problem, including why developing countries persistently resist economists' advice. Although political scientists and sociologists have long incorporated violence into their views, they start in the wrong place. Most theories of the state follow Weber (1947) and begin with the assumption that the state has a monopoly on violence.[4] By employing this assumption, these models start at the end of the development

---

4. See, e.g., Barzel (2001); Bates, Greif, and Singh (2002); Bueno de Mesquita et al. (2001); Levi (1988); Myerson (2008); North (1981), ch. 3; Olson (1993); Tilly (1992).

process, when states have come to satisfy the Weberian monopoly-of-violence condition. Models that assume a Weberian monopoly control over government are incapable of explaining the origins of the state and its role in the developing countries with dispersed access to violence.

In most developing countries qua limited-access orders in today's world, violence potential is distributed. The state may assert a monopoly on violence, but this does not hold in practice. The lack of such a monopoly is clear in states, such as Colombia and Peru, where local drug lords rule parts of the country, but it also holds throughout most of Latin America and sub-Saharan Africa, where the military is nearly always a potentially independent actor. Similarly, the prevalence of ethnic conflict and civil wars in developing countries around the developing world demonstrates the distributed violence potential.

Consider Mexico, one of the richer developing countries where coups have not been a problem. Violence potential is distributed among many groups. Pemex, the state-run oil monopoly, has its own violence potential: a reform-minded government that attempts to withdraw the enterprise's privileges risks being forced to confront this violence potential. More generally, organized labor in Mexico has the power to create disorder, which it uses when necessary. Drug lords represent another obvious source of violence in Mexico. All this shows that violence is distributed in Mexico.

One important conclusion is that violence in limited-access orders need not be manifest for it to have a profound effect on the society and the economy. In the presence of distributed violence potential, major political, economic, and social actors adjust to the potential for violence in a way that lowers its likelihood of breaking out. These adjustments, in turn, have important effects on the nature of politics and the form of the economy, including the incentives to foster development. As Powell (1999) shows, even when violence is not manifest, states make choices in the shadow of violence. By ignoring the problem of violence, standard approaches to development miss these effects, including the effects on the economy and economic growth.

To understand limited-access orders, we study how they deal with the problem of distributed access to violence, particularly how they limit violence. The NWW approach shows that most societies solve the problem of violence through limited access. Limited-access orders restrict rights to valuable economic and social activities, granting control over them to individuals and groups with violence potential. These restrictions and privileges have two immediate consequences. First, they produce valuable rents. Second, because these rents are distributed to the individuals and groups with violence potential, they provide the groups with an incentive to cooperate and refrain from violence. Violence disrupts the flow of rents, so rents and privileges produce incentives for these individuals and groups to maintain peace. Limited-access orders therefore create rents not because of rent seeking by organized groups—individuals and groups in both limited-access and open-access societies seek rents and privileges—but because rents solve the problem of distributive violence, allowing the societies to capture substantial gains from cooperation represented by the limited-access order's ability to suppress violence.[5]

Limited-access orders therefore create a coalition of interests among those with violence potential that we call the dominant coalition. Members of this coalition hold both the violence potential and the valuable rents and privileges. Systematic rent creation to limit violence, however, requires that economic policymaking becomes a tool for political organization and social stability in these societies.

This system is hardly perfect. Some groups, for example, may use violence as a means of improving their advantage relative to other groups. Moreover, various shocks advantage some coalition members and disadvantage others, leading to demands by those gaining power for a reallocation of rents. If reallocation negotiations fail, violence is a possibility. But on average, limited-access orders provide a means for social cooperation that limits, if not fully suppresses, manifest violence and allows for a degree of specialization and exchange. Most limited-access orders are vastly richer than those societies experiencing extreme violence, the so-called failed states.

Because the limited-access order is the dominant form of social organization throughout the world today and because, until two hundred years ago, it was the sole solution to distributed violence, NWW calls it the *natural state*. Seen from the perspective of distributed violence, natural states are successful because they limit violence. The appropriate

---

5. Our perspective therefore emphasizes rent creation rather than rent seeking. The former emphasizes the role of rents in solving problems of violence, while the latter concept holds that the political system supplies rents because of the power of the groups demanding them.

comparison is not with open-access orders of the developed world, but with failed states experiencing disorder and violence. Natural states provide a means of organizing society that limits violence and allows substantial social cooperation, including far more specialization and exchange than the alternative hunter-gatherer societies or societies experiencing ongoing violence.

This perspective also explains why the problem of development has proven so difficult for the developing world; that is, why underdevelopment is so persistent. As the solution to the problem of distributed violence, the natural state systematically restricts rights and privileges, including limits on access to political and economic organizations. Natural states therefore create an equilibrium development trap. Privileges make powerful individuals and groups with access to violence better off when they cooperate peacefully than when they use violence. But the policies implementing these privileges and rents necessarily restrict competition in both politics and economics. Limited access limits entry and competition; it creates monopolies, privileges, and corruption; and it prevents Schumpeterian creative destruction. From the perspective of modern development economics, the policies that help to maintain peace and prevent disorder appear as "market interventions." Economists are right in their observations that natural states manipulate markets for political purposes; but they are wrong in their understanding of the reasons for this manipulation.

In the face of seemingly massive market intervention, economists and donors recommend that a natural state establish property rights, open access to organizations and corporations, foster greater economic and political competition, provide good governance and rule of law, and remove privileges and monopolies. Without realizing it, however, they are actually recommending that the society dismantle the mechanisms that create order and prevent violence. The reforms economists advocate therefore threaten the social organization based on rent creation that promotes order and prevents violence.

Economists argue that their brand of economic reform is Pareto optimal: that it can make everyone in the society better off. But this conclusion fails in the presence of distributed violence. The economists' reform package of open access and competition, removing privilege and rents, threatens the natural state's stability. By attempting to dismantle the system of rents holding the natural state together, typical economic reforms threaten to make the society worse off, not better off. Taking away rents removes the glue that holds these societies together and limits violence within them.

This logic explains why developing countries so persistently resist reform: social order with rents and limited competition beats violence and disorder. It also explains why international donors, despite huge levels of resources and numerous reform packages since World War II (Easterly 2006), have failed to create many success stories.

The NWW approach redefines the problem of economic development as the *transition* from the limited-access to the open-access order. Making this transition is both rare and difficult. The first movers (Britain, France, and the United States) began the transition in the late eighteenth century and completed it in the nineteenth. In the twentieth century, most of western and southern Europe made the transition, most recently including Ireland, Portugal, and Spain. Besides the European nations, Australia, Canada, New Zealand, and the United States, the only countries to make significant progress in this transition are Japan, South Korea, and Taiwan.[6]

A central feature of the transition involves incremental increases in access. Under some circumstances, the natural state's dominant coalition has an incentive to open access incrementally. Security is one motive for this increase in access, when natural state elites perceive that reductions in rents associated with increases in access are more than compensated for by increases in security. In the mid-eighteenth century, Great Britain, for example, transformed its system of naval supply. In the beginning, Britain used a natural state rent-creation system for supplying the navy by awarding supply contracts to valued members of the coalition, often members with no knowledge or comparative advantage in this task. Britain replaced this system with one of competition among large firms that gave suppliers incentives to reduce costs and to innovate. The result was a dramatic increase in Great Britain's ability to keep ships at sea, which helped it to defeat the fleet of its archrival, France (NWW, ch. 5). In another example, U.S. president Andrew Jackson and his supporters sought in the late 1820s and the 1830s to limit the opposition's

---

6. In recent years, Chile and several countries in Central and Eastern Europe (e.g., the Czech Republic and Poland) have made significant progress in the transition to an open-access order.

ability to secure political support through granting privileges to special corporations. Instead of simply transferring privileges from the opposition to their own constituents, Jackson and his supporters changed the game by replacing the system of privilege with open access to the corporate form through general incorporation laws. This allowed anyone to use this form of organization without special legislation, which often involved an exchange of support for privilege.

Competition among states in Western Europe was a major motivation fostering the transition among the first movers. Indeed, Tilly (1992) argues that war drove all major innovations in the states in Western Europe during the past thousand years.[7] Systematic military competition over long periods gave natural state elites the incentive to devise the means to finance larger and longer wars. As the naval supply story illustrates, the desire to finance larger, more intense, and longer wars drove European states to replace natural state rent-creation mechanisms with ones that relied more on open access, competition, and impersonal relations (Bates 2001, NWW, and Schultz and Weingast 2003).

A final useful concept in the NWW framework is the idea of *double balance*. Stable societies exhibit a balance between the degree of openness in their political and economic systems. Limited-access orders limit both political and economic access; open-access orders foster open access in both politics and economics. If one of these systems is considerably more open than the other, then the society lacks balance. Various forces press for a return to balance. Too much political openness relative to economic openness allows interests outside of the elites to press for relaxing economic rents and privileges. This imbalance may lead either to increasing economic openness or to a reduction in political openness, brought about by those seeking to preserve their rents.

Similarly, too much economic openness relative to political openness fosters economic growth in the short and medium term. As firms become more complex, however, they seek more complex support from the government, in turn requiring greater credible commitments from and constraints on government. And citizens who get richer typically press for democracy, freedom, and protections against arbitrary political action. Here too the imbalance can lead to changes in either direction: to

---

7. This theme is echoed in a great many works. See, for example, Bates (2001) and Scheve and Stasavage (2010).

greater political openness to match the degree of economic openness, or to a reaction that limits economic openness as a means of preserving benefit flows provided by the status quo. We emphasize that no teleology exists that pushes states toward increasing access; incremental increases in access can either continue or result in a reaction that reverses the increases. Although some societies may be out of balance during the transition, over the long term, double balance holds. As we will argue, development requires open access in both the economy and the polity.

Korea's Transition toward an Open-Access Order: Three Turning Points

To make progress toward an open-access system, a society must increase both political and economic openness. What is important to the study of development is the sequence of increases in political and economic openness that a particular country follows (Huntington 1987). Do countries achieve political and economic openness at the same time? Or does progress in one area come first and then the other area catches up? The case of Korea shows that a developing country is prone to falling out of balance as it attempts to promote and balance political and economic openness, and even a successful developer is likely to experience a series of turning points that work to rebalance the system. Korea's transition to development since the Korean War is marked by three such turning points: the military coup of 1961, the transition to democracy in 1987, and the economic crisis of 1997. As Figure 1.1 shows, three transitions marked qualitative changes in economic performance. The transition to an export-led industrialization strategy in 1961 resulted in a rapid increase in the openness of the Korean economy, as measured by the share of trade as a percentage of GDP, and a continuous rise in per capita income. The impact of democratization can be seen most clearly in the steady fall in the rate of economic growth since 1987. The Korean economy suffered the biggest decline in per capita income in the aftermath of the 1997 economic crisis.

In this book we use the new framework outlined above to provide a unified perspective explaining the events central to South Korea's successful economic and political development. We do so by focusing on the three turning points. For each turning point, our approach has three pieces: we discuss the instability of the regime during the crisis; we explore

Figure 1.1. Korean Economic Performance through Three Transitions
Source: Korean Statistical Information Service: http://www.kosis.co.kr.

why the regime reacted as it did, including the incentives underlying those reactions; and we explain the dynamic forces of change that undermined the stability created after the previous crisis.

The conventional view holds that no significant development took place in the first postwar period (1953–1961) under President Syngman Rhee's regime, which is often depicted as a "predatory state." Despite huge subsidies from the United States, this regime failed to produce sustained economic growth. Some scholars argue that President Rhee began to formulate a coherent development plan toward the end of his rule (Haggard, Kim, and Moon 1991), but the plan was not actively implemented before the new government came to power in 1961. Despite huge American subsidies, this regime was unstable and faced demonstrations and the threat of disorder, leading to Rhee's resignation.

A military coup in 1961 ended the ineffectual political economy of the 1950s. The coup was carried out by General Park Chung Hee, the leader of a group of reform-minded young officers. After winning the presidency as a civilian candidate in 1963, following two years of military rule, President Park formulated and implemented an export-led growth strategy that changed the nature of the Korean political economy. The system Park put in place would later be called the "developmental state"

(Johnson 1982, Amsden 1989, Evans 1995, Wade 1990). Park's developmental state was a huge economic success; the Korean economy grew an average of 8 percent a year during his presidency (1961–1979). Ultimately, however, the relative economic openness, in combination with political repression, caused problems of instability. The basic structure of the developmental state remained intact after Park's death in 1979.

The developmental state began to unravel in the mid-1980s. Although previous demonstrations advocating democracy had been repressed in the early 1970s and in 1980, those in the mid-1980s were bigger and harder to put down. A new crisis emerged, forcing democratization in 1987, our second turning point. The newly elected leaders maintained most of the economic policies of their predecessors, continuing Korea's economic growth.

Over time, new problems emerged under democracy. In contrast to the previous authoritarian regimes, the democratic government lacked the ability to channel credit to its favored industries and to suppress the demands of labor and other alienated economic sectors. What replaced the developmental state is not clear, however. Although weakened, the developmental state did not disappear. The mercantilist idea of supporting and protecting strategic industries remained popular, justifying regulatory controls by bureaucrats. While democracy weakened the bureaucrats, it strengthened and emboldened organized private-sector actors, workers and big business being two principal examples. For corporatist purposes, the developmental state had organized labor and business organizations. Thus when democratization began, labor and the *chaebol* (Korea's largest corporate conglomerates) were in a good position to take advantage of the new political openness because they were already organized. As democratization evolved, workers and big business became more assertive and began to have a significant impact on economic policies.

The 1997 financial crisis in East Asia hit South Korea hard, revealing that the initial Korean political economy under democratization was not sustainable. The crisis forced Korea to undertake extensive economic and political reforms, our third turning point. The main goal of the reforms was to move Korea closer to the competitive market economy—that is, closer to open access in its economic system. But economic and political reforms did not take place simultaneously. In the first five years after the 1997 crisis, the Korean government under President Kim Dae

Jung focused mainly on issues closely related to the genesis of the crisis: notably, corporate and financial restructuring and reforms. Although progress since then has been uneven, most observers agree that these reforms put in place the basic institutional foundations for a competitive market economy. Significant political reforms, however, had to await the government of the next president, Roh Moo Hyun, who held office from 2002 to 2008.

Existing theories of development fail to explain South Korea's transition. Most theories tend to be outcome oriented and ignore the transition process of development, even though many acknowledge that development consists of multiple goals, including economic growth, equity, democracy, good governance, autonomy, and stability, which are not necessarily compatible with one another (Huntington 1987). Modernization theory, for example, delineates the powerful historical pull toward development but fails to explain both the different paths to that end taken by the successful nations and, more important, the reasons why most developing countries fail to develop. Also inadequate are theories of economic or political development that focus on a particular aspect of development or a specific period of development. A major question in democratization theory, for example, is whether democracy can arise in a capitalist economy, assuming that capitalism is already in place (Rueschemeyer, Stephens, and Stephens 1992).

The arguments in the literature provide useful insights into South Korea's economic development, and we draw on many in what follows. But they do not fully explain it. A great many scholars emphasize the communist threat, for example, but they do not connect this idea with the logic of why the Korean regime was able to sustain market-enhancing policies when the vast majority of developing countries fail to do so. Many other states face security threats and fail to produce either economic growth or the transition from a natural state to an open-access order, as illustrated by North Korea, for example.

Amsden (1989) and Wade (1990), among others, emphasize the role of an independent, meritocratic bureaucracy in implementing prodevelopment policies. The meritocratic bureaucracy is clearly central to Korea's experience, but here, too, traditional approaches are missing an essential element of the explanation: How did South Korea sustain this meritocracy when so few developing countries can do so? For a meritocratic bureaucracy to survive, the state must follow impersonal bureaucratic rules, an element of the rule of law, rather than the personalistic logic of limited-access orders. Most developing countries qua natural states cannot sustain impersonal rules but instead exhibit considerable corruption in their administrations.

Kohli (1994) emphasizes the Japanese colonial experience. Undoubtedly, aspects of the Japanese experience proved lasting—including education and the formal bureaucracy—but was this experience a sufficient condition for growth, as Kohli seems to imply? In criticizing Kohli's interpretation, Haggard, Kang, and Moon (1997) observe that this perspective fails to explain the poor performance of the Rhee regime of the 1950s.

Similarly, a large number of studies, especially among those by economists, focus on the particular policies chosen. These studies explain why the policies positively affected economic development, but they do not explain how the Korean political economy could sustain those policies. Most developing countries receive aid from donors in conjunction with reform packages but fail to implement the reforms in a way that fosters development. Something about Korea differs from most developing countries, and we need to look beyond the characteristics of Korea's policies (such as the meritocratic bureaucracy) to understand the reasons why it chose those policies and especially how it sustained them. Finally, Campos and Root (1996) emphasize the importance of shared growth in gaining sufficient support for the regime among a broader constituency.

Each of these ideas represents a piece of the puzzle, and we draw on each in what follows. But these separate elements lack a framework that adds up to a satisfying explanation. We need an explanation for South Korea's growth that explains not only what policies fostered long-term economic growth but also why officials in the political and economic systems chose and then sustained them.

Applying the New Approach to South Korea

The perspective developed in this book provides a new account of the South Korean experience. We first address conceptual and empirical issues related to the application of the NWW framework to the case of Korean development (Chapter 2). In applying the NWW framework, we present an integrated account of Korean development, concentrating on the three critical turning points in Korea's transition: Park's creation of the development state beginning in the early 1960s and into the 1970s (Chapters 3 and 4), democratization in 1987 (Chapter 5), and the genesis of and reaction to the 1997 economic crisis (Chapters 6, 7, and 8).

At each turning point, Korea took a significant step toward creating an open-access social order. But the turning points themselves indicate that Korea has not completed the full transition to an open-access order: after each one, the political economy that developed proved unsustainable and needed further change. We argue that the main source of instability in the Korean political economy has been unbalanced development in its economic and political systems—that is, a mismatch between political and economic openness. Nonetheless, in fits and starts Korea has moved ahead in its transition from a natural state to an open-access order.

The first crisis/transition, discussed in Chapters 3 and 4, moved South Korea from the unstable natural state under Rhee in the 1950s to that of the Park era (1961–1979), in which began elements of the transition: namely, the process of impersonal allocation of policy benefits and the gradual opening of economic access, and, with them, sustained economic growth. The Rhee regime represents a classic natural state with limited access in both economics and politics. The Park regime expanded economic access, with entrepreneurs increasingly free to start new businesses, and government programs fostering small and medium-size companies. Although the large chaebol gained significant privileges and influence, those companies that were among the largest changed over time.[8] At the same time, the regime maintained tight constraints on both political organizations and organizations that could become political, such as unions (H. Chang 1999). This regime had significantly more open economic access than the Rhee regime. We also represent the Park regime, especially during its first ten years (1963–1973), as offering somewhat greater political access than Rhee. This political openness reflects Park's much greater emphasis on sharing the benefits of economic growth, including education, rural infrastructure, and open access to markets and jobs in both the economy and the government.

As a natural state, the Rhee regime that dominated the 1950s provided an array of rents, and also created an environment of privilege and cor-

---

8. In contrast, Diaz-Cayeros (2012) shows that a list of the largest companies today in Mexico, a natural state, is almost identical to the list of the largest companies in 1960.

ruption. This regime survived in part because of the American presence, which provided both military security and dollars to support the South Korean budget (Woo 1991, Cumings 2005). If the Americans withdrew their funds, this system could not be sustained; South Korea would risk succumbing to the communist threat, both domestic and from the north. Responding to this threat and to the Americans' threats to withdraw their support, the new regime after 1961 faced different incentives. Political officials realized that for security, South Korea had to gain the capacity to defend itself.

In a series of stages, the regime began to open access in the economic realm, focusing initially on creating efficient export firms that could compete in international markets. The Park regime initiated this process almost from the start, but pressed ahead in earnest after the withdrawal of American support at the end of the Vietnam era (Kang 2002, Kim 2004, Woo 1991). The communist threat, combined with Korean insecurity about American support, gave Koreans the incentive to sacrifice short-term rents generated through privilege. This incentive manifested itself in the development of export firms that could succeed in competitive international markets, thereby helping to foster long-term economic growth. The communist threat also gave the regime incentives to create shared growth (Campos and Root 1996; see also Acemoglu and Robinson 2006b); that is, to share the gains of economic growth more widely than among the narrow elite typical of developing countries qua natural states. Shared growth increased support for the regime and blunted the attractiveness of communism. To this end, the Park regime pursued public goods such as universal education and rural infrastructure.

Our view also reveals new insights into the Korean meritocracy. This type of bureaucratic system is rare in the developing world. How was South Korea able to sustain one? In contrast to the literature, we argue that the meritocracy was sustained not because it was insulated from politics but because it produced the results desired by officials in the political system—namely, export-led growth and, with it, security. In Chapter 4, we explain the incentives for political officials and bureaucrats to cooperate in sustaining a meritocratic bureaucracy.

Despite its economic achievements, the developmental state was not a long-term, stable political equilibrium. While President Park increased the openness of the economy through export promotion and private-public cooperation, he took the opposite position on democracy and political openness. Park maintained aspects of elections in the first ten years of his rule but suspended constitutional rule in 1973, introducing a draconian authoritarian rule with no limit on the presidential term (Im 1987). These changes resulted in an imbalance between political and economic openness that grew worse over time. As the economy continued to grow, this imbalance created strong pressures from many sources for greater political openness, including democratization. Park's traditional political opponents did not let up their attacks on his rule, and they were increasingly aided by the emergence of a progressive middle class and the organization of Korean labor. Even big business began to press for more decentralization and autonomy. The mounting pressures for democratization finally achieved a breakthrough in 1987, and we explain the timing and process of democratization in Chapter 5.

We then study the consequences of democratization for Korea's economic and political development. We divide the post-1987 period into two time frames: democratic economic management in the decade before the 1997 financial crisis (Chapter 6), and the political economy of the crisis, reactions to it, and reforms (Chapter 7). This is followed by a discussion of the most recent era, 2003 to 2008 (Chapter 8).

South Korea began its democratization process in 1987 with the legacy of a substantial period of economic openness but limited access in politics. This imbalance in openness fostered the growth of powerful economic organizations while inhibiting the growth of the civil society. In particular, too few organizations existed to counterbalance the influence of chaebol conglomerates, in the sense of providing support to political officials to promote policies against the interests of powerful economic organizations.

We argue that the onset of democracy changed the incentives of politicians. To win elections, officials now needed campaign funds, which the chaebol supplied. This gave the chaebol a new source of power over political officials that they had lacked in the previous regime, setting up a classic natural state exchange, with funds from the economic organizations going to political officials who provided policy benefits favored by those organizations.

The new electoral incentives fostered a cozy political relationship between the chaebol and elected officials, one with major political and economic consequences. Politicians' dependence on the chaebol for campaign funds limited the government's ability to discipline the chaebol as it had under the previous regime's developmental state. The democratic regime proved powerless to prevent the chaebol from taking on greater financial risks and accumulating larger and larger debts, thereby greatly increasing their exposure in the case of an economic downturn. Because political officials viewed the chaebol as too big to fail (TBTF), the chaebol had incentives to increase their debt, and as the economy continued to grow, they earned large profits. But if the economy faced a big downturn, the government would be forced to bail out these firms. The risky financial behavior of the chaebol therefore weakened the soundness of the Korean economy. This situation created a classic common-pool problem that put the entire economy at risk, setting the stage for the financial crisis of 1997.[9]

With this greater exposure to risk, the absence of strong political oversight combined with the huge chaebol debt to exacerbate the financial crisis of 1997, forcing the government to bail out many enterprises— and to a greater degree than would have been necessary had the chaebol been less exposed. In reaction to the crisis, Korea also undertook extensive political and economic reforms that changed the relationship between the political and economic systems. These reforms helped further South Korea's transition to an open-access order.

In terms of our theory, the main point is that the authoritarian era (1961 to 1987) greatly increased economic openness but tightened constraints on political access. Thus when the democratization era began in 1987, the system was out of balance, with far greater economic openness than political openness. During this period large numbers of economic organizations grew powerful, especially the chaebol but also labor. Economic interests gained significant political influence in both the authoritarian period and during democratization.

Overnight, democratization created an electoral system, enfranchising millions of voters. Political officials were suddenly accountable to a mass electorate. But political organizations did not immediately come into being to counterbalance the long-standing and powerful economic

---

9. Wildasin (1997) provides an analysis of TBTF incentives. Incentives of this type underpin a range of financial problems, including, in the United States, the savings-and-loan crisis of the 1980s and the 2008 bank crisis. Similar incentives in a very different setting underpinned the fall of the Soviet economy following Gorbachev's reforms (see Kornai 1992).

organizations. A complex web of economic organizations existed in 1987 that could draw on vast resources, but no comparable set of political organizations existed. The civil society was therefore relatively weak.

The lack of political and social organizations caused the double balance to fail in the initial phase of democratization. Paradoxically, the role of the chaebol in campaign finance increased the conglomerates' political influence following democratization, creating greater advantages for incumbent organizations and effectively reducing the degree of openness.

Political officials were forced to cater to mass electoral politics with a lopsided set of organized interests. Inevitably, this biased policy toward organized groups. The pre-crisis democracy (1987 to 1997) was characterized by a significant increase in political access from the Park era and, reflecting the increased chaebol influence, a modest decrease in economic access.

The influence of the chaebol during the first phase of democracy came at a big price. During the Park era, the state was able to constrain the chaebol so that the TBTF incentives never became a major factor. Close scrutiny and government-enforced discipline kept a check on firms' explosive risk taking. In the Park era, companies that appeared to take advantage of the TBTF incentives by mounting too many losses or taking too many risks found it harder to get new subsidies and often faced forced reorganization. After democratization, this situation changed. Elected officials came to rely heavily on campaign financing from large firms, and constraining those firms proved far more difficult for political officials. Without constraints, corporations followed their natural incentives and increased their risk, making them more vulnerable to a crisis.

Even without these problems 1997 was likely to have been a difficult year for the South Korean economy, but the political incentives of the new democracy greatly exacerbated the crisis. Although not apparent during this painful period, the economic crisis of 1997 may have positively affected Korea's democracy and economy over the long term. Following the crisis environment, the government carried out long-overdue economic reforms, followed by a series of political reforms. When the reforms were completed, Korean politics and the economy became much more open and competitive.

Building on the post-crisis economic reforms of President Kim Dae Jung, President Roh Moo Hyun further expanded political and economic reforms. Roh expanded the openness of the Korean political system by mobilizing and promoting a younger generation of politicians, the so-called 386 generation, and by weakening regionalism through electoral reforms. The rise of these new interests and the new post-crisis environment combined to give the government both the means and the political support to go against the chaebol. Decentralization of economic power was the main objective of President Roh's economic policy. He believed that too much power was concentrated in the hands of large chaebol, at the expense of balanced development. As we discuss in our concluding chapter, it remains to be seen whether the post-crisis economic and political reforms will prove sufficient to allow Korea to balance the political power of the chaebol and complete the transition to an open-access order.

In the following chapter we present a theoretical overview and an analytical framework of Korean development. The theoretical lens we use to explain the major turning points in the Korean political economy relies on the concepts of the transition from limited- to open-access order and double balance. A system in transition that is unbalanced in its political and economic openness is unstable. To make progress toward an open-access system, an unbalanced country is likely to experience a series of turning points that work to rebalance the system, and it faces considerable risk of backsliding toward a natural state rather than progressing toward open access. After developing this theory, we present case studies of the three turning points, first looking at the Rhee regime, including the crisis that caused his downfall (Chapter 3), and the transition to the developmental state under the Park regime (Chapter 4). We next study the events leading up to and including the second turning point, democratization in 1987 (Chapter 5). And we cover the third turning point, the financial crisis of 1997 and its aftermath in Chapters 6, 7, and 8. We conclude with a look ahead in Chapter 9.

CHAPTER 2

An Analytical Framework for Understanding

South Korea's Transition

South Korea is one of the few countries succeeding in the transition to a developed economy. How has it accomplished this difficult task? The case of South Korea warrants a serious theoretical inquiry, not only to test existing theories of development but also to draw appropriate lessons for other countries. In this chapter, we provide a framework for understanding South Korea's transition.

We focus on the political economy of South Korea as the primary dimension and force of development.[1] South Korea's political economy has evolved in several stages, and the character and logic of the system in each stage explains not only the economic performance of the system but also the subsequent path of regime change.

There is no comprehensive theory of change that explains why and how one system follows another. We argue, however, that over the long run the open-access order is the only durable means of development, and that this order seems stable only when both economics and politics are sufficiently open and competitive. We propose a new, integrated analytical framework for deriving a typology of South Korea's different political economies based on NWW's concept of economic and political openness, and for analyzing the performance and stability of each

---

1. An approach based on the political economy includes a broader range of organizations, including (purely) political organizations, than an economic view, which tends to focus on organizations directly engaged in economic activities.

system. This framework affords new insights into the key turning points in South Korea's postwar history.

In this chapter, we first review the NWW framework, with particular emphasis on variants of social order and the dynamics of change between social orders. We then turn to the issue of operationalizing the concepts of social order. Limited-access and open-access orders differ in their levels of political and economic openness, and we offer several indicators of economic and political openness. We then apply openness indicators to demonstrate which types of social order prevailed in the various phases of the South Korean political economy, and to trace the evolution of the South Korean social order toward open access.

Social Orders and the Dynamics of System Change

The literature on the Korean political economy shows that in its movement toward an open-access order with a competitive market economy and competitive polity, Korea has experienced at least four systems of political economy: the predatory state, the developmental state, economic populism (to a degree), and plutocracy. But it is not clear how one differentiates, conceptually, one political economy from another and, more important, how we derive measurable criteria for deciding which system has prevailed in a particular period of time. This section addresses these questions by drawing on the NWW framework sketched briefly in Chapter 1.

LIMITED-ACCESS AND OPEN-ACCESS SOCIAL ORDERS

Following NWW, we first distinguish two types of social order: limited access and open access. The social order describes how a given society organizes its politics, economics, religion, military, and other component systems. Developing and developed countries fall into different social orders, each with its own way of organizing the polity, economy, and society.

An important distinction between limited- and open-access orders: is how they accommodate and control violence. All states must solve the problem of violence. Limited-access orders do so through rent creation: granting privileges to those with violence potential gives them an incentive to cooperate, for violence would lower the stream of rents associated with privileges. Open-access orders limit violence through institutions that support the rule of law, competition, and open access itself. The methods by which a society controls violence have striking implications for markets and long-term economic development: limiting access hinders such development while open access fosters it.

When a society persistently restricts access to valuable rights, privileges, and organizations to a relatively small group of elites, it is a limited-access order. When it instead sustains widespread access to those rights and privileges in the form of civil rights and rule of law, it is an open-access order. A specific type of access is of central importance to the difference between the two social orders: who has access to organizations and can rely on the state to enforce the organizations' contracts. Limited-access orders explicitly limit access to organizations in all component systems: politics, economics, and society. Citizens do not have the right to freely create formal organizations but typically must gain the permission of the state. This limited access to organizations, in turn, limits the degree of competition in both politics and economics. Limited access therefore constrains those who would use organizations to compete. Open-access orders allow access to organizations of all types so that citizens may form organizations for a wide range of economic, political, and social purposes without acquiring official permission. Open-access therefore results in competition in each system.

Another difference between the two social orders concerns personal versus impersonal exchange. Nearly all relationships in limited-access orders are personal: how an individual is treated depends on who they are and, especially, their position in the social hierarchy and the dominant coalition. Economic exchange is also personal, requiring face-to-face interaction for the vast bulk of transactions. The absence of legal institutions that sustain the rule of law limits impersonal exchange that relies on contracts enforced in the courts. As economic historians of the transformation from personal to impersonal exchange explain, the reliance on personal exchange limits the ability of citizens to capture gains from specialization and exchange (North 1981, Greif 2006).

Open-access orders, in contrast, foster impersonal exchange. Rule-of-law institutions support extensive impersonal contractual relationships. These institutions also enforce the rights of all citizens, not just those of the elite, allowing people to capture gains from exchange in a wider range of circumstances than they can in limited-access orders characterized by personal exchange. The transformation to impersonal exchange and relationships based on explicit and enforceable contracts greatly expands the ability to capture gains from specialization and exchange.

Although limited-access orders differ in many ways (see North et al. 2012)—resource-rich versus poor, which groups are most powerful, whether they are fragile and prone to frequent mass violence, or whether they support private organizations—they share common characteristics:

- Violence is a persistent possibility. Limited-access orders control violence through elite privileges. The central state rarely has a monopoly on legitimate violence, as many members of the elite may retain violence capabilities. When allocated to those with violence potential, privileges reduce their incentive to exercise violence.
- Limited-access orders create limits on access to trade, markets, and the exploitation of natural resources. They therefore impose restrictions on entry and exit in economic, political, religious, educational, and military organizations. The state manipulates markets in service of controlling violence and maintaining the dominant coalition.
- Limited-access orders typically provide relatively strong protections for elite privileges and relatively weak property-rights protections for nonelites. To the extent that a limited-access order has rule of law, it is rule of law for elites.

Central to natural state stability is the control of violence in an environment where violence potential is distributed. By granting privileges to those with access to violence, natural states give powerful individuals and groups incentives to cooperate and maintain peace. Put simply, fighting lowers the stream of rents from privileges. Nonetheless, some groups with access to violence may be repressed by a more powerful coalition that retains privileges. Of course, to succeed, the coalition's ability to repress must be sufficient; if not, the target group will cause the coalition—and natural state—to fail.

Limited-access orders are successful states given their environment of distributed violence. People living in them are far better off than in hunter-gatherer societies or societies experiencing violence and disorder. In particular, they are typically better off than failed states or those just emerging from violence. Nonetheless they have several obvious deficiencies in comparison with open-access social orders. First, natural states reduce but do not eliminate violence. Consequently, important exchange relations among people have an inherent personal quality. Everyone must know whom they are dealing with, because if disorder breaks out, arrangements between individuals in different factions can suddenly fall apart. Natural states also rely on personal exchange mechanisms to enforce contracts and organizational arrangements: repeat play and face-to-face dealings are the principal mechanisms for enforcing exchange agreements. As a result, nearly all exchange is personal exchange; the natural state cannot support a wide range of impersonal exchanges or the deep specialization and division of labor that supports more successful, thriving markets.

Second, natural states provide insufficient security for property rights and thus insufficient incentives to nonelites. Because nonelites cannot credibly affect the dominant coalition, the dominant coalition need not provide them with unbiased justice or honor any promises. Insecurity of property rights lowers levels of investment in physical and human capital by nonelites, which hinders economic growth.

Third, natural states use economic policymaking as a tool for structuring the social order, creating rents and binding coalition members to one another. They cartelize or monopolize many markets, limiting competitive markets and lowering social welfare. And yet the problem of market intervention in most natural states goes deeper than monopolies. Elites often do not create rents by charging monopoly prices; instead, natural states supply many goods and services (such as water or electricity) at low nominal prices in return for political support. From the perspective of open access, limited-access orders exhibit too much market intervention and control. Natural states thus severely constrain markets and the price mechanism's ability to coordinate economic and social behavior.

All natural states have some markets, and many have elections. But having some markets is not the same as having open access in economics, and having elections is not the same as having open access in politics. Natural states create privileged access to markets, hindering market competition. In the same way, natural states that hold elections often hinder political competition by constraining opposition parties, by constraining the media and the free flow of ideas, through corruption and fraud in elections, and by curtailing open access to organizations, thereby preventing representation and diminishing the power of many opposition groups. Similarly, elected legislatures in natural states tend to be weak in comparison with the executive, so they cannot constrain the executive in ways familiar to open-access orders, as Spiller and Tommasi (2007) demonstrate for the case of Argentina. In many natural state electoral democracies, the president can rule through decrees independent of the legislature, which lacks a veto over legislation, spending, and taxation. For example, in many natural states, the executive commands the military and uses this force to threaten others, limiting their ability to constrain the executive's power. As another example, natural states lack basic rule-of-law institutions, so a major way in which legislators control the executive (see McCubbins, Noll, and Weingast 1987, 1989)—provisions in legislation that constrain executive action and policymaking—is simply unavailable in natural states. Indeed, courts in most natural states are corrupt and fail to provide standard public services available in open-access orders: justice, rule of law, efficient enforcement of contracts, and the security of property rights.

A final deficiency of limited-access orders is their environment, which forces the natural state to adapt to changing conditions. Relative prices, broadly conceived to reflect the effects of technology, demographics, and weather disasters in addition to market prices, all change over time. For natural states, these changes affect the relative balance of power. Changes in power, in turn, require that the dominant coalition adjust the distribution of rents and privileges. Standard problems in bargaining, however, complicate negotiations over these changes (see Powell 1999, ch. 1). Asymmetric information (for example, about how power has shifted) plagues these bargains, as does the natural state's limited ability to make credible commitments. For this reason, limited-access orders are more prone to crises, breakdowns, and violence than are open-access orders, which more easily adapt to changing circumstances.[2]

In short, institutions work very differently in open-access orders than in limited-access natural states. Markets and elections both work differently in the absence of competition and the presence of systematic privilege, as

---

2. Cox, North, and Weingast (2012) develop the difficulties facing limited-access orders in adapting to changing circumstances.

in the natural state, than they do in the open, competitive environments of open-access orders.

THE TRANSITION

The distinction between the two social orders redefines the problem of development as the transition between limited and open access. Most types of incremental change—including most so-called reform efforts—do not lead to the transition. Nonetheless, a few countries do seem to initiate the transition: namely, those that achieve the so-called *doorstep conditions*. The doorstep conditions posit that limited-access orders with a particular configuration of institutions are capable of making the transition, although these institutions do not imply that the transition is inevitable. The three doorstep conditions are: (1) rule of law for elites; (2) a perpetually lived state with support for perpetual organizations for elites; (3) centralized elite political control of military force.

Rule of law for elites arises in a natural state when stable relations among elites lead to the creation of legal institutions capable of rendering unbiased and impersonal decisions about certain agreements reached among members of the elite.[3] Examples in European history include laws regarding the ownership and transfer of land in England (NWW, ch. 3), the canon law in the medieval Catholic church (Fukuyama 2011), and the merchant courts that developed in European cities. Another example is the enforcement of contracts among business firms in Korea and Taiwan during the authoritarian transition of the late 1960s through the early and mid-1980s. An important implication of the rule of law for elites is that it facilitates and extends the process of impersonal exchange and thus increases the size of the economy.

Another important aspect of rule of law for elites is the connection with organizations. Modern business corporations, for example, require perpetuity; that is, the lives of these organizations extend beyond the lives of the individuals who create them. Firms, and organizations more generally, without this characteristic face higher costs in raising capital,

---

3. We use the phrase "rule of law for elites" in the following sense: the rules for elites become impersonal and perpetual rather than personal. Elites may have rights, even if nonelites do not. Of course, in this sense, rule of law for elites differs considerably from the more general rule of law, which applies universally to all citizens.

pooling risks, and making long-term contracts and investments. Indeed, Kuran (2004) argues that the opposite condition—that partnerships must be dissolved on the death of any partner—has crippled the economy in the Islamic world, where most business organizations are partnerships.

Because the existence and the rights of organizations depend on the survival of the particular coalition in power, limited-access orders typically cannot sustain perpetually lived firms and organizations. Creating perpetually lived organizations requires the state to credibly commit to perpetual agreements. These commitments require a transformation in the state itself: namely, that it is perpetually lived as well. In the absence of a perpetual state, a coalition or leadership change can result in changes in the rules, possibly abrogating agreements that created organizations. The transformation to a perpetual state is associated with the doorstep conditions.

Perpetually lived organizations rely on the state to enforce internal agreements among members and external agreements between organizations and other individuals, and many of those agreements need to continue beyond the lives of individual members. Thus the ability of the state to enforce agreements, in turn, requires features of the rule of law. In this way, the logic of the first two doorstep conditions is intertwined. Similarly, protecting corporations from expropriation requires that the state have the ability to make credible commitments—again, a feature of the rule of law.

The third doorstep condition—political control of the military and other organizations with violence capabilities—is probably the most difficult to achieve. In many limited-access orders, a single faction within the dominant coalition may temporarily obtain a monopoly on military force; indeed that would seem to be every rational ruler's goal. But a monopoly on elite violence is unlikely to be sustainable (along with the rule of law for multiple elite organizations) if it confers a true ability to coerce other elite members. In that case, other elites have a strong incentive to keep themselves armed and to restore a rough balance of power within the elite. Controlling the military requires not only a state monopoly on violence, but also a set of agreed-on rules that control the circumstances under which violence is used, particularly against citizens. Absent credible limits on the use of violence, the state will invariably use it against citizens.

Elites within the dominant coalition will voluntarily surrender their access to violence only if they are confident that, collectively, they can control the military organization that specializes in violence, regardless of which coalition or party holds power. Such a system also requires a well-developed rule of law for elites and a system of strong, sophisticated, and perpetual elite organizations. The existence of strong non-military elite organizations makes credible the state's promise not to use the military to reallocate resources.

The two most notorious cases of failed transitions are Germany and Japan in the first half of the twentieth century. In both cases political control of the military became problematic, resulting in pathological natural states, then totalitarian dictatorships and World War II.

A final factor in the doorstep conditions is stability. We have noted that all natural states are unstable and that the developmental state is a form of the natural state. But natural states differ. As they progress through different stages of complexity, they become more stable (see NWW, ch. 2). On attaining the doorstep conditions, they are the most stable of all natural states, and so the developmental state in both Korea since 1960 and postwar Japan, at different dates, was relatively stable.

All developing countries today are limited-access orders, and few meet the doorstep conditions. Nothing in the logic of limited-access societies compels them to move toward the doorstep; no teleology pushes limited-access orders toward the transition. Limited-access orders are stable in the sense that, though they may experience violence and reorganization, they remain natural states. Several countries in Latin America over the past century and a half have moved closer to the doorstep conditions, only to slip away when crises have brought a return of the military to politics and undermined rule of law, even for elites. The key implications for developmental policy involve the dynamics of limited-access orders and how to move them toward the development doorstep.

DIFFERENTIATING LIMITED-ACCESS ORDERS

We now use the NWW framework to address the question of differentiating among types of political economies. Even though the concept of access identifies the most important dimension of a social order, the degree of access by itself cannot account for significant institutional differences within either limited-access orders or open-access orders.

The framework emphasizes power but leaves abstract the types of groups in society that have power. Political economy research also emphasizes power but attempts to determine the sets of powerful interests in a given society. Rueschemeyer, Stephens, and Stephens (1992), for example, point to three types of power relations—balance of power among classes and class coalitions, state-society relations, and transnational relations—that determine whether democracy can emerge and stabilize.

Consistent with this tradition of emphasizing power relations, we argue that the distribution of power among principal stakeholders (e.g., the government, capitalists, farmers, merchants, and workers) is the most important determinant of institutional variation. Limited-access orders under the capitalist system can then be divided into the predatory state, the developmental state, macroeconomic populism, and plutocracy, depending on which actor or actors most strongly influence economic decisions. The government is the dominant actor in the first two systems, while private actors and labor and business dominate in macroeconomic populism and plutocracy, respectively. The main point is that different configurations of interests and power across limited-access orders result in different patterns of political and economic behavior.

In both the predatory state and the developmental state, government elites control access to political and economic organizations. The difference between these two states is that government elites in the predatory state prey on the weak society to enrich themselves, their cronies, and their clients, while in the developmental state, bureaucratic elites use their power to push and guide private economic activities to achieve developmental goals (Johnson 1982). In plutocracy and economic populism, government leaders are subordinate to powerful societal interests, serving as their agents. A plutocracy is a political economy ruled by a class of wealthy people. Plutocrats seek to further their advantages by restricting access to political organizations. Under plutocracy, politics tends to become less democratic over time.

In economic populism, the working class (possibly with other mass-based groups, such as government employees) dominates politics. Economic populism, especially in the Latin American context, for example, often develops when populist leaders try to bring the urban masses—the middle and working classes—into the political system. Under a populist regime, working-class interests become the primary concern of government elites. As a limited-access order, a populist regime promotes neither economic nor political development. Populist leaders, who are usually authoritarian, with little interest in advancing democracy, tend to favor expansive macroeconomic policies that may benefit the working class in the short run but in the long run often damage most people's interests (Dornbusch and Edwards 1991). These regimes typically pursue unsustainable macroeconomic policies that provide short-run benefits but cause macroeconomic imbalances and crises in the long run.

These categories of states are not mutually exclusive. For example, populism and plutocracy can exist in tandem, as they did in Latin America in the 1970s and 1980s. In Latin America, business elites dominated the domestic market, using trade barriers to protect themselves from foreign competition, while populist governments kept on winning national elections. This combination of macroeconomic populism and state-conferred monopoly-industry privileges was the key feature of Latin American natural states in those decades.

Some limited-access orders experience economic growth. In fact some, such as developmental states, are characterized by a strong commitment to growth. But sustainability is another matter. Growth statistics reveal that developing countries on average experience many years of growth, often at higher rates than developed ones; but in comparison with developed countries, developing ones experience more years of negative growth, and when they contract, they do so more quickly than developed societies (NWW, ch. 1, table 1.2). Most limited-access orders experience substantial periods of growth but also significant crises and periods of negative growth. Limited-access orders therefore fail to deliver long-term political and economic progress.

Less emphasis is placed in our study on institutional variations across open-access orders, even though there has been a growing interest in them (Hall and Soskice 2001; Baumol, Litan, and Schramm 2007). One reason is that South Korea has not yet reached the status of an open-access order. More important from the perspective of development, institutional variations among developed economies are of secondary importance in comparison with the transition from limited- to open-access order.

DOUBLE BALANCE AND THE TRANSITION

A final concept in our analytical framework is that of *double balance*, the idea that, over the long term, the degree of openness in the economy tends to match that in the polity, and vice versa. The two typical examples are limited-access orders that limit access in both the political and economic systems, and open-access orders that enjoy openness and competition in the market economy and in politics.

Political openness must, over the long term, parallel increases in economic openness. When a government retains natural-state features it cannot acquire or sustain the constitutional features of credible commitments, perpetuity of the state and organizations, and impersonal rule of law. Yet these constitutional features are necessary if institutions are to survive leadership successions so that the state can maintain property rights, enforce contracts, and open access to organizations. An expanding economy requires increasingly complex sets of contracts and investments, and greater specialization and exchange. To support this expansion, the state must create mechanisms for supporting the rule of law. At the very least, maintaining economic openness for a generation or more, even without political openness, requires the doorstep conditions—rule of law for elites, a perpetual state with perpetual organizations, and control of the military. Policymaking in natural states, in contrast, reflects the absence of these conditions.

Major changes in the environment alter power relations among the dominant coalitions. Changes in relative prices, technological change, demographic growth, the appearance of an external security threat—all of these factors advantage some groups over others. Because in the natural state policy benefits and privileges must be roughly proportional to power, significant changes in power imply that the dominant coalition must adjust policy. Sometimes this occurs smoothly, through bargaining. But many times bargaining breaks down, as when, for example, the natural state cannot produce the relevant credible commitments to sustain the bargain or because the bargaining parties face asymmetric information (see Powell 1999, ch. 1). Bargaining failure often results in violence and the violent takeover of power. These episodes of violence typically result in major changes in policy and the reallocation of privileges, often with considerable expropriation and the abrupt transfer of privileges from one individual or group to another.

Violent takeovers and the attending changes in institutions and policies mean that most natural states cannot sustain development policies over the long term. A move toward openness could easily be reversed, a process easily recognized in many Latin American and African states.

The inability of a natural state to make credible commitments to economic reform is part of the reason so many natural states undergo periods of sustained growth followed by major contractions. The commitments necessary for extensive and ongoing economic reform arise in states that initiate the doorstep conditions.

Nonetheless, double balance does not require that political and economic openness move in lock step. Some states remain out of balance for considerable periods—say, a couple of decades. These states may have considerably more openness in their economy than their polity, for example. Over the long haul, however, it is hard to maintain such imbalances. States that lack balance tend either to increase openness in the realm with limited access, or to reduce it in the realm with greater access.

DIFFERENTIATING POST-TRANSITION POLITICAL ECONOMIES

The most important dimension of the polity and the economy is their openness, that is, the degree to which individuals have access to organizations. The type of political economy that emerges after a state's initial transition depends on its levels of political and economic openness.

One possibility is that a competitive market economy may emerge immediately following the transition. By definition, the structure of the economic system is open in a competitive market economy. The concept of double balance suggests that limited-access orders cannot sustain a competitive market economy; at the very least, such an economy requires the doorstep conditions. Further, it is widely recognized that a competitive market economy is more likely or sustainable in the presence of an open political system. A predatory state, representing the polar opposite of the competitive market economy, typically exists only when a country's political and economic systems are both closed.

It is more difficult to predict the relationship between the type of the political economy and the structures of the economic and political markets when one or both of the economic and political structures take an intermediate value of openness. Nevertheless, it is still possible to associate popular types of political economies with certain combinations of political and economic openness.

Take the example of the developmental state: the developmental state is essentially a political economy in which leaders make the economic system open and competitive while keeping a tight grip on political freedom. Therefore, a developmental state is characterized by an economy that is more open than the political system. When the political system is more open than the economy, either economic populism or plutocracy (or both) is a persistent possibility. When the economy is closed and the political system is open, economic resources (and organizations) are likely to be controlled by a small number of individuals or groups; and when these plutocrats control the government, they will use government policy to benefit their private interests. When plutocrats lose political power, populists, typically representing the interests of farmers and workers, often step in to replace them, leading to a cycle of expansionary macroeconomic policy and economic crisis.

Empirical Indicators of the Character of Social Orders: Economic and Political Openness

So far, we have argued for a close relationship between the character and durability of a political economy and its levels of economic and political openness. To operationalize this hypothesis, we need to develop measures of political and economic openness.[4]

NWW defines political openness in terms of an individual's ability to access political organizations and the institutions protecting rights and privileges. To have this access, individuals must possess basic, impersonal political rights and civil liberties. Political rights allow individuals to participate in formal political processes, including elections and policymaking processes, and also ensure their access to impersonal, incorrupt courts and administrative bureaucracies. Civil liberties, such as freedoms of speech, assembly, and religion, are needed for effective participation in the political process. These liberties are also necessary for protecting private realms, including personal, religious, family, and business interests, from government interference. Authoritarian regimes formally deny political rights and civil liberties to their citizens, so they lack political openness.

---

4. NWW does not propose explicit measures of openness versus limited access. What follows is very preliminary, and is meant as an indication of these distinctions rather than a definitive approach to measure their differences. More precise measures await future research.

So-called electoral democracies—that is, states holding regular elections—exhibit considerable variation in their level of political openness, even though they all claim to protect the political rights and civil liberties of their citizens. Moreover, electoral democracies differ greatly along the dimension of how free and fair are the elections. Some of these regimes impose draconian restrictions on the opposition, for example, limiting its ability to organize or to have access to the media. Some jail the opposition leaders, preventing them from competing. Holding free and open elections to choose leaders is typically the first step in the democratization process. Whether a political system allows and upholds regular, open elections is therefore a first (but not the sole) indicator of political openness.

Looking beyond elections, we consider whether individuals win meaningful political participation in an electoral democracy. Even if elections are regularly held, they may not be competitive, thus preserving one party's monopoly on power. Many developing countries qua limited-access orders limit the degree of competition in elections, through restricting access to the media, for example, restrictions on the opposition's ability to compete (including, in some cases, its ability to organize as a party), and limits on the ability of citizens to form opposition organizations to coordinate their members and to advocate for their interests. One-party or dominant-party systems are all too common in the developing world (see Magaloni and Kricheli 2010). These states are rarely democratic, either because they lack open access with respect to electoral competition or with respect to the rights of individuals and minorities. Even where the dominant party does not openly abuse its power, it tends to survive by manipulating political institutions and policies to entrench its political interests. An open political system must have both free elections and a competitive party system, including open access to the media, to organizations, and to the right of assembly.

One criterion of a competitive party system is that an opposition party has a reasonable chance of winning power (Przeworski et al. 2000). In theory, this competitive pressure (eventually) gives individuals more access to political organizations, as parties must compete to win their votes by offering such benefits as more access. But it is wrong to assume that the benefits of competitive electoral pressure reach individuals automatically.

Political parties may fail to respond to electoral pressure for several reasons. First, existing parties may form oligopolies to share power; they may alternate being in power, for example, without the need to respond to the electorate or to minority interests. Second, even if existing parties represent a sufficient number of interests in society, party leaders may not act in a manner accountable to party members, for example if access to organizations is restricted so that citizens cannot effectively mobilize against party or political officials. Third, the legislative branch may be so weak relative to the executive that political parties have little influence over the executive-dominated policymaking process. Fourth, limited-access orders have only a limited ability to promulgate impersonal policies. Instead of providing public goods, they provide private goods, for example through patron-client networks, often perverting policies nominally aimed at public goods for patronage purposes. In all these cases, political parties do not—or cannot—adequately represent or temper individual political demands. Thus, strong parties are another, higher-level requirement for an open political system.

Party competition in open-access societies differs from that in limited-access ones for two other reasons, reflecting two characteristics of the doorstep conditions: impersonality and perpetuity. These characteristics allow their states to provide various public-goods programs, especially social insurance programs that mitigate the effects of markets on individuals and thus reduce the incentives for massive redistribution (NWW, ch. 4). Personalistic, limited-access orders have difficulty providing these policies; when attempted, they often become just another source of patronage.

The last requirement for an open political system is a strong civil society, including a wide range of organizations independent of the state.[5] To counter the undue influence of both private firms (often bolstered by official privileges) and government, individuals must enjoy autonomy in their private realms. Organizations allow citizens to defend their interests against adverse reactions. Groups in civil society include not only nongovernmental organizations (NGOs) but also more traditional organizations such as religious groups, the media, and intellectuals. A strong civil society relies on a strong rule of law protecting individual liberties, which in turn requires an effective system of checks and balances with a

---

5. Students of the civil society include Lipset (1963); O'Donnell, Schmitter, and Whitehead (1986); Putnam (2000); and Tocqueville (2000 [1835]).

strong independent judiciary (Weingast 2010). Requirements of a strong civil society are not only institutional but also cultural. Citizens who possess pluralistic values are more comfortable organizing themselves for their common private interests and are less likely to respond negatively when others do so.

We expect the relationship between our measure of political openness and other measures of democratic development to be closely related. The most common measure of democracy and political freedom is the Freedom House survey, which rates countries on two categories of democratic development, political rights and civil liberties. Political rights allow people to participate freely in the political process. Civil liberties are the freedoms to develop views, institutions, and personal autonomy independent from the state. It is important to recognize that the measures of political openness and democracy are likely to diverge in cases where the protection of basic rights fails to create a high level of political competition or a strong civil society.

The second variable in our framework is the level of economic openness. Like political openness, economic openness is defined in terms of an individual's ability to gain access to economic organizations and to the third-party enforcement institutions of the state. The more access individuals have to economic organizations and third-party enforcement, the more open the economic system.

As with political parties, the internal accountability of economic organizations cannot be taken for granted. Malfeasance, rent-seeking, and the neglect of responsibility are as common in banks and corporations as in political organizations. Therefore, an economic system cannot be truly open without a strong system of corporate (and financial) governance, along with the political means to enforce the rules.

The last requirement for an open economic system is a diffuse distribution of economic power. Citizens face lower threats from corporate privileges, monopoly market powers, and plutocracy if economic powers in the economy are diffusely distributed. This condition is also necessary to unleash Schumpeter's process of "creative destruction," whereby new market participants have the potential to upstage and replace older ones, for example by creating new products or producing existing ones at cheaper prices. The diffusion of economic power involves more than a high level of competition at the industry level. It also involves two sources of balance: first, there must be a balance of power among major economic sectors, such as the corporate sector, the financial system, labor, and the civil society; and second, the polity must balance the economy so that economic actors cannot dictate the rules. The corporate sector may, for example, be concentrated, but its power to reduce opportunities may be limited if other sectors—such as financial institutions, unions, NGOs, and citizen organizations—perform their functions effectively and have the ability to counter attempts by the corporate sector for privileges.

The concept of economic openness is closely related to that of economic freedom. The Fraser Institute publishes an index of economic freedom, called Economic Freedom of the World (EFW), which seeks to "measure the extent to which rightly acquired property is protected and individuals are engaged in voluntary transactions."[6] The five areas that the Fraser Institute considers important to economic freedom are size of government; legal structure and the security of properties; access to sound money; freedom to trade internationally; and regulation of business, labor, and credit. Although economic freedom and economic openness are closely related, they are not identical. As we have seen in the case of political openness, giving freedom to individuals does not automatically create new opportunities for them. In fact, existing economic organizations—such as business groups, banks, and unions—may use newfound freedom to gain even more economic power over unorganized economic actors. Therefore, a sufficient level of market competition is needed to keep the market more open. Markets do not become competitive automatically; the government must work diligently through effective competition policy to keep the market competitive.

Using Openness Indicators to Trace Changes in Korea since 1961

Let us now examine how political and economic openness have evolved since 1961 in Korea, as suggested by the openness indicators that we have presented. We will supplement the openness indicators with time-series data on annual Freedom House (FH) and EFW scores (Table 2.1, Figure 2.1). Since FH and EFW scores are likely to correlate with the concepts

---

6. For more on the EFW index, see the Fraser Institute's Economic Freedom Network: http://www.freetheworld.com.

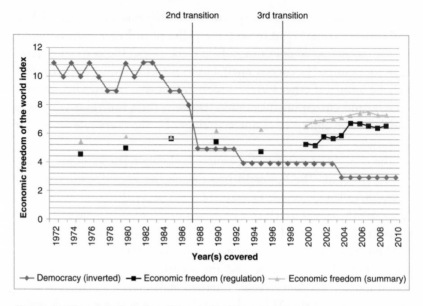

Figure 2.1. Korea's Political and Economic Openness since 1971
Source: Data are from Economic Freedom of the World (EFW): http://www.freetheworld.com;
Freedom House (FH): http://www.freedomhouse.org. (Insufficient data provided for the first
transition [1963].)

of political and economic openness, they give us some indication of how
the levels of political and economic openness have changed over time.
An important advantage of the EFW index compared with others is that
the EFW data are available for Korea from 1980 to the present, affording
an analysis of historical patterns over an extended period of time.[7]

The political economy in effect in Korea before democratization was a
developmental state. Unfortunately, the data do not go back far enough
to allow us to say anything about the first transition, from the unstable
Rhee regime in the 1950s to the Park regime of the 1960s and 1970s,
which launched the developmental state. We argue below that an important factor that led Park and his coalition to create the developmental
state over time was the security threat from North Korea (and its allies),
in combination with the withdrawal of the United States from Asia, and

---

7. Again, we observe that no satisfying measures of the various concepts in NWW
exist. What follows is intended to give an indication of the large, overall changes, rather
than a detailed and precise characterization of them.

Table 2.1. Freedom House (FH) and Economic Freedom of the World (EFW) Ratings for Korea since 1970

Year	Democracy (FH ratings)			Economic freedom (EFW ratings)					
	PR	CL	PR+CL	Govt. size	Property rights	Sound money	Open trade	Regulation	Summary
1970				8.11	5.84	5.28	5.43	—	6.17
1971									
1972	5	6	11						
1973	4	6	10						
1974	5	6	11						
1975	5	5	10	6.60	4.86	4.56	6.62	4.58	5.44
1976	5	6	11						
1977	5	5	10						
1978	4	5	9						
1979	4	5	9						
1980	5	6	11	5.97	6.52	5.29	6.20	5.05	5.81
1981	5	5	10						
1982	5	6	11						
1983	5	6	11						
1984	5	5	10						
1985	4	5	9	6.24	4.16	6.41	6.26	5.65	5.74
1986	4	5	9						
1987	4	4	8						
1988	2	3	5						
1989	2	3	5						
1990	2	3	5	6.49	5.45	6.59	7.22	5.47	6.24
1991	2	3	5						
1992	2	3	5						
1993	2	2	4						
1994	2	2	4						
1995	2	2	4	6.42	5.62	8.05	6.79	4.80	6.34
1996	2	2	4						
1997	2	2	4						
1998	2	2	4						

(*continued*)

Table 2.1. (continued)

Year	Democracy (FH ratings)			Economic freedom (EFW ratings)					
	PR	CL	PR+CL	Govt. size	Property rights	Sound money	Open trade	Regulation	Summary
1999	2	2	4						
2000	2	2	4	6.26	5.97	8.27	7.09	5.31	6.58
2001	2	2	4	6.25	6.35	9.32	7.31	5.25	6.90
2002	2	2	4	6.38	6.23	9.23	7.10	5.84	6.96
2003	2	2	4	6.81	6.37	9.42	6.97	5.68	7.05
2004	1	2	3	6.74	6.33	9.53	7.19	5.91	7.14
2005	1	2	3	6.66	7.01	9.53	6.51	6.80	7.30
2006	1	2	3	6.62	7.51	9.54	6.91	6.73	7.46
2007	1	2	3	6.98	7.26	9.63	7.15	6.56	7.52
2008	1	2	3	6.92	6.76	9.47	7.14	6.44	7.35
2009	1	2	3	6.82	6.61	9.49	7.12	6.58	7.32
2010	1	2	3						

Note: FH ratings are based on a scale of 1 to 7, with 1 representing the most free and 7 the least free. PR = political rights; CL = civil liberties. EFW scores are given on a scale of 0 to 10, where 0 represents the least free and 10 the most free.

from South Korea in particular. This withdrawal meant that South Korea had to provide its own security.

The data suggest that, by the 1970s, the developmental state had a relatively high level of economic openness. In Korea, the government allowed some level of economic openness in order to support export-led economic growth, in turn requiring impersonal policies that did not play favorites. Companies were allowed to compete freely both in domestic and international markets. To increase competition, the government used a variety of means to prevent large companies from exercising too much market power. The government periodically forced weak companies out of the market; it also provided impersonal incentives, such as subsidized loans and foreign exchanges, to induce companies to meet their performance targets.

Over time the developmental state in Korea became progressively more authoritarian. By the time the developmental state ended in 1987, it had reached the point of martial law. But the developmental state was not totalitarian; it was an electoral authoritarian regime (Magaloni and Kricheli 2010). The regime held regular and relatively free legislative elections. The ruling Democratic Republican Party was much like a Leninist party in its organization (though not in its ideology), organizing political actions down to the village level. Although citizens faced many restrictions on their political activities, most enjoyed a high level of religious and other social freedoms.

FH and EFW data for the years of the developmental state were largely consistent with our characterizations of political and economic openness for the system. Between 1980 and 1987, the period of the developmental state for which we have data, both political rights and civil liberties were very weak and were given FH ratings of 5 to 6.[8] But the economy was relatively free, especially in such areas as the size of government, property rights, and openness to international trade, with summary scores of 5.8 (out of 10) in 1980 and 5.7 in 1985. The exceptions were access to sound money and the level of regulation. Inflation in 1980 was high owing to the effects of large, unsuccessful investments in heavy industries and the second oil crisis. Restrictive regulations on business, labor, and credit reflected the government's use of those regulations to support strategic industries.

Korea's developmental state successfully promoted rapid economic growth for almost two decades. But ultimately it proved to be vulnerable to internal contradictions. A sustained period of economic growth with widespread inclusion, public goods, and sharing of the gains created a large middle class whose demands for political freedom grew over time. Authoritarianism also proved to be a significant barrier to further development of the economy, as more individual initiative and creativity were needed to move industries up the technology ladder.

In terms of our framework, the developmental state lacked double balance and relied on an asymmetric combination of political and economic openness. This asymmetry in openness implied instability, reflected in the growing pressure for democratization. An interesting question is whether the developmental state might have been more durable if its

---

8. FH ratings are based on a scale of 1 to 7, with 1 representing the most free and 7 the least free. EFW ratings are based on a scale of 0 to 10, where 0 represents the least free and 10 the most free.

leaders had made politics more open over time, on a par with the level of economic openness. But Korean leaders did just the opposite: the developmental state became more oppressive in its political dimensions.

Two additional factors are relevant for the lack of balance that undermined the developmental state in the 1980s. First, support for democratization grew over time, coming to include the middle class and thereby making the prodemocracy movement more difficult to suppress. Second, the United States stood aside while the regime suppressed the prodemocracy movement in 1980. But then, in 1987, the United States signaled it would not tolerate such violence against prodemocracy demonstrators. Although these factors were not definitive, at the margin they affected the choices of major actors in Korea.

The political economy of the pre-crisis democratic period began in 1987 and lasted ten years, ending with the economic crisis of 1997. The crisis revealed that the Korean state was out of balance and could not be sustained.

Two sources of imbalance existed in the pre-crisis system. One was a lack of balance and competition among organizations and interest groups. South Korea began democratization in 1987 with a legacy of economic openness but limited access in politics. This meant that powerful economic organizations existed within the larger environment of a stunted civil society (Chang 1999). Many organizations existed, but their range and depth were limited. Too few interest groups existed that could counterbalance the influence of the chaebol. In particular, no set of organizations existed to counterbalance the influence of powerful chaebol conglomerates.

The level of political openness rose significantly following democratization in 1987. Democratic reforms in 1987 allowed the direct election of the president. Moreover, national elections became competitive. But it is important to note that the postdemocratization level of political openness did not reach the level of advanced democracies. In addition to the weak civil society, political parties also remained weak and were often the personal instruments of powerful political leaders, such as the "three Kims."[9] New organizations, such as NGOs and other groups of political activists, were slower to develop.

---

9. The leaders known as the three Kims were Kim Young Sam, Kim Dae Jung, and Kim Jong Pil.

Political reforms during the pre-crisis period were not significant—at least not enough to make politics more open. One reason is that those in power had little interest initially in serious political reforms. The first president after democracy, Roh Tae Woo, won the first post-transition presidential election in December 1987 as the candidate of the ruling party of the authoritarian regime and did not have a strong political-reform agenda. Expectations were so low that some even give him credit simply for not reversing the transition to democracy and for leaving office peacefully at the end of his term.

Moreover, politicians compromised the reform process by using it to settle political grievances instead of creating an open political system. Political reform did reach the top of the reform agenda of Kim Young Sam, who in 1993 became the first civilian president since the 1961 military coup. Kim's main reform measures were the 1993 enactment of the Public Servants' Ethics Law, which required public disclosure of assets by senior officials, and the 1994 political and electoral reforms to reduce campaign spending, consolidate electoral laws, strengthen enforcement and increase penalties for violations, and transfer more power to local governments. On the political side, Kim engineered in 1993 a purge of senior military officers with close ties to the Chun Doo Hwan government, and the 1996 prosecution and jailing of two former presidents, Chun Doo Hwan and Roh Tae Woo, on bribery and sedition charges.[10]

The second source of the imbalance was between political and economic openness. Even though political reforms were limited in scope, the level of political openness increased significantly during the post-crisis period. Nonetheless, the opening of the economy did not move as fast as that of politics. The developmental state was able to keep domestic markets relatively competitive often by fiat.

FH ratings during the pre-crisis period support our claim that politics did not become more open after the initial jump immediately following the transition to democracy in 1987. In 1988, however, the ratings for political rights and civil liberties improved to 2 and 3, respectively, from 4 and 4 a year before. They did not change much after that, except for a one-point gain in civil liberties in 1993.

---

10. Chun engineered a coup in December 1979 following President Park's assassination. He ran an authoritarian regime until 1987.

EFW data also show that the Korean economy did not become more open during the pre-crisis period of democracy. The summary score on economic freedom did increase from 5.7 in 1985 to 6.4 in 1995, but the economic gains were relatively small if we compare them with the FH ratings for political gains, which improved from a score of 9 in 1985 to 4 in 1995. Among areas of economic freedom, property rights became more secure, inflation came under control, and markets became more open to international trade. But the size of government and the level of government regulations hardly changed, suggesting that markets may have become less competitive because big business and labor used their economic power to influence government regulations to their advantage.

The imbalance between economic and political openness had significant effects. Under the developmental state, the government possessed the ability to control adverse behavior by firms; notably, to prevent excessive leverage, to limit risk-taking by the chaebol, and to deal with ailing firms before they became crises. We show that the government lost this ability under democracy, which allowed the chaebol to gain political power and also to take greater risks. The absence of balance—in particular, the lack of a vibrant civil society to counter the chaebol influence—exacerbated the crisis (Haggard and Mo 2000).

Unsurprisingly, the reform mood shifted to the economy under President Kim Dae Jung (in office from 1997 to 2002), when recovery from the 1997 economic crisis became the top priority for his government. As the economy recovered by 2000, Kim Dae Jung shifted his attention to North Korea. In this environment, political reforms did not attract much attention. Some reforms were put through: notably, the legalization of two formerly illegal unions (the teachers' union and the radical association of trade unions), the allowing of union political activities in 1998, the passage of the Anti-Corruption Law, and the establishment of the National Human Rights Commission.

Two other important political developments occurred that had significant implications for political openness and competition. First, the election of Kim Dae Jung in 1997 marked the first time that an opposition party won a presidential election, showing a significant level of political competition at the electoral level.[11] Second, civil groups became

---

11. Many measures require the peaceful transition of power in order for a system with elections to be called a democracy. See, for example, Przeworski et al. (2000).

active in electoral politics (e.g., in a 2002 campaign to "blacklist" what they considered antireform National Assembly candidates).

Under the Roh Moo Hyun government following the 2002 elections, democratic reform again became the focus of reform politics. Accordingly, Roh chose "Participatory Government" as the slogan or theme of his administration. Roh's main political objectives were twofold: to broaden political participation by bringing a new generation of political leaders (e.g., the so-called 386 generation) into government and politics and by decentralizing political and government powers, and to fight the persistence of regionalism. For the 2004 National Assembly elections, the ruling Uri Party nominated a large number of young politicians and reformed election laws to help get them elected, including a ban on corporate campaign contributions. To reduce the influence of regionalism, an important political cleavage in Korean politics, Roh increased the number of party-list seats in the National Assembly and proposed large electoral districts so that parties would have at least one person elected in regions dominated by their opponents.

Most analysts also give Roh credit for democratizing the presidency and improving political openness. For example, he decentralized many powers concentrated in the presidency and the central government. Roh also vowed not to abuse his executive powers by using the security and law enforcement agencies, such as the intelligence, tax, police, and prosecution agencies, against his political opponents. Roh's political reforms also included sharing power with the prime minister, giving independence to the ruling party, and decentralizing power to local governments.

Post-crisis economic reforms in Korea have been extensive and significant. The level of economic openness clearly increased from the pre-crisis level. Companies and banks became much more accountable to their shareholders. The economic structure has also become more diffuse as foreign investors have taken over the commercial banking sector and some multinational companies have become large enough to challenge the chaebol in some industries, notably, automobiles. Nonetheless, the chaebol remain dominant in the market, and corporate governance is still weak.

Political openness has also increased, especially since Roh Moo Hyun became president. But whether it has reached the level of a mature democracy is debatable. Significant progress has occurred, such as the system of checks and balances, the independence of security and law enforcement agencies, and notably the rise of the civil society. Nonetheless, political parties remain very weak. Nor is it clear that the civil society is gaining strength; a large number of NGO leaders went into politics or the Roh Moo Hyun administration, undermining public confidence in NGOs as independent political actors.

The economic crisis of 1997 has made the Korean political economy system more open both in politics and economics. Political and economic progress has also become more balanced. But it is equally clear that South Korea has not reached the state of long-term double balance, as its political and economic systems are not yet fully open and the gains made so far are not yet consolidated.

FH ratings are consistent with our evaluations of political openness after the economic crisis. FH scores did not change under the Kim Dae Jung government, but they improved in 2004 under the Roh Moo Hyun government. The economy became much more open under both the Kim and Roh governments. By the end of the Kim government, the summary economic freedom rating increased to 6.9 in 2001 from 6.34 in 1995. The Roh Moo Hyun government also saw the summary rating increase, to 7.3 in 2005. Among areas of economic freedom, business regulation has seen the most drastic change, moving from 4.9 in 1995 to 6.8 in 2005. A similar improvement was recorded for the security of property rights and the access to sound money. But the size of government and openness to international trade remained largely unchanged.

These improvements also show that the Korean political economy is far from becoming a competitive market economy. As stated before, Korea still has significantly less economic freedom than other advanced market economies. Since it took about ten years for Korea to increase its EFW summary score by one full point, to 7.3, it may well take another ten years to reach an 8.5 score threshold, even if Korea carries out economic reforms at the same pace that it did in the past ten years.

One should bear in mind that the indicators discussed in this section do not represent exact measures of our concepts of political and economic openness. Nonetheless, we believe they adequately indicate the broad patterns we have discussed.

We draw the following conclusions about the trajectory of political and economic openness since 1987, as shown by FH and EFW ratings in Table 2.1. First, both politics and economics in Korea have become increasingly open since 1987. It is remarkable that amid the political turmoil of the late 1980s and the economic crisis of the late 1990s, economic and political openness did not suffer the setbacks common in the developing world.

Second, even though Korea has made continuous progress with respect to the twin goals of political and economic openness, progress in political openness has been faster and more significant than economic openness. By 2004, political rights were given an FH rating of 1, the highest category, while civil liberties rated 2, the second-highest rating. In contrast, the EFW rating for Korea's level of economic freedom was in the range of 6 to 7 points in 2006, still significantly lower than scores for advanced market economies, which were rated around 8.5 to 9.0.

Third, the relationship between political and economic change since 1987 has followed a politics-first, economics-second pattern. In the early 1980s, Korea was significantly more open in terms of its economy than its polity. Between 1987 and 1996, politics became significantly open while economics, especially the level of business, labor, and credit regulations, hardly changed. During this period, Korea was relatively open on both dimensions but remained significantly below the maximum values on both economic and political openness measures.

Fourth, the data suggest that, in the political arena, Korea has moved faster to improve political rights than civil liberties. After 1987, political rights were stronger than civil liberties during two different periods, 1988 to 1992 and 2004 to the present. When political rights are stronger than civil liberties, democracies become more vulnerable to economic populism and plutocracy because expanded opportunities for participation, without a comparatively strong system of laws, strengthen the groups suppressed under the authoritarian regime, such as workers, and the groups organized at the time of democratization, such as big business and farmers.

Fifth and finally, areas of economic freedom, such as business regulation, which started from a low base, were slowest to change between 1980 and 1995, indicating that the developmental state–type control of the economy did not abate during the pre-crisis period.

CHAPTER 3

Leading Up to South Korea's First Transition:
The Crisis of 1960–1961

South Korea's transition to sustained development began in earnest in the 1960s when the new military-led government of President Park Chung Hee carried out fundamental economic and political reforms to support its export-led development strategy. But the modern history of South Korean development did not take place in a historical vacuum; nor did these changes take place overnight. Rather, the turning point in South Korea's development strategy was the end point of a longer political transition that began with the political crisis of 1960–1961, when the unstable political regime in place before Park came to an end.

This historical perspective suggests that Park's reforms in the first half of the 1960s and the subsequent consolidation of his developmental regime were largely reactions to the political and economic failures of the previous regime. Thus, we precede our study of the transition to the Park regime by discussing why the status quo ante proved to be unbalanced and unstable.

The regime before Park featured a patriarchal leader, President Syngman Rhee, who was in power for twelve years (1948 to 1960). Rhee had been South Korea's first president since the founding of the South Korean state in 1948. Rhee showed considerable diplomatic skill as an international leader, as he kept his country together and intact through the early years of the Cold War and a devastating war with North Korea. But domestically he failed to put together a majority coalition and faced repeated political crises when opposition parties, the military, and student activists mounted strong challenges to his government. Political instability reached a climax in 1960–1961, when the students revolted and forced Rhee to resign in 1960, and then the military overthrew the government of Chang Myon, who succeeded Rhee in 1961.

The events leading up to the political crisis of 1960–1961 set the stage for the emergence of a new policy regime under President Park. The framework described in Chapter 2 provides new insights into this regime, and we interpret it through that lens. We emphasize at the outset, however, that this chapter on the Rhee era is intended as background for the subsequent regime change. We do not provide a complete explanation for the character of the Rhee regime or for the coup that took place and initiated the Park regime. We wish to explain, instead, why the natural state of the 1950s was unstable and out of balance, even with the huge subsidies from the United States, and how that instability contributed to the demise of the Rhee regime.

In this chapter we discuss how the final crisis began and evolved, leading to the replacement of the ancien régime with the new military-led system. We place particular emphasis on the political and economic instability inherent in a young democracy, imposed from outside on a society lacking the social and economic foundations for democracy. Among the sources of instability, such as weak political parties and the lack of intermediate organizations, we argue that the imbalance between military and civilian power within the Rhee regime requires special attention. The military emerged from the Korean War as the most powerful and efficient organization. But Rhee denied the military a significant role in his government and instead used the military politically, as a source of political funds and votes.

The exclusion of the military from the inner circle of the government turned out to be a constant source of instability, as various military leaders plotted coups repeatedly. When the military finally took over the government in 1961, it moved in the opposite direction; that is, toward the overmilitarization of the government. These reversals show the tendency of civil-military relations in Korea to move from one extreme to the other. The crisis of 1960–1961 makes clear the importance of the South Korean military in shaping the character of the new regime as well as the old.

In the following sections we discuss the breakdown of the Rhee regime and existing interpretations of its collapse, as well as the role of the

South Korean military in shaping the character of both the old and the new regime. The chapter ends with a new account of the Rhee regime based on the framework developed in Chapter 2.

The Breakdown of the Rhee Regime and Its Immediate Successor

General Park Chung Hee's military coup in May 1961 toppled the democratically elected Chang Myon government. Just a year earlier the Chang government itself had replaced another "democratic" regime led by President Syngman Rhee. We call the Rhee government (1948–1960) democratic because it did not renounce or reject outright the democratic constitution of 1948, even though the regime admittedly became more authoritarian toward the end of its rule.

Democracy came to South Korea under U.S. military rule (1945–1948). The American occupation forces sought to build the infrastructure for a strong democracy and to install a democratic government in South Korea. Under American auspices, South Korea held its constitutional assembly election in May 1948. The newly formed National Assembly drafted a constitution in July 1948 and elected the officials who formed the first government in August 1948; Syngman Rhee was chosen as the country's first president.

Korean party politics in the beginning was chaotic. Thirteen parties won at least 1 seat in the 200-seat National Assembly in 1948, with the largest party (the NARRKI) winning only 22.5 percent of the seats. Further, 85 independent candidates also won seats. The proliferation of political parties continued in the second National Assembly election of May 1950 in which 11 parties and 126 independents won seats.

Over time, however, a two-party system emerged, with the Liberal Party led by Syngman Rhee as the ruling party, and the Democratic Party, made up of conservative politicians opposed to Rhee, as the main opposition party. President Rhee, who was not formally affiliated with a party in his first term, founded the Liberal Party in 1951 to run in the 1952 presidential election; unlike in 1948 when the National Assembly chose the president, the president was directly elected by voters in 1952. The Democratic Party was formed in 1955 as a merger of several opposition parties that joined together to better compete against the ruling Liberal Party. Rhee had handily won the wartime presidential election of 1952 with 74.6 percent of the vote. In the 1954 National Assembly election, the Liberal Party won an outright majority of seats, 114 out of 203, against the badly divided opposition. The largest opposition party won only 15 seats in 1954.

Once the opposition united in the Democratic Party, it quickly emerged as a viable alternative to the Liberal Party, turning Korean party politics into a competitive two-party system. The two parties collided for the first time in the 1956 presidential election. In that hotly contested election, the Democratic Party came very close to unseating President Rhee but saw its chances evaporate when its candidate, who was leading in the polls, died of natural causes ten days before the election. But the Democratic Party captured the vice presidency when its candidate, Chang Myon, narrowly defeated his Liberal Party rival, Yi Ki Pung, by 46.4 to 44.0 percent. The outcome of the 1956 election was particularly disappointing and threatening to the Liberal Party because Rhee won only 70 percent of the final vote, in spite of the absence of a Democratic Party candidate. Fully 30 percent of the voters supported Cho Bong Am, a progressive politician who ran as an independent, instead of President Rhee. In the National Assembly election two years later, the Democratic Party proved its competitiveness again by winning 34 percent of the vote and 79 out of 233 seats. Although the Liberal Party won a National Assembly majority with a 42.1 percent vote share and 126 out of 233 seats, the size of its majority shrank significantly from the level of the previous assembly.

Increased competitive pressure from the Democratic Party was not the only cause of the Liberals' electoral decline after 1955. Anti–Liberal Party sentiment grew among voters who were concerned about the steady erosion of democratic principles under Liberal Party rule, especially after the Liberals rammed through a constitutional amendment in 1954 to allow Rhee to run for a third term. Political opposition to the Rhee government was not limited to ballot boxes. Students, intellectuals, labor unions, and civil-society groups such as church organizations grew increasingly impatient with the abuses of power by the Rhee government. In the authoritarian 1950s they did not openly protest against the government, but their discontent was growing. Among them, Cumings (2005) singles out two groups, university students and intellectuals, as leaders in the nascent anti-Rhee social movement.

Student protests in Korea have a long history. In premodern Korea, Confucian students often demonstrated in groups against government decisions or officials that they disapproved of. Schools were also the hot-bed of the independence movement during Japanese rule. Cumings points out that "student protests drew upon wellsprings of Confucianism that demanded or even required the educated to be moral exemplars, conscientious sentinels of the nation" (Cumings 2005, 344). Other circumstances in the 1950s also rendered university students restless. University and high school enrollments rapidly increased after 1948. By 1965, Korea had a higher percentage of its population attending college than Britain did. But good jobs were not easily available to the students after graduation. Also, universities at that time generally maintained low educational standards, thus affording students time for political activities. According to Cumings, this combination of factors led many university students to student activism.

Journalists and intellectuals represented another social group that turned against the Rhee government. Intellectuals were and still are influential in Korea because Confucian tradition fosters a vibrant intellectual community. Also thanks to Confucianism, intellectual dissent is ingrained in Korean political culture (Hahm 1999; Kihl 2005). Given such a strong intellectual community, journals, magazines, and newspapers flourished in the late 1950s; according to one survey more than 100,000 people claimed to be journalists in 1960 (Cumings 2005). The main outlet for leading intellectuals in the late 1950s was the intellectual journal *Sasanggye* (World of Thought), which the government frequently shut down in reaction to the journal's criticism of the regime.

As public pressure on the Liberal Party grew, party leaders turned increasingly to authoritarian tactics to maintain power. In a desperate effort, the Liberal Party committed massive electoral fraud during the March 1960 presidential election. The blatant acts of fraud set off nation-wide demonstrations against Rhee in April 1960. Student groups led many of these demonstrations, calling for the nullification of the March election outcome and President Rhee's resignation. The government responded harshly to the protests by declaring martial law, but it could not stop them. When student protests turned violent in front of the presidential mansion, President Rhee saw he had no choice but to resign.

Rhee left Korea to seek asylum in the United States after tendering his resignation, and his government collapsed, unable to maintain law and order. To protect constitutional rule and placate the protesters, the National Assembly announced a plan to constitute a new government and installed an interim administration to manage the transition. The Democratic Party then swept to victory in the May 1960 National Assembly election mandated by the transition plan. In June, the Assembly passed a new constitution whose main feature was the adoption of a parliamentary system. Under the new constitution, the National Assembly elected Yun Po Son as president and Chang Myon as prime minister in August 1960.

Unfortunately, the Democratic Party failed to restore order and normalcy to Korean society. This time the opposition parties were not the cause of instability; the Democratic Party faced virtually no opposition in the National Assembly. The problem was internal divisions within the ruling Democratic Party. The Democratic Party had long been divided into two factions, the "old" and the "new" faction. Prime Minister Chang led the old faction, while President Yun was the leader of the new faction. The conflict between the old and the new factions was torn wide open as they clashed openly over appointments, nominations, and party control (Han 1974).

The specter of nonstop demonstrations and strikes added to the sense of paralysis. After helping to throw out the Rhee regime through their collective action, student and other civil society groups gained confidence and became more aggressive and confrontational in voicing their grievances and in making demands on the new Democratic Party government. Labor leaders, who had long been suppressed by the Rhee government, mobilized workers to resurrect the labor movement. Teachers also became active, organizing their union for the first time. Some student groups even began to advocate an openly leftist agenda, such as immediate unification with North Korea.

Having watched the onset of disorder from the sidelines for more than a year, the Korean military decided to intervene, and it overthrew the Chang Myon government in May 1961. At the time of the military coup, Prime Minister Chang's government was only nine months old. A military junta led by General Park took over and ruled the Korean government directly for the next two years. Although the military restored civilian rule in 1963, it did not stop interfering in civilian government. In fact, the military would remain a significant political actor in South Korean politics for the next thirty years. Military influence continued even after Korea made its transition to democracy in 1987, significantly diminishing only when President Kim Young Sam, who was the first democratically elected civilian president, purged the military of the entire faction of politically active officers in 1993.

Existing Interpretations of the Rhee Regime

Scholars often point to structural limitations when explaining the failure of Korean democracy under President Rhee and Prime Minister Chang. According to Henderson (1968), the main structural weakness of Korean democracy in the 1950s was weak political parties. As a result of the weak political party system, Rhee had to rely on personal networks and charisma to maintain power, which proved to be highly unstable. Henderson attributes the weak party system to the nature of Korean society at that time—what is called a mass society, which, due to its homogenous and centralized character, lacked intermediate organizations and interest groups that could mediate the interactions between individuals and the government and produce political leaders. In this environment, individuals relied on personal relations and education, not on organized groups, hampering the development of true political parties. The Korean political parties in the 1950s can be thought of as temporary associations of individuals whose desire for personal power was much more important to them than party continuity.

Han (1974) identifies the deep ideological divide in Korean politics between the left and the right as the main source of political instability in the short-lived Second Republic. This divide may not be apparent when one side or the other is predominant, but the differences surface whenever political control becomes weaker. "The Korean War, which magnified the ideological divide that had been apparent before 1950, at the same time helped mask the division by enabling the orthodox right to silence completely any dissenting voice . . . the leftist voice, indeed chorus, would noticeably amplify whenever the government relaxed its grip, as in 1960 after the student uprising" (Han 2000, 1–2).

Rhee and Chang's governance failures involved not only political but also economic mismanagement. According to Haggard (1990) and Haggard, Kim, and Moon (1991), the economic policy that the Rhee government pursued after the Korean War ended in 1953 was a strategy of import-substitution industrialization. The success of this economic strategy required three policy outcomes: securing U.S. aid, keeping exchange rates overvalued, and maintaining macroeconomic stability. But economic policymakers lacked the capacity to implement the required policies effectively. "Korea in the 1950s exhibited political characteristics that were clearly inimical to development planning. The government was poorly insulated from the demands of the private sector and was penetrated by patron-client networks. The economic bureaucracy was subject to political interference from both the executive and the ruling party" (Haggard, Kim, and Moon 1991, 875). As a result, economic conditions deteriorated significantly toward the end of the 1950s. Having reached a 9 percent growth rate in 1956, economic growth slowed steadily thereafter, falling to 3.9 percent in 1959 and 1.9 percent in 1960.

The Role of the Military during the Transition from the Rhee Regime

Facing adverse social and economic conditions, the Rhee regime took on the characteristics of a natural state. And like many natural states, Rhee's turned out to be highly unstable and eventually succumbed to internal pressure for regime change.

From the perspective of balanced development, we can identify at least two sources of imbalance in Rhee's natural state. The first and more obvious is the political dominance over economic and bureaucratic spheres. In Rhee's natural-state system, political interests represented by the president and the ruling party held a privileged position over bureaucratic and business interests. Politicians controlled not only key economic policies but also the recruitment and promotion of bureaucrats (Henderson 1968). The business sector depended on the favors doled out by politicians, such as import licenses, foreign exchange, and bank loans. In creating a system of favors and privileges, the regime valued political support and loyalty over economic performance.

Rhee's main reliance on the political party rather than other agents, such as the military and the bureaucracy, may have reflected his institutional constraints. For historical and political reasons, he had to maintain an electoral democracy. The American imposition of and insistence on electoral democracy worked to the advantage of political parties and their leaders among the potential power centers of the ruling bloc. Based on this elevated position vis-à-vis other power centers, political leaders were able to rule largely unchecked and ended up mishandling both the economy and democratic politics.

Civil-military relations represent another imbalance within the Rhee regime. Throughout his rule, Rhee never quite found a comfortable balance between civilian and military powers. His first confrontation with the military came in 1952 when the military refused to send troops to support Rhee's attempt to force a constitutional amendment on the wavering National Assembly. After losing trust in the military through this incident, President Rhee tightened his personal control of the military, often compromising its independence and professional standing in the process.

The Korean military, having fought a major war and now receiving large amounts of American aid and support, grew into the most powerful and professional Korean institution in the 1950s, making it semi-independent from the government (Henderson 1968). Cumings (2005, 302–303) offers this description: "Standing above all the disorganization and human fragments of post-1953 Korea was a Korean military that had swelled from 100,000 in 1950 to well over 600,000 by 1953. It was now the strongest, most cohesive, and best-organized institution in Korean life, and it would soon make its political power felt."

But the military's potential to maintain stability was not utilized in the 1950s. The Rhee regime excluded the military from its inner circle, and military elites were also socially alienated from other elites, as most of the military officers came from rural and poor backgrounds. As a powerful stakeholder in Korean society, the military had a legitimate role to play. Given the underdevelopment of the bureaucracy and civil society, it could have been an alternative source of expertise, resources, and support to national leaders embarking on national development.

The military became increasingly discontented with the Rhee government's encroachment on its professional prerogatives (Kim 2004). Rhee used a divide-and-conquer method of controlling the military. He openly promoted factional competition among senior officers, which eroded their morale and professionalism. Afraid of and suspicious of the military, Rhee tried to control it directly by placing military security and police forces under his direct control. The Rhee regime also directly mobilized the military for political purposes. A large portion of the military budget was siphoned off to fund the ruling party. In the 1956 and 1960 elections, the Rhee regime asked military officers to support the campaign and to pressure soldiers to vote for the ruling party.

Predictably, the exclusion and alienation of the military had adverse consequences for the stability of the Rhee regime. Rumors of a military coup were frequently circulated, suggesting that a military intervention was a constant possibility. In fact, some senior officers plotted a coup against the Rhee government during the 1952 constitutional crisis.

The military finally stepped in in May 1961, ushering in the era of the military-led developmental regime. This outcome was not preordained. The military did not intervene during the student revolution of April 1960, for example.[1] Why did the military decide to take over in May 1961, but not in 1960? One possibility is that the military felt that it lacked sufficient legitimacy in 1960. With the popular Democratic Party ready to take over, the public would not have supported military intervention at that time. But 1961 was different. By then, the public was disillusioned with politicians and party politics in general. Looking back, the decision to intervene in 1961, not in 1960, worked out well for the military. After witnessing the failure of the Chang Myon government, the public was more willing to support a military intervention, as it perceived it as necessary to save the country from plunging into chaos.

After the takeover, military leaders went on to run the government for the next two years. By most accounts, the military performed its job rather competently. Law and order were quickly restored. More important, the military put into place a basic institutional framework for growth-oriented economic policy that continued under the subsequent civilian government.

Haggard, Kim, and Moon (1991) note three institutional changes that contributed to the new framework. First, the military government took power away from the political parties and concentrated it in the executive and his bureaucracy. Second, the new government restructured business-government relations to strengthen the link between business performance and government support. Third, economic decision making within the bureaucracy was centralized in the Economic Planning Board. The military also supplied a critical corps of professional managers: many military officers left the military and became managers in both the private and the public sector (Se-Jin Kim 1971). President Park

---

1. In 1960 the military could have intervened for the Rhee government, not against it. Certainly, leaders of the Rhee government desired a more resolute response by the military against the demonstrators. However, military leaders refused to fire at the students. Apparently some military officers were sympathetic to the student protests against the Rhee government, and the United States may also have pressured the Korean military to refrain from military action (Kim 2004).

(formerly General Park), who retired from the military in 1963 and won the presidential election as a civilian candidate, picked up the task of national development where the military left off.

From the perspective of balance in the structure of governance, the military's postcoup performance is revealing because it suggests what President Rhee might have achieved if he had forged a more satisfactory balance between civilian and military powers in the 1950s. By concentrating power in the ruling party and shunning the military, Rhee may have missed an opportunity to mobilize other sources of policy expertise and political support, such as the military's leaders and technocrats. As Samuel Huntington (1968) emphasizes, the success of a rapidly changing society depends on its ability to accommodate newly socialized citizens through political institutions. The many upwardly mobile young men in the military in the 1950s represented such a newly socially mobilized group, but without a political avenue that could accommodate them.

The Political and Economic Failure of a Natural State: A New Account of South Korea under Rhee

As Haggard (1990) and Haggard, Kim, and Moon (1991) emphasize, an explanation for the political failure of democracy in the 1950s and in 1960–1961 must take into account the interaction between politics and economics, especially the natural-state practice of manipulating economic policy for political purposes. Indeed, Syngman Rhee headed a government that was in many ways typical of natural states during this era; in this case, it practiced a form of clientelism based on personal exchange, with loyalties based on families, regions, and other traditional personal ties. Korea differed from other natural states, such as the Philippines, in that important elements of the old guard had been removed. Rural landlords in some developing countries hold the power to block reform efforts. Korean landlords, often branded as pro-Japanese collaborators, had lost influence through a major land reform that took away the economic basis of their power.

Haggard (1990, 55–61) provides one of the best descriptions of the Rhee years, and it closely conforms to the NWW natural-state approach.[2] Haggard describes the wide range of policy instruments used in

---

2. Other works on the Rhee regime include Cho (1996) and Cumings (2005, ch. 6).

service of politics and coalition maintenance. The Rhee regime overvalued the Korean won, making foreign exchange scarce. The politically induced excess demand for foreign exchange allowed the regime to distribute it to favored constituents. Domestic firms received protection from imports. Limited import licenses and scarce financial credit, including that from U.S. aid, were also given out to favored constituents rather than on the basis of merit. "Rhee's control over imported grains and other goods allowed him to distribute largesse directly to government employees and others, protecting them from inflation" (Haggard 1990, 57). Consistent with this assessment, Jones and Sakong (1980, 304) suggest that a major source of chaebol growth under Rhee was "privileged access to government controlled markets." Although the Rhee government's policies in the 1950s included education and rebuilding the economic infrastructure lost in the two successive wars, economic policymaking lacked a clear vision and policy goals (Cho 1996), as economic policies were made in the service of maintaining political support and the regime's survival.

Another feature of this period was the immense inflow of resources that accompanied the American presence. In addition, a great many new businesses arose to supply the Americans, including several companies that would join the ranks of the chaebol in the coming years (Cumings 2005). Thus, parts of the economy did grow under the Rhee natural state.

During the 1950s, the U.S. government actively sought reform in Korea based on "a return to the export-oriented economy of the Japanese occupation." But Rhee and his government continued to steer a different course, without following a coherent economic logic. "Rhee's objections [to the U.S. policy alternatives] were above all political . . . Policies that appeared a complex and confusing patchwork in economic terms can be explained by . . . Rhee's use of the instruments of economic policy— allocation of foreign exchange, bank credit, important licenses—to sustain political support" (Haggard 1990, 57; see also Jones and Sakong 1980, 44–46).

In natural-state fashion, the regime also pursued a variety of subsidies, import substitutions, and trade protections as a means of providing privileges and benefits to help keep the coalition in power. Korea during this period was heavily dependent on American aid (Cumings 2005), sometimes characterized as "addicted to dollars," with as much as 60 percent of the government's budget derived from U.S. funds. The state used this aid for economic rebuilding, funding the military, and supporting well-connected elites. Bureaucrats' low salaries were typically supplemented by gains from corruption. Reflecting the natural state's personalistic orientation, appointments went to the well connected rather than to those with talent and merit.

Although many analysts focus on the failures of this regime—inflation, economic stagnation, and corruption—Woo (1991, ch. 3) observes that Rhee had a "method to his madness": namely, that he sought to maximize the resource flow from the United States while attempting to avoid the constraints the Americans sought to impose as conditions on aid (see also Cumings 2005, ch. 6). More important, Rhee sought to deflect the Americans' goal of having the Korean economy help bolster Japan's (Cumings 2005, ch. 6).[3]

Despite the ability to allocate huge flows of American aid, the Rhee regime failed to produce substantial economic growth and lost legitimacy over time. As we have noted, following major riots protesting electoral fraud and corruption, Rhee was forced to resign in April of 1960 (Haggard 1990, 60).

The short-lived Second Republic attempted to promote economic reform and an export orientation. But this government was both ineffective and unstable. "Though reformist, the new government had no way of containing the conflicting demands placed on it by newly mobilized social forces" (Haggard 1990, 51). The instability of the Second Republic suggests that Rhee was right to ignore the American advice for economic reform. The result—which emerged from the shadow of poor economic performance, declining public support for the regime, and the military's dissatisfaction—was the 1961 military coup.

---

3. Neither Woo nor Cumings addresses the issue of whether Rhee's manipulation of the United States affected Americans' willingness to continue that aid.

CHAPTER 4

Initiating South Korea's Transition, 1961–1979

To underscore South Korea's remarkable economic development over the past half century, many look back to 1950 or 1960 and compare Korea with Africa. At that time, Korea's economic development was, at best, even with Africa's. Expectations in the development community were that Korea would not fare as well.

This comparison is inapt, however. During the Japanese colonial era (1910–1945), Korea experienced rapid industrial growth (Haggard, Kang, and Moon 1997; Jones and Sakong 1980, ch. 2; Kohli 1994; Myers and Peattie 1984). World War II and the Korean War devastated Korea, however, which is one reason why income levels were low in the 1950s. As Rodrik (1995) suggests, Korea's conditions in 1960 were more favorable for economic growth than those of most developing countries. The Korean economy under Japanese rule had grown rapidly during the 1920s and 1930s, and Korea's system of compulsory education had produced a much more educated population than Africa's. Korea thus had a high level of human capital relative to physical capital, in large part because of the devastation caused by the two wars. South Korea also had relatively equal income and wealth distribution, a circumstance that many economists argue is favorable to economic growth (Alesina and Rodrik 1994). Similar conditions held in Taiwan at this time, for example, but not in Africa.

Any explanation for South Korea's success must explain why Korea pursued policies that produce remarkable growth when the vast majority of poor, developing countries fail to do so. Moreover, the explanation must be universal, not based on arguments tailored to the Korean experience. The NWW framework shows that developing countries qua natural states have strong incentives to pursue policies that create rents and privileges, limit access to both politics and economics, and fail to provide secure property rights, rule of law, and various public goods necessary to support thriving markets and long-term economic growth.

The principal question of this chapter is: Why did the Park Chung Hee regime focus on producing growth instead of managing a more typical natural state or, worse, a boldly kleptocratic natural state, such as Idi Amin's Uganda? South Korea's remarkable growth demands an explanation for how Korea, unlike other developing countries, could break free of the typical natural-state incentives.

In addressing our principal question, we also address other important secondary questions about why the developmental state took the form it did. In particular, how did the various pieces fit together? A great many observers emphasize the importance of the meritocracy (see, for example, Amsden 1989, Johnson 1982, Root 1996, Wade 1990). As impersonal meritocracies are rare in the developing world, how was this system sustained in South Korea?

South Korea began its independence following the Korean War as a natural state, as discussed in Chapter 3, not particularly different from a great many others in the developing world at the time, especially in the 1950s. In standard natural-state fashion, the regime used economic policymaking in service of political goals, creating sufficient political support to keep the ruling coalition in power for most of the decade following the Korean War. The regime was characterized by clientelism and personal exchanges linked to family, regional, and other traditional ties. Over time, however, it lost legitimacy and proved unstable (Cumings 2005, ch. 6; Haggard 1990, ch. 3).

Two related features of its environment differentiated South Korea from most developing countries qua natural states. First, Korea faced a double threat of communism: from North Korea and China in the international realm, and from potential supporters of communism among its own population (Campos and Root 1996, ch. 1; Haggard 1990, ch. 3; Kang 2002, 29; Nam 1994; Vogel 1991, ch. 3; Woo 1991, 8–11).[1] Indeed, as

---

1. As noted in Chapter 2, scholars have long emphasized the importance of security threats as incentives to develop.

Nam (1994) shows, the threat from the North was ongoing.[2] And although Rhee's government was anticommunist, many South Koreans were not. At the time, perceptions around the world tended to view North Korea as better off than the South (Kang 2002, 34–35). The egalitarian nature of communism appealed to many of the poorest South Koreans, including many peasants. In addition, by the end of the 1950s the United States began searching for ways to lower dramatically its subsidies to Korea. Given this combination of factors, many South Koreans felt their society was threatened. Koreans would have to defend themselves.

Park Chung Hee's 1961 military junta built a new support coalition whose goal was to transform South Korea. Although they created an authoritarian regime, Park and his supporting coalition pursued a different path from the typical natural state, including that of the previous South Korean natural state. As a means of providing security, Park sought to change Korea from a backward, agrarian nation to an industrialized state, one capable of rivaling or surpassing Japan. The approach evolved over Park's tenure. Tenuous at first, the new regime gradually grew stronger, especially after the decline in American subsidies at the end of the Vietnam War forced the regime to provide for its own security independence.

The central feature of this regime was that Park and members of his coalition came to believe that Korea could not rely on the United States for its security, especially by the late 1960s and early 1970s (Kang 2002). They also believed that South Korea could provide its own security only

---

2. Nam (1994, 19n7) observes that it is internationally recognized that the North started the Korean War and that South Korea had, until recently, unilaterally suffered from armed provocations and terrorism inspired by Pyongyang. As evidence of the continued threat, Nam lists the following: "the kidnapping of Korean passenger planes in February 1958 and again in December 1969; attacking navy vessels twice, killing 69 soldiers, in January 1967; hijacking the U.S. Navy ship *Pueblo* in January 1968; and the ax murder of the U.S. soldiers in the DMZ in August 1978; dispatch of the ill-fated 31-man death squad who made their way close to the Blue House to assassinate President Park Chung-Hee; the second attempt to assassinate President Park in 1974, in which a bullet killed his wife; discovery of three underground tunnels in the DMZ dug by the North for military use; the attempt to assassinate President Chun Doo-Hwan visiting Rangoon, Burma, in 1983, which killed sixteen top officials and one reporter accompanying President Chun; and the bombing of a KAL plane in 1987 by a secret mission sent by Pyongyang to obstruct the 1988 Olympic Games, killing 115 passengers."

through economic independence. Failing to do so in the context of the threats of communism risked the collapse of South Korea. To counter the communist threat, the regime embarked on a set of policies involving shared growth: "The wider population was given the opportunities to reap long-term, lasting benefits from the resulting economic expansion" (Campos and Root 1996, 2). This involved various types of economywide public goods, such as education, infrastructure for markets, potentially rising incomes as the economy grew, and open access in the private and public sectors of the economy. Earlier policies of land reform were also relevant. Those reforms had at once destroyed the political base of the traditional landlords, provided a great number of poor rural farmers with land, granted would-be entrepreneurs a resource base from which to launch new enterprises, and significantly reduced rural inequalities in wealth. Although the regime suppressed labor organization, wages rose, on average, 8 percent per year from 1970 to 1989 (Haggard, Cooper, and Collins 1994).

A natural state based on personal relationships, Korea in 1960 met none of the doorstep conditions; it gave no hint of beginning the transition to a developed, industrialized democracy. Yet Park's regime initiated that transition, creating the doorstep conditions in a manner that diverged from the path historically followed in Western Europe. Part of the transition involved changes in beliefs among the population, and part involved the extension of rights to include a much wider set of citizens than in the natural state, exemplified by the regime's shared growth and policies that opened up economic access. The embodiment of inclusion in the West, rights extended to all citizens, almost always had a political component, such as the American Declaration of Independence's "All men are created equal" and the French Revolution's "Liberté, égalité, fraternité." Inclusion in East Asia differed, at least initially, as it was based on expanding economic rights, economic opportunities, and shared growth but downplaying political and civil rights (Campos and Root 1996).

Korea's situation differed from that of most natural states in the post–World War II era because of the direct and powerful communist threat. This existentiac threat changed the incentives for Korea's dominant coalition. Inclusion and shared growth became credible because failing to include them risked the regime's future through increased domestic support among the masses for communism, in addition to the communist threat from the North. The devastation of the economy during World War II and the Korean War, combined with the lack of a resource base, meant that domestic resources were far too small to ensure Korea's survival absent the huge American military and resource presence. Inclusion and shared growth held the promise of generating the resources for security while gaining domestic support for the regime.

In what follows, we focus on the wide range of interrelated mechanisms created by the regime that simultaneously began to pull Korea into the transition from a society based on personal connections to one based on impersonal rights and laws. The export-led growth system created a new series of incentives for firms, bureaucrats, citizens, and the military, all based on impersonal rather than personal characteristics (for example, favoring firms that exported the most instead of those that had the best political connections). The regime used its management of portions of the economy, particularly credit and subsidies, to provide incentives for firms to produce efficiently and to innovate (Campos and Root 1996; Jones and Sakong 1980; Rhee, Ross-Larson, and Pursell 1984; Woo 1991). The focus on export growth created impersonal targets and expectations for firms: to obtain subsidies and rents, they had to perform well in a competitive, international market rather than living off rents from the domestic economy.

The regime also created a range of impersonal incentives for bureaucrats, such as exams and meritocracy, but these were not independent from politics. As with bureaucracies in every country, politics controlled the Korean bureaucracy, but Korea's political leaders valued implementing objective, impersonal goals instead of personalistic and clientelistic ones. To the extent that political officials gave the bureaucracy room to become a meritocracy with the appearance of independence, it was because the bureaucracy produced the results sought by those officials (Haggard, Cooper, and Collins 1994; Jones and Sakong 1980; see also Amsden 1989 and Wade 1990). Bureaucratic rewards were based in part on the success of the sectors they managed. The regime also kept the military out of policymaking, in the sense that it could not treat the economy as a source of rents. Although many members of the military served in political positions, they did not do so in uniform or as representatives of the military. In exchange for the absence of direct military input into policymaking, the regime financed the military's development into a modern force capable of providing national security. Sustained growth would allow significant increases in military resources, equipment, manpower, and technology. The final piece of our argument involves citizens, who, as we have emphasized, shared in Korea's growth and opportunities and supported the regime in exchange.

We divide our discussion into static and dynamic aspects of Korea's development—first discussing how South Korea maintained the developmental state as an equilibrium state, and second, how that state came about through an incremental process. In the next section we look at Park's initiation of the transition, emphasizing the interlocking incentives for firms, bureaucrats, the military, citizens, and the government. We then discuss the developmental state and the doorstep conditions, and finally the evolution of the South Korean regime over time.

Initiating the Transition: Creating a New, Integrated Set of Incentives

After a brief nationalization phase, President Park Chung Hee's new regime began the transition and established the developmental Korean state, sometimes referred to as "Korea, Inc." (Hutchcroft 2011; Woo 1991, 2). As Amsden (1989) and Wade (1990) observe, the Korean developmental state did not attempt to "get prices right" but pursued significant management of the economy, specifically by "getting prices wrong" (Amsden 1989, 13–14) through such policies as rationed, subsidized credit; various other subsidies; discretionary import licensing and enforcement of regulations; foreign exchange controls; and achieving dominance in strategic industries (Root 1996, 20).

Park organized a support coalition to sustain a systematic transformation process in the state and the economy, one capable of producing the twin goals of development and security. "Park openly stated that the supreme object of his military coup was to fight poverty through economic development and to protect the country from North Korean aggression" (Nam 1994, 14–15). In terms of the NWW framework, Park's coalition helped initiate a series of incremental steps—the doorstep conditions—in the transition from a natural state to an open-access order, a process that began slowly but gathered momentum as Park engineered increasing economic openness from the mid-1960s through the 1970s. Increases in political openness lagged, but followed in the late 1980s and 1990s. Korea's transition is still ongoing.

The initial transition involved a systematic transformation of the policies pursued by the government; of the bureaucracy implementing those policies; of the organization, environment, and incentives facing firms; and of the relationship of the population to the state and the new economy. We will discuss each of these transformations in turn and then show how they fit together to create a political and economic equilibrium capable of sustaining economic development. The new system involved a set of interlocking incentives supporting open access and competition, thereby producing sustained economic growth.

The transformation of each sector represented a move from personal exchange and clientelism to impersonal exchange, more open economic access, greater competition, and relationships based on contracts, with greater emphasis on the rule of law. As Jones and Sakong (1980) explain,

> Under Rhee a major source of chaebol growth was privileged access to government controlled markets, and the resulting transfers produced relatively few benefits for society as a whole. Entrepreneurs were thus largely involved in zero-sum activity . . . Under Park, zero-sum transfers remain, but largely as add-ons to productive positive-sum ventures. In part this followed from the elimination of some zero-sum opportunities (for example, the shift to non-discretionary allocation of foreign exchange). More important, it follows from insuring that bureaucratic discretion is exercised so that resources are allocated to reasonably productive users. (304)

The transformation resulted in a marked increase in impersonality, objectivity, and open access in both economic and public organizations. As Root (1996, 30) summarizes, "Perhaps [Park's] outstanding contribution to Korea's modernization was the management of the transition from a society of personal networks to one of impersonal contracts, enforced equally regardless of an individual's or a firm's status . . . Park's regime can be identified with universal application of rules and laws. He insisted that if rules are bent, the integrity of the system will break down." Park also took deliberate steps to control the military, especially to keep the military out of the government's economic policymaking process (Root 1996, 24).

Several aspects of Korean history and culture affected the choices made by Park and his coalition. First, the Japanese colonial period, including Park's close association with the Japanese in the 1930s and during World War II, helped provide a model for creating economic growth. Elements of the Japanese experience, including the structure of the bureaucracy, aspects of land reform, and the emphasis on mass education, influenced Korea after independence. Close economic ties to Japan, beginning with the normalization of relations in 1965, brought access to subsidies and technological know-how. In many ways, the Park era emulated the structure of Japan prior to World War II.[3] Second, the Confucian culture emphasized values of hard work, goal achievement, pragmatism, and education. Third, the Korean military had been exposed to the modern management techniques of the United States Army. This experience affected the thinking of many junta members. Indeed, some observers have likened the South Korean developmental state to a state mobilizing for war.

To survive in power, Park assembled a coalition of direct supporters among the military, exporting firms (including the chaebol), and conservatives in the rural population. Although the system was authoritarian, Park and his coalition had to be mindful of the communist threat and domestic sympathy and potential support for the North. In contrast to a typical natural state, survival for this regime required retaining the support of a major portion of the population. The dominant coalition therefore had incentives to widen the distribution of benefits beyond a narrow elite to include a large portion of the citizenry.

The regime pursued a variety of policies for sharing the benefits of economic growth more widely than the typical natural state's concentration of benefits among a small elite. In the process, it extended economic rights and access in a way that at once created more competition in the economy and allowed firms and the bureaucracy to draw on a much larger pool of potential talent. Recent events aided the formation and success of this coalition. The two wars had not only devastated the country but also wiped out many entrenched interests; nearly everyone had been displaced at some point (Cumings 2005, ch. 6). Land reform following the Korean War removed most of the traditional rural elites, many of whom were branded as collaborators because of their cooperation with the Japanese. Moreover, South Korea did not possess a large

---

3. Haggard, Kang, and Moon (1997) and Kohli (1994) emphasize the legacies of Japanese colonialism in the Park regime and in South Korea's success more generally.

number of firms that grew up around a set of privileges they would fight to protect. These factors—security risks and fewer entrenched interests— differentiated South Korea from other natural states of the era, such as Mexico and the Philippines. In what follows, we examine the incentives facing all major sets of actors: the government, firms, bureaucrats, the military, and citizens.

GOVERNMENT COALITION INCENTIVES

To make the developmental state work, the government moved, first, to create new policies and incentives for other actors. As we have argued, the government had a pivotal role in creating and maintaining the developmental state: it provided national security; it set the incentives for the meritocratic bureaucracy; it provided public goods and rising incomes for citizens; and it provided incentives for firms, creating a cooperative venture in developing new, international markets for Korean exports.

We therefore begin by investigating the government's incentives to foster this type of state. Both the government and the dominant coalition had to have incentives to institute and maintain the new system of impersonal exchange. What prevented the government from using standard natural-state forms of reneging? How did Korea avoid the more typical natural-state problem of privilege and expropriation?

Part of the answer is that the central strategy for long-term political security and economic growth—reliance on export-led growth—shaped government incentives in striking ways, creating fiscal incentives for the government to succeed.[4] Export-promoting policies used international markets for prices and other impersonal signals of success. Haggard, Cooper, and Collins (1994) show that the emphasis on export-led growth relied on international markets as a self-correcting device. Initiatives that failed to succeed in international markets, such as the move into chemical and heavy industries, adversely affected an array of domestic financial variables, including the balance of payments, exchange rates, and domestic budget deficits: "Despite some successes, the misallocation of resources under the Heavy and Chemical Industry Drive, and its inflationary consequences, translated into a loss of competitiveness in

---

4. Weingast (2009) provides a short survey of a growing range of works on fiscal incentives and governmental behavior in the context of federalism.

international markets—an important signal to decision makers that policy adjustments were required. Korea's export orientation not only contributed to economic growth directly; it also contributed to a virtuous policy cycle. Significant departures from the pursuit of competitive advantage quickly became apparent to both business and the government" (Haggard, Cooper, and Collins 1994, 15).

Export growth for a small, peripheral trading state required success in markets beyond the exporting country's manipulation. Giving natural state–style subsidies to inefficient enterprises that lacked the ability to compete in international markets would drain the treasury, add inflationary pressures, and turn exchange rates against successful exporting firms. Costly initiatives to expand exports become major drains on the budget when they fail to generate the desired revenue from overseas sales. The integrated export and financial system therefore created strong financial incentives for the government to succeed and penalized it for granting subsidies to favored constituents rather than to firms that had a chance at succeeding. South Korea's strategy differed from most natural states, which do not attempt aggressive, export-led growth. Succeeding on the international market necessitated secure property rights and a government capable of impersonal policies.

The Korean system also differed dramatically from the typical natural state, where privilege and credit are allocated on a personalistic basis. For example, the description in Haber et al. (2007) of the banking system in Mexico reveals behavior typical of natural states in the developing world. Mexico created such a small number of banks that, although the banks were inefficient, they made considerable profits through rents generated by restricted competition. A major portion of loans went to finance the government rather than business enterprises. And loans to finance enterprises typically went to insiders and politically connected people. Moreover, the Mexican government could not sustain this system: it followed periods of rent creation for bankers with episodes of expropriation and then new periods of rent creation. Personalistic natural states face great difficulties financing a thriving, entrepreneurial sector. In contrast to the impersonal Korean system, the personalistic Mexican banking system depended on a closed economy; Mexican banks were not required to succeed on the international market in order to receive their benefits.

The export-led growth strategy provides another part of the answer to why the Korean government ignored opportunities to renege on opening the economy and expropriate firm investments. First, especially to produce security, the export-led growth strategy created direct incentives for the regime (Haggard, Cooper, and Collins 1994). As we have seen, allocating subsidies based on personalistic ties rather than impersonal performance criteria would have failed to create internationally competitive industries and would have led to budget deficits, exchange-rate problems, and inflationary pressure. Second, the security threat implied that any attempt by the regime to renege on one component of the system would threaten all the other components, and with them, the regime's survival. In the presence of the appeal of communism and the threats from the North, failure of the regime to make good on its promises for shared growth risked the regime's support, legitimacy, and future.

In combination, these two factors generated incentives for members of the dominant coalition that differed from those facing the typical natural state. Allocating privileges and rents to cronies, or tolerating rampant corruption, would upset the incentive system supporting export growth, leading to fiscal problems in the short term and problems with security in the long term. Reneging on firms' rights—for example, by expropriating assets or applying confiscatory taxes—would have the same effect.

A security threat is hardly a sufficient condition for economic success. A large number of countries have experienced threats and failed to create the institutions necessary to survive. In previous centuries, those states were often absorbed by more powerful ones. Yet in South Korea's case, the security threat—combined with the individual, organizational, and social capacities of Park's leadership—worked to initiate the transformation to economic openness and impersonal policymaking and to maintain a bureaucratic meritocracy. Moreover, once the government started on this course, the security threat provided the incentive to maintain it.

INCENTIVES FOR FIRMS

Park and his coalition did not create a wholly new system but adapted the old one. The new regime had many sources of rents and privileges, but these were no longer distributed solely on the basis of natural state–style personal relations within the dominant coalition. The paramount drive to create security independent of the United States helped to focus policymaking on creating economic self-sufficiency. And the economic focus on export-led growth introduced a more objective, impersonal component based on success. Korea lacked many raw materials, such as oil, and it could pay to import them only through increasing exports and reducing other imports, such as food.

To reduce food imports, the regime sought to create self-sufficiency in food production. Korea pursued policies favorable to agriculture in the late 1960s and early 1970s. Policies promoting rural development thus had two separate political benefits for the dominant coalition: directly, they expanded support for the regime and blunted potential sympathy with the North; indirectly, they reduced imports and thus helped the regime's export efforts.

To induce business to cooperate, the state created three "carrots" through its economic policymaking: loans, credit, and licenses. One of Park's early economic policies was to nationalize the banks (Amsden 1989, 16). Control of the banks granted the regime the power to allocate credit. Subsidized credit, sometimes with negative interest rates (interest rates below the rate of inflation), fostered highly leveraged firms; that is, firms were far more debt financed than equity financed.

Controlling credit gave the state critical leverage over firms. Highly leveraged firms are vulnerable to changes in the availability of funds because when short-term and medium-term notes come due, they need to replace them with new loans. The government's control over the banks allowed it to issue new credit to firms that cooperated with its goals and to withhold it from firms that failed to cooperate; to survive, firms in sectors targeted by the regime had to cooperate. Besides receiving credit, firms gained in other ways. For example, the authoritarian regime suppressed organized labor, helping to keep firms' labor costs low and obviating their need to deal with unions and strikes. Such policies combined to give firms high-powered incentives to produce exports.

The principal feature of the new system was a systematic set of impersonal incentives, another step toward the doorstep conditions. Benefits bestowed by the regime—credit, licenses, and tax refunds, for example—went to firms that met their export targets; that is, the regime exercised discretion based on impersonal rather than personalistic or clientelistic criteria. According to Jones and Sakong (1980), both the Rhee and Park regimes allocated credit on a discretionary basis. But, they point out, "under Rhee political and personal gain seem to have played a major role. Under Park, such considerations are by no means absent but are clearly subordinate to economic priorities" (295). For example, taxes on imports were reimbursed when firms met their export criteria (Root 1996, 28); firms that failed to meet those targets received diminished subsidies. As Root shows, "non-performing firms were quickly dropped from the list of beneficiaries" for subsidized credit (27). Firms that did perform, however, received considerable rents from this system.

An especially critical component of the system was the relative absence of bailouts and soft budget constraints on firms. Common among natural states, the prospect of bailouts creates a soft budget constraint: because firms can perform poorly and still survive, they lack incentives to produce efficiently. Instead, the Park regime's emphasis on performance and objective, impersonal indicators of success created a hard budget constraint (Campos and Root 1996). The evidence bears this out: only three of the top ten chaebol in 1962 remained among the top ten in 1987 (Gong 1993); moreover, instead of bailing out ailing firms, the government forced them to close or merge with successful ones. Unsuccessful firms were not allowed to keep their government benefits. Instead, as new firms became top performers, they replaced previously successful firms.

The difference between the Rhee regime's allocation of policy benefits and Park's reflects the movement from a natural state's discretionary allocation of benefits, rents, and privileges to a system that allocates them on the basis of impersonal criteria, such as export promotion. Failure to perform on international markets meant a firm received fewer benefits and faced potential reorganization. The impersonal aspects of this system created elements of the rule of law, at least for elites—the first doorstep condition.

To understand the logic of the incentive system, consider the idea of tournaments, a variant on the standard principal-agent problem (Lazear and Rosen 1981). In this setting, a principal (e.g., a firm manager) wants multiple tasks performed: in particular, the same task performed in different areas (say, in different departments of a firm or in facilities located in different regions). To accomplish these tasks, the principal hires several agents and puts them in competition—a tournament—for rewards. The principal sets the rewards so that the biggest rewards—for example, high salaries and promotions to the next level of management—go to the most successful agents. By allocating the highest reward to the best competitors, the system provides incentives for multiple agents to further the principal's goals. For this system to work, the principal has to distribute rewards based on objective, impersonal criteria. In contrast, when a natural state plays favorites by allocating rewards based on personal rather than impersonal criteria, it fails to achieve the desired incentive effects of tournaments.[5]

The tournament approach helps us understand the nature of the incentives facing South Korean firms in the Park era: competition for scarce financing, subsidies, and other policy benefits joined with the competitive nature of global markets to force exporting firms to be efficient and innovative.[6] A lack of efficiency and innovation meant an absence of international demand for their products. Firms that failed on either dimension failed to move on to the next round of the tournament. As we have seen, credit was a central instrument in the reward structure. Firms that met their targets continued to receive subsidized credit; firms that failed to meet them failed to get that credit. Given the larger firms' highly leveraged financing, a systematic loss of credit risked bankruptcy. The bottom line is, the chaebol became huge organizations, and they did so largely through excellent export performance in competitive international markets, rather than, in a more typical natural-state fashion, through holding privileged positions within a domestic economy, protected from international competition.

Competitive markets were another important feature of the system. Within the administrative and regulatory system that controlled some markets (especially financial and import markets), firms gained considerable economic freedom (Nam 1994).[7] Open access for small and medium-size companies increased competition in many domestic industries. Land reform (prior to the Park regime) not only redistributed assets but also gave many potential entrepreneurs sufficient capital to

---

5. Lazear and Rosen (1981) explore the abstract logic of tournaments. Nellis (1996) demonstrates the applicability of tournaments for understanding Korea's development. Breton and Wintrobe (1986) present a related idea to explain the success of the Nazi bureaucracy.

6. This discussion draws on Nellis (1996).

7. According to Nam (1994, 16), "the real engine of growth . . . has been the market-oriented economic system itself, under which Korean businessmen and workers enjoyed fairly wide freedom to pursue their own interests. The working of the system, however, was largely conditioned by the active role of the government . . . Thus, the role of the economic engine and that of its operator, the government, have been, in my opinion, the most important factors in Korean development."

launch new enterprises. Universal education complemented these economic achievements.

In many ways, the administrative system paralleled the market. Although South Korea deliberately got some prices wrong, as Amsden emphasizes, this is not the whole story. The Korean economic management differed dramatically from socialist central planning, which also got prices wrong but which replaced rather than complemented market incentives. Because Korean firms received rewards for performance in international markets, they had an incentive to set and meet ambitious goals: that was the way to garner greater resources and subsidies from the bureaucracy. In contrast, enterprises in socialist systems had incentives to hide their productive capacity and to set low targets that they could surpass (Kornai 1992; Rhee, Ross-Larson, and Pursell 1984, 16).

The success of this system is well known. During Park's first decade, the South Korean economy grew at a rate of more than 8 percent per year, with GDP increasing by a factor of five between 1965 and 1978. During the 1970s, industrial production grew by approximately 25 percent per year. Exports also increased by an average of 45 percent a year in the mid-1970s.

BUREAUCRATIC INCENTIVES

As Amsden (1989) and Wade (1990) emphasize, bureaucrats were essential to the implementation of export-promoting and other economic policies. They set targets for firms and industries, evaluated their performance, and allocated various rights, credit, subsidies, and other public benefits. The Economic Planning Board (EPB), created in 1961, sat at the top of the bureaucratic hierarchy and served as the link between the president (and his coalition) and the bureaucracy.

Our approach suggests a new interpretation of the Amsden-Wade thesis that an independent, meritocratic bureaucracy provided the central pillar of South Korea's success. The meritocratic features of bureaucracy are evident and beyond dispute: exams for positions; promotions based on objective and impersonal criteria; creating impersonal targets for firms that promote growth, based on realistic expectations; and allocation of rewards, subsidies, licenses, and tax refunds based on impersonal criteria rather than on the natural state's innate corruption and personalistic criteria. In Amsden and Wade's view, the bureaucracy accomplished these goals because it was insulated from politics.

Yet the Amsden-Wade view fails to answer a central question: How was the meritocratic system insulated from politics? In particular, what prevented Korea's authoritarian regime from perverting the meritocratic bureaucracy, as occurs in so many developing countries? Also missing from their accounts is an understanding of the bureaucracy's incentives to reward performance rather than corruption. Privilege and bureaucratic corruption are so rampant in the developing world that a sustained meritocracy is a phenomenon we must explain. In nearly all natural states, politics and corruption have a direct impact on bureaucratic decisions. In India, for example, corrupt bureaucrats sold ration cards that were supposed to be given to the poor. In Mexico, political officials allocated funds for alleviating poverty to areas where they hoped to gain votes, rather than to the poorest areas (Magaloni 2006). And in Africa, critical medicines, such as those for treating malaria, have not been distributed free to the target population, as intended, but have been sold through black-market channels. So how did Korea sustain its meritocratic system?

The answer is that the meritocratic system was not insulated from politics (Haggard, Cooper, and Collins 1994). The Korean bureaucratic system differed from bureaucracies in most natural states because Korean politics differed from that of most natural states. As we have emphasized, survival in the face of pervasive communist threats forced the state and the dominant coalition to sacrifice short-term rents in favor of a system capable of providing security. Park and his coalition built the new merit system to replace the more traditional clientelistic one because only a meritocratic one held the hope of fostering economic growth and security.[8] Meritocratic decision making survived because it produced the outcomes sought by political officials and the dominant coalition, not because the independent bureaucracy was able to insulate its policy choices from the meddling of political officials. Our account suggests that the Korean bureaucracy of Park's developmental state was meritocratic in the sense that it used impersonal, objective indicators

---

8. Perhaps it is better to say that Korea under Park *rebuilt* the meritocratic system, given that the Japanese used such a system to administer all of Korea (see Kohli 1994 and Haggard, Kang, and Moon 1997).

rather than corrupt practices; it seemed to act independently of politics only to the extent that it produced desired results.

So why did the bureaucratic system produce policies supporting export growth? Here too the system of incentives was important. Bureaus and bureaucrats that fostered growth expanded and gained rewards, while those that failed to foster growth did not. Haggard, Cooper, and Collins (1994), Jones and Sakong (1980), Campos and Root (1996), and Root (1996) all provide evidence for bureaucratic rewards based on performance. Root (1996), for example, discusses the "shuffling and reshuffling of ministers" as reflecting performance evaluations. The bureaucracy was highly regarded among political officials precisely because it carried out their goals (Jones and Sakong 1980, 47–48). As Jones and Sakong reported (ibid., 291), "The Korean civil service, with its high selection standards and inculcation of Confucian hierarchical tradition, is admirably equipped to respond" to Park's policy concerns for growth and security. "As a result, virtually the entire executive branch has been mobilized to make decisions based on expected economic outcomes."

Information was a central aspect of the impersonal system for allocating credit, subsidies, and other privileges. For the system to work, allocation decisions had to be based on accurate and verifiable information so that it was clear that the government allocated credit on the basis of impersonal, objective indicators (such as export targets and a firm's success in meeting them) rather than personalistic criteria or corruption. Part of the solution was to rely on relatively simple indicators, making verification easier, more transparent, less subject to judgment, and, especially, less subject to the covert manipulation that tends to occur under a natural state. Deliberative councils, discussed below, were another part of the solution. Organized by industries, these councils allowed firms to collect, share, and verify various forms of information (see Campos and Root 1996, ch. 4). To prevent corruption and personalistic decision making, information had to be common knowledge—available to all, including the relevant bureaucracy and the various firms competing for subsidies and export growth.

Nam, reflecting on his experience as a high governmental official in the Park era, explained the incentive system in this way: "The progress of the program and projects was regularly evaluated in a Conference for Evaluation and Analysis, which was attended by all ministers and top business leaders and presided over by the President. If some projects were found to be lagging behind schedule, the causes of the delay were analyzed and a decision on corrective action was taken, often on the spot. One result was that every official had to be alert to ensure that a project on his authority did not become an object of negative attention at the meeting and in the presence of the President" (Nam 1994, 9). Nam's observation about negative attention emphasizes the importance of incentives: officials had incentives to ensure that the projects under their authority made progress, lest they be singled out for public criticism and negative attention from the president, the ministers, and top businessmen.[9]

Several features of the Korean system generated incentives that limited corruption. As one example, Korea instituted a pension system for bureaucrats in the mid-1960s. As a means of increasing bureaucratic compensation, this system had two advantages. First, in contrast to higher wages, pensions deferred compensation, providing the regime with more funds in the short term for investing. Second, the system gave the regime leverage, in that it could threaten to deprive corrupt officials and wrong-doers of their pensions. To work, the regime had to allocate these rewards on the basis of impersonal criteria rather than personal, clientelistic ones.

Direct scrutiny by President Park provided another incentive against corruption. For example, Root (1996, 24) recounts the story of how Park visited a minister at his lavish home and asked him how he could afford such luxury on his ministerial salary. The minister could not provide a good answer and was fired the next day.

In combination with competition among firms for rewards, the deliberative councils also helped limit corruption. By providing an organization within which to share and verify information, deliberative councils allowed all firms in an industry to observe whether bureaucrats made decisions by the rules or whether they played favorites. The transparency and openness of these participatory organizations also allowed firms to monitor bureaucratic decision making, to flag problems, and to coordinate reactions against decisions not consistent with the rules. Competition among firms was necessary for this system to work; if, instead, all firms were allocated privileges and each obtained its share, they would have little incentive to police nonmeritocratic bureaucratic actions. This

---

9. Rhee, Ross-Larson, and Pursell (1984, 16–17) make the same point.

system complemented the political rewards for bureaucrats to provide them with strong incentives to promote the public goal of exports. These councils also gave the government a forum within which to make announcements to all firms at the same time, as opposed to playing favorites through the selective release of information to politically favored firms.

Open access in the economy not only created competition, it also created mutual monitors. Competition for credit was transparent in the sense that all participants in an industry could tell whether bureaucrats used impersonal criteria to allocate credit. The open, competitive environment therefore reduced the ability of bureaucrats to be corrupt or to make decisions favoring particular firms.

This system was not perfect, as Kang (2002) underscores. We do not claim that the regime succeeded in suppressing all corruption; undoubtedly, substantial corruption existed during this era.[10] Our point is, instead, that the regime was able to dampen the incentives for corruption so that they were not the dominant bureaucratic incentives.

The Korean system has interesting parallels with that of early-reform China, especially in the 1980s and early 1990s. Here, too, literature on corruption (see, e.g., Manion 1996) fails to explain China's success. The Chinese created competition and tournaments in a very different manner from South Korea, and failed to create a bureaucratic meritocracy. Instead, they created what has been called "federalism, Chinese style"— competition among provinces and lower jurisdictions for success in foreign investment and in exports in international markets (Montinola, Qian, and Weingast 1995). Township and village enterprises became the engine of early Chinese economic growth. In the context of interjurisdictional competition among provinces, too much corruption would cripple a province's ability to compete, both with neighboring provinces and with other firms internationally. When officials drew excessive rent from enterprises in one township, for example, they would grant neighboring ones a competitive advantage (Ang 2012). In both the Chinese and the South Korean systems, competition limited (but did not eliminate) the rent extraction and corruption.

---

10. Indeed, the relatively frequent corruption scandals in all open-access orders suggests that the presence of major corruption cannot be a reliable test of whether a state is a natural state or an open-access order.

These competitive incentives contrast with systems in India and the Philippines. India's centralized system under the dominant Congress Party reflected typical natural-state behavior. Bureaucratic and firm incentives did not reward performance but emphasized bestowing benefits on clients, insiders, and those with personalistic ties to policymakers. In contrast to China's market-preserving federalism, India created a far more centralized federalism that limited the independence of state governments. Centralized federalism allowed the dominant coalition—the Congress Party from independence in 1947 to 1989—to allocate budgetary subsidies to clients, to limit access in various industries to create rents, and to erect trade barriers to protect favored industries (Parikh and Weingast 2003). In the Philippines, Marcos created a system based on privilege and rent creation, focusing on a relatively small number of elite families, landowners, and larger firms (see Hutchcroft 2011, Montinola 2012).

In short, Korea's focus on exports gave firms and bureaucrats impersonal, objective indicators on which to base and coordinate their behavior. This system helped align everyone's objectives: Park's, the dominant coalition's, the bureaucracy's, and the chaebol's.

MILITARY INCENTIVES

Park rose to power through the military. His regime's new system favored the military in some ways, but placed limits on it in others. Korea's independence from the United States and its survival in the face of security threats required not just a large military but an effective, professional one. Security required the allotment of substantial resources to the military to finance its operations, including first-rate equipment and plentiful weapons, equipment, and personnel. Park and his coalition knew that in the face of pervasive threats, failing to maintain an efficient, effective military force could prove disastrous.

The regime also prevented the military from having a direct presence in policymaking, the bureaucracy, and the management of firms. In contrast to China during its first two decades of economic reform, for example, the Korean military was not engaged directly in economic matters. As noted, many former military officers served in political and bureaucratic positions, but not as representatives of the military.

Moreover, the regime pursued goals desired by the military: a well-equipped and professional military force, national security, and long-term economic growth. Because of the regime's success in achieving these goals, the military faced relatively few temptations to interfere with politics and policymaking.[11]

The result was that the military was simultaneously a source of political support for the regime and security for the nation during this era. Importantly, the regime was able to control the military, so disputes among coalition members were unlikely to result in internal violence. In NWW's terms, the regime thus approached the third doorstep condition: consolidated political control of the military.

CITIZENS' INCENTIVES

The Korean system bestowed a mix of benefits and costs on its citizens. Koreans lived in a repressive, authoritarian regime and lacked fundamental political and civil rights. The regime suppressed democracy, political freedom, and the right to organize. More generally, whereas the regime fostered open access in many markets, it limited access in politics, suppressing a range of organizations and the civil society that otherwise would have flourished.

On the positive side, the regime provided most citizens with a variety of benefits, and although not democratic, it responded to citizen interests. The communist threat meant that failing to maintain the support of the majority of citizens risked the regime's security. Park and his coalition made economic growth "the legitimizing goal" of his regime (Jones and Sakong 1980, 293). They did so by creating greater openness— through inclusion and sharing—than is typical of a natural state. Specifically, the government provided a range of valued public goods, including security, education, economic opportunity, and shared growth. The new openness in the economy and the public sector meant jobs and opportunities for many. Universal education opened these opportunities to a much wider set of players than before. And fostering the national market made most citizens, including formerly self-sufficient peasants, part of the system, in which wages rose significantly over time. All these

---

11. The American military presence represented a final factor affecting Korea's military. As in Germany and Japan in the aftermath of World War II, the American military maintained a large number of troops in South Korea after the Korean War. The Americans not only aided in security but also undoubtedly tempered the Korean military's activism and especially its use of violence.

public goods and services relied on the government's ability to deliver impersonal benefits, implying that the regime had begun to satisfy aspects of the first doorstep condition, rule of law for members of the coalition. Indeed, in the face of the driving security need to suppress potential support for an insurgency, the regime extended aspects of these benefits to most citizens, including education, open access to economic organizations, and use of state institutions to support them.

The citizens under the authoritarian Park regime lacked political freedom, but it is not clear that democratic responsiveness in natural states offers a great advantage for pursuing economic growth or long-term, stable democracy.[12] The NWW framework emphasizes that natural states that hold elections contrast starkly with democracy in open-access orders. These natural-state democracies often fail to provide public goods and policy responsiveness, and to protect citizens' rights. Further, democratic natural states are often far more responsive to organized constituencies. For example, they frequently provide overvalued salaries that the state can ill afford to groups like labor, teachers, and government workers, while failing to implement standard public goods necessary to support growth. Natural-state programs nominally designed to provide justice, health care, and poverty relief frequently fail to do so.

Park's regime emphasized shared growth (Campos and Root 1996). To this end, the regime provided public goods complementary to markets rather than direct transfers or rents to citizens and organized interests. Infrastructure improvements, such as the 1960s programs that built roads to reach markets, helped transform rural South Korea. Before, subsistence farmers producing largely for themselves or for small local markets had very limited economic opportunities. The new infrastructure gave them access to larger regional and national markets, allowing for investment, specialization, and exchange, and producing richer

---

12. With the exception of states in Europe (such as Spain, Portugal, Greece, and Ireland, which rely on the guidance and incentives of the European Union), no state since 1960 in the developing world has gone from a natural state to an open-access order through simultaneous democratization and marketization. The successful states, such as South Korea and Taiwan, have begun marketization first and then moved on to political liberalization. China has taken the first path, though it remains to be seen whether it will also take the second.

farmers.[13] Education, combined with new economic opportunities, meant that their children had a wide range of employment options in business and the public sector. The openness in both public and private realms provided new opportunities, allowing talent to rise. Land reform carried out in the 1950s also granted many rural residents the ability to finance enterprises and become entrepreneurs. These policies resulted in an efficient agricultural sector that produced enough food that South Korea did not have to use scarce foreign-exchange resources on food. As a result of these changes, most citizens were able to share in the growing economy and take advantage of new opportunities. Authoritarianism remained the one problem, and as Korea grew richer, it became an increasing problem.

IMPLICATIONS

The complex set of incentives created by Park's economic and political policies reveals a mutually supporting system. All major players had incentives to play their role. The government pursued new policies of economic openness, especially in sectors it sought to encourage. It also opened access to the bureaucracy, transforming it from a more personal, cronyism-based system to one relying more on performance and impersonal criteria. Government management of critical aspects of the economy, such as finance and subsidies, fostered incentives for firms to produce for markets, especially export markets. Successful performers received high rewards and earned substantial profits (and their leaders received prestigious honors). The massive chaebol were one result. Firms that lagged behind fell by the wayside—or the government forced their owners to give up control. Central to implementing a wide range of economic policies, bureaucrats handed out benefits, subsidies, and tax refunds based on impersonal export-performance characteristics. The government's fiscal incentives strongly favored impersonal policies that promoted growth; acts of political favoritism risked budget deficits, adverse exchange-rate changes, and inflation. Bureaucratic corruption was thus limited, reducing its incidence. Although they lacked political

---

13. This process parallels the transformation of the English countryside from the late sixteenth century through the eighteenth. As London grew, it required more food and fuel, leading to greater markets within England and thus producing the richest peasants in Europe (see, e.g., Thirsk 1957).

rights, citizens received a series of public goods, access to jobs, rising incomes, and more broadly shared economic growth. Delivery of benefits proved sufficient to allow the regime to suppress the potential for a communist insurgency and support for the North. The military had strong incentives to cooperate with the regime, and thanks to successful incentives for economic growth, the regime was able to finance adequate national security.

Both the dominant coalition and the government had strong incentives to maintain this system. Financially, the system of export-led growth and international openness meant that paying subsidies to firms and industries that failed to become competitive on international markets harmed the balance of payments, the exchange rates, and budget deficits. Politically, the drive to provide security required a successful economy that generated sufficient support among the population, preventing a rise in support for communism and sympathy for the North. Significant deterioration of the system into crony capitalism based on privilege and insulated domestic markets would jeopardize the coalition and the regime's survival.

Park's program for "Modernization of the Fatherland" combined with the incentives to support economic reform. His approach weakened opposition to reform, since it could be branded as unpatriotic. Park created a support coalition based on producing both economic prosperity and political security from the communist threat. As Nam (1994, 3–4) concludes, "The communist security threat from the North . . . helped the government forge national cohesion and consensus in favor of economic development as well as prolong its authoritarian political power."

Most participants favored open access to jobs. Although each set of participants would have preferred a program of rents focused on them, given the presence of the new system, nearly all preferred to support and sustain open access to jobs, an outcome firms fostered through competition and the desire to produce efficiently. Having open access to the bureaucracy was essential for the meritocratic system. Citizens sought opportunities and careers, and therefore supported access in both the economic and the public sectors.

The paramount incentive, the need to create security in the face of a dangerous world, underpinned the entire system. This incentive drove the government and the dominant coalition to support a political economy that provided for economic growth, economic openness, a merito-cratic bureaucracy, and control over the military.

The Developmental State and the Doorstep Conditions

The developmental state was the first stage in the process of South Korea's transition from a natural state in 1960 to an open-access order, a process that is well along today, though not yet complete. South Korea made progress on achieving all three doorstep conditions during Park's regime.

Consider the first doorstep condition, rule of law for elites. South Korea began fulfilling this condition with respect to business elites. Privileges, in the form of export licenses, access to credit, and foreign exchange, began to become impersonal and were increasingly subject to well-established rules. Property rights and contract enforcement became more secure. Moreover, impersonality and perpetuity underpinned the drive for export-led growth. At the same time, widespread sharing of economic growth implied not only greater inclusiveness, reaching be-yond a narrow elite to include a large proportion of the citizens, but also the extension of impersonality to many aspects of the economy and public goods, including education and the meritocracy.

With respect to the second doorstep condition, perpetuity for the state and organizations more generally, the incentives discussed above show the means by which the state made various credible commitments to maintain policies and institutions that supported the developmental state. Failing to do this would have risked both security and economic growth, as well as the widespread support and legitimacy enjoyed by the regime.

The third doorstep condition, centralized elite political control of the military, is the least understood, both theoretically and as applied to South Korea. On the positive side, as evidence that Korea had achieved the third condition, military leaders did not serve directly in the govern-ment or the private sector, and the public sector directly controlled mili-tary resources. Moreover, maintaining security and long-term economic growth required impersonal rules, and ruled out the use of organized state violence to harass major portions of the economy (labor was an obvious exception, reflecting the regime's political repression). Nonethe-less the influence of the military was widespread, if indirect. The military's lack of independent political action in part reflects the fact that government policies promoted goals shared by the military, namely, security and development.

The incentives studied in the previous section underpinned South Korea's movement toward the doorstep conditions. The goals of security and economic growth led to greater inclusion and openness, the need to provide impersonal policies and rule of law for parts of the economy, and control over the military and other forms of violence. To succeed in a small country, these goals demanded greater inclusion: access for more people to public goods, education, and jobs in both the private sector and the bureaucracy, and an absence of arbitrary action by the government.

Dynamics: The Evolution of the South Korean Regime under Park

The discussion thus far has been largely static, providing an explanation for the policies that South Korea used to initiate its transition and the incentives that helped sustain that system. It has missed the important dynamics of the evolution of the system over time. As NWW emphasizes, initiating the transition has to be consistent with the logic of the natural state. In 1961 South Korea was a natural state, and as such, Korea's reforms following the military coup had to be consistent with that logic. The initial setup, including the beginnings of incentives for export-led growth, was a form of natural-state rent distribution. The new system emerged over the next fifteen years, rather than being fully formed from the start. In the beginning, the small number of players made the system highly personalistic. Gradually, however, impersonal elements of the doorstep conditions emerged as the regime regularized and systematized its approach to supporting enterprises and export-led growth.

In the 1960s, the regime and its support coalition were less focused and more personalistic, in part because substantial levels of American aid subsidized their survival. Following the United States' failure in Vietnam, however, President Richard Nixon not only removed subsidies for the South Korean military presence in Vietnam but also, initiating a policy now referred to as the Nixon doctrine, began a new policy of withdrawing American aid supporting South Korea. Park and his coalition became far more focused at this time on economic self-sufficiency and export-led growth as offering the principal hope for Korea's survival (see Haggard 1990; Kang 2002; Woo 1991, ch. 1). South Korea's economic performance improved in the 1970s. As Cumings (2005, 316) summarizes, "If this system worked intermittently in the 1960s, it worked like clockwork in the 1970s and became the essence of the 'Korean model.'" Moreover, long-term economic growth led to an economywide rise in income, fostering considerable and sustained support for the regime.

Another important dynamic aspect of Korea's transition concerns the chaebol. The system of financial incentives gave them strong incentives to be highly leveraged: highly subsidized credit, often with negative interest rates (that is, interest rates below the rate of inflation), made debt financing much more attractive. A consequence of this system was that it fostered politically induced economies of scale. Medium-size and large firms had incentives "to become large enough that the possibility of bankruptcy would pose a social threat." This incentive led to the chaebol's "excessive concern . . . with expansion rather than with the soundness of their financial base [which bred] instability for the Korean financial system" (Woo 1991, 13). Put differently, firms had incentives to be so excessively large that they would be too big to fail, thus forcing the government to bail them out during periods of financial shortfalls. Over time, Korea's many huge conglomerates were the result.

As we discuss in Chapter 6, the growth of the chaebol created a problem that would loom larger under democracy. Open access in the economy combined with biased subsidies to create a range of very powerful economic organizations that could mobilize to defend and further their own interests, but restrictions on open access in politics and social organizations led to the absence of a comparable set of organizations to mobilize citizens whose interests differed from those of the chaebol.

The South Korean system became more institutionalized over time. The number of players was small enough in the beginning that it could be run informally, retaining its personalistic aspects. But as it grew larger and more institutionalized, this helped foster the three doorstep conditions: rule of law for elites and beyond, a perpetual state and perpetual organizations, and consolidated control over the military.

Over time, the regime also expanded inclusion through shared growth. Although the government suppressed political rights and democratization, it did ensure that the benefits of growth were widely shared, and worker income grew at a fast pace. Moreover, and in contrast to most developing countries, South Korea focused on providing a wide range of public goods whose benefits were widely shared, including education, infrastructure, and open access to jobs in both the government and the growing economy.

Citizen demands on the government also evolved. The middle class grew, and workers, farmers, and professionals all grew richer. The rural infrastructure program succeeded in turning poor, self-sufficient peasants into market participants whose children became educated, and many left the country to take jobs in business or the bureaucracy. The power of urban labor grew significantly. As the middle class expanded, demand for democracy grew. Organized demonstrations advocating democracy were held in 1973 and 1980; both were repressed. By the mid-1980s, the middle class had become much larger and much more willing to participate in demonstrations, making repression more costly and potentially less effective.

Conclusions

We have examined the logic by which the Park regime initiated—but did not complete—the transition from a natural state to an open-access order. Under Park, the government focused largely on access in the economy and the bureaucracy; political access remained severely constrained. The Park regime suppressed democracy, including a range of political and social organizations that it believed might pose a threat. Open access in the economy created a range of powerful economic organizations that were able to mobilize to defend and further their business interests, but restrictions on access in politics and social organizations meant there was no comparable set of citizens' organizations to defend their interests.

Park and his coalition sought security for the country through economic independence and by widely sharing the benefits of economic growth. To this end, Park created a systematic pattern of incentives to support a new set of policies favoring greater economic openness. Each of the major components of state, economy, and society played a direct role in the transition. The regime set the broad policy goals of economic reform based on export-led growth, including new economic openness. The bureaucracy implemented those policies with a relatively low level of corruption, and bureaucrats faced explicit incentives to further the regime's larger policy goals. The bureaucracy did not allocate valuable public resources and rights—such as credit, import licenses, subsidies, refunds of import taxes, and foreign exchange—in a typical natural-state, personalistic fashion, bestowing privileges on valued political constituencies. Instead it allocated them based on impersonal criteria and competition among firms to build up exports. Firms that met ambitious export targets were far more likely to receive policy benefits. This process provided firms with incentives to invest and to become more efficient in producing products that would sell on the competitive international markets. Symbolizing the regime's new incentive system, the monthly planning and review meetings, presided over by Park, helped review both bureaucratic and firm performance, rewarding outstanding performers and punishing those who lagged (Rhee, Ross-Larson, and Pursell 1984, ch. 3).

Park and his coalition also included a large proportion of Korea's citizens as beneficiaries of its policies, in stark contrast to most natural states that concentrate privileges on the elites. The regime launched a new phase of shared growth, widely sharing the benefits of a growing market. To maintain its power in the face of the communist threat, the regime provided a range of benefits to citizens in the form of public goods, jobs, and access to markets. Continuing a tradition under Rhee, Park's regime emphasized education, which provided new opportunities for citizens. Rural roads constructed to reach markets provided infrastructure that transformed a great many formerly self-sufficient, subsistence farmers into market specialists. As labor markets grew tighter with industrialization, the general equilibrium effects raised farmers' incomes as well. Growing industrialization and bureaucracy also provided many new opportunities for the average citizens.

Finally, the government and members of the dominant coalition had strong incentives to maintain this system, preventing them from reneging, expropriation, or moving back to a natural state. Failure along any of those dimensions would have compromised the drive for economic independence and prosperity that offered the best path toward political security, away from insurgency and the North Korean threat.

All of these features of the South Korean situation differ from those typical of developing countries qua natural states. In contrast to Korea's open access with respect to the economy, most natural states are clientelistic, based on limited access and rent creation. Most natural states have highly protectionist economies, and if they export, it is typically primary products, such as coffee, copper, or sugar. Natural states generally cannot grant public goods and public benefits based on objective or impersonal characteristics, such as building roads where they are most needed, allocating poverty relief to the poor, or granting subsidies to the best performers rather than those with the right personal connections. Instead, these regimes tend to respond to citizen demands through expensive transfer policies that they can ill afford, such as paying above-competitive wages to government employees, teachers, and unions, or highly subsidized prices for public services, such as water and electricity. Few natural states are able to create competition for regime benefits in ways that foster economic efficiency and growth.

For example, South Korean policies contrast with those of the sub-Saharan natural states as described by Bates (1981). Few of those postindependence African regimes sought export-led growth. Instead, they acted as typical natural states, creating privilege and taking advantage of most citizens. In addition, the absence of a security threat allowed the African regimes to be far more extractive and to systematically take advantage of farmers (Bates 2001). As a result, a "continent of farmers" could not feed itself, and the states were forced to import food.

The logic of the Korean system is underscored by a point made by Hutchcroft (2011). In comparing Park with his contemporary Ferdinand Marcos, president of the Philippines from 1965 through 1986, Hutchcroft argues that if the two men had traded places, they could not have succeeded with the same strategies that they used at home: specifically, Park's strategy for export-led growth and the transition most likely would not have succeeded in the Philippines, and Marcos's more typical natural-state strategy would likely not have survived in South Korea. The latter seems apparent, as the natural state under the Rhee regime failed, despite huge American subsidies. Hutchcroft's point about Park is more interesting. We have argued that security concerns drove Park and his coalition to focus on economic self-sufficiency. This focus changed the trade-offs facing coalition members. Attempting to garner too many rents would have compromised not just the system but the regime's survival; restraint arose not simply because Park demanded it but because coalition members faced incentives to be restrained. Because these incentives were not present in the Philippines, Park's strategy would have been unlikely to succeed. Absent an immediate security threat, nothing would have stopped powerful coalition members from demanding more rents, and Park would likely have responded as Marcos did—or he would have risked being deposed.

Our approach to understanding Korean economic development shows that part of South Korea's economic success was in initiating the transition from natural state to open-access order, a process that is still under way. Achieving the doorstep conditions proved central to the transition. The Park regime extended the rule of law to a wide group of citizens, including land law and contracts. The regime gained the ability to allocate goods based on impersonal criteria, and thus to provide public goods. Maintaining control of the military and security from the threat of communism reduced the possibility of disorder. The regime also initiated elements of perpetuity, for example in land rights and with respect to corporations.

The transition toward open access was also central to the new regime. The new policies created considerable economic openness and competition among firms; competition proved essential to the success of the new export strategy, and this required open access. The regime also made the transition from personal exchange to impersonal exchange with respect to bestowing public goods, rights, and services. Moreover, almost all parties supported open access to jobs in both the public and private sector. The regime and firms both sought both aspects of open access as a means of drawing on a wider talent pool and increasing performance. Citizens supported this as a means of expanding their career opportunities, gaining jobs that, in natural states, too often go to insiders and those with the right personal connections.

Yet Korea's transition differs considerably from the historic Western European pattern described in NWW.[14] In those transitions, the doorstep conditions—rule of law for the elite, control of the military, and a perpetual state—emerged as a separate step antecedent to the transition proper. In Korea, lines between these steps were blurred. The need to provide security generated incentives for the regime to expand inclusion and sharing beyond that of the first movers (France, Great Britain, and the United States) when they went through the transition. Many later movers on the periphery of Western Europe (for example, Spain, Portugal, Greece, and Ireland) also seemed to differ from the historic pattern

---

14. See North, Wallis, and Weingast (2009), ch. 5 and 6.

in that aspects of the doorstep conditions were created simultaneously with extending rights and rule of law to the entire citizenry. But unlike South Korea, those states attempted a transition to open access in both the economy and politics at the same time.[15]

Another important difference between South Korea's transition path and those of the first movers in the eighteenth and nineteenth centuries is that Korea initially focused on economic openness while suppressing political openness, turning to the latter only two decades after economic openness began. England, for example, initiated the transition with political reform for elites following the Glorious Revolution of 1688, reforms that solidified the parliamentary representative system, placing new constraints on royal legislative powers and fiscal independence (North and Weingast 1989, Cox 2012).

Put together, the incentives facing South Korea supported initiation of the transition from a natural state to an open-access one, at least in the economic dimensions. Government policymakers transformed the system of allocating rights and subsidies from a natural-state, clientelistic basis to a competitive one reflecting major economic policy goals, such as exports. On the political side, the regime remained repressive during the early transition, suppressing political openness, for example, by placing limits on political voice, elections, rights of protest, and unions.

The result was a remarkable economic success, differentiating South Korea from all but a handful of other developing countries, mostly also in East Asia. By 1979, South Korea was well along the path to becoming an economic powerhouse and a rich society.

Nonetheless, problems loomed on the horizon. Although the chaebol did not dominate the economy, they were growing quickly in both size and influence. Pent-up demand among the citizenry for consumer goods and political rights remained unfulfilled. The idea of double balance suggests that, at Park's death, South Korea may have been in a short-term stable equilibrium, but it was not in a long-term equilibrium.

---

15. Moreover, as we discussed in Chapter 2, these states also received considerable aid from the European Union in the form of subsidies, access to vast markets, labor migration to jobs outside the country for many of the nations' poorest, security, and prescriptions for political institutions that constrained domestic political choices and forced a choice between full liberalization (open political and economic access) and failing to join Europe (see also Cox, North, and Weingast 2012).

CHAPTER 5

The Political Economy of the Democratic Transition

Despite its economic successes, Park Chung Hee's developmental state did not prove to be durable. Throughout the developmental-state period (1963–1987), the ruling party faced constant pressure for political reform from within and outside of Korea. Inside pressure arose through domestic opposition groups—such as opposition parties, dissidents, and student activists—which eventually became more politically significant. Outside pressure groups included international human rights groups and the U.S. government. Although the United States did not openly undermine the authoritarian government in power, it made it clear that it favored democracy in South Korea. Under the weight of mounting pressure, the authoritarian regime finally gave in to democratic demands in 1987, ushering in the period of democracy that lasts to the present day.

In this chapter we argue that the developmental state was structurally unstable because it remained unbalanced by maintaining economic openness without political openness. Indeed, some argue that this imbalance was an inherent feature or consequence of the Korean development model (Johnson 1989). Economic openness and political openness, however, exhibit complementarities. If greater progress is made in one dimension than in the other, the system is in disequilibrium and some corrective processes ensue.

As predicted by double balance, the economic openness of the developmental state had several consequences that kicked off the corrective process toward more political openness. First, economic openness produced substantial growth. Second, widespread sharing of the gains made Koreans better off. Third, the first two factors, in turn, combined to foster the growth of the middle class, the civil society, and a stronger opposition, resulting in demands for greater political openness. All three factors set the stage for dramatic negotiations in 1987 that produced democratization.

The transition to democracy that year was the second important turning point in the Korean political economy since the 1950s. By all accounts, the 1987 transition marked a structural change in the Korean economy. The average growth rates before and after 1987 are significantly different. A similar structural change can also be observed in time-series trends in wage levels, the size of the government, and social welfare spending (Kim and Mo 1999).

In explaining how democratization was negotiated in Korea, we first describe what happened in 1987, the year when the transition to democracy formally began. We follow that with a historical account of the political developments leading up to 1987; a historical perspective is necessary for understanding the timing and context of the political crisis in 1987 that led to the transition. Many competing explanations for the success or limitations of the Korean transition have been proposed over the years, and we group them into two categories: theories emphasizing political variables and those employing economic variables. To explain the character and process of Korea's democratic transition in 1987, we argue that accounts based on structural variables are insufficient to explain democratization. As an alternative, we propose an elite bargaining framework that identifies major actors who participated in negotiations over the rules of the transition and takes into account their preferences and bargaining power. We conclude by drawing on our larger theoretical perspective to offer an integrated account, with particular emphasis on unbalanced development produced during authoritarian rule.

The 1987 Transition to Democracy

The spring of 1987 marked a definitive period in Korean politics. With the end of President Chun Doo Hwan's presidential term approaching in February 1988, the Korean nation faced a critical juncture in shaping the direction of the democratization process. President Chun had pledged to leave office voluntarily when his term expired; this would represent the first peaceful transfer of presidential power in forty years of modern constitutional rule in Korea. Much less clear, however, were the terms of his departure. The opposition demanded a constitutional revision to restore direct presidential elections, which Park had suspended in the Yushin constitution of 1973.[1]

Insufficient support for the status quo system of indirect election of the president meant that it was unlikely to continue. Realizing that some sort of accommodation was necessary, President Chun agreed to open a constitutional debate in 1986. In the negotiations that followed, the two opposing positions were held by the ruling Democratic Justice Party (DJP), which insisted on the adoption of a parliamentary system, and the opposition New Korea Democracy Party (NKDP), led by Kim Dae Jung and Kim Young Sam and supported by prodemocracy activist groups, which demanded continuation of the presidential system but with a directly elected president.

When the negotiations bogged down, President Chun announced on 13 April 1987 that a negotiated settlement was not possible and that he would start the process of turning over power to his hand-picked successor, Roh Tae Woo. The announcement prompted a surprisingly large and negative reaction. Prodemocracy groups rose up en masse, and Korea experienced the biggest civil uprisings and demonstrations in its history in May and June 1987. When Chun realized that he had overplayed his cards, he reopened negotiations with the opposition parties over the new constitution. These negotiations resulted in the famous June 29 Declaration, in which the Chun government acceded to a constitutional amendment for the direct election of the president.[2]

The National Assembly quickly passed a new constitution in August 1987, paving the way for the first presidential election under the new

---

1. The key feature of the Yushin constitution (1972–1980) was the indirect election of the president. The president was indirectly elected, for an unlimited number of six-year terms, by the National Conference for Unification (NCU), a body of between 2,000 and 5,000 delegates whom voters elected for a six-year term. See Im (1987) for an account of the rise of the Yushin system.

2. Other opposition demands accepted by the authoritarian regime were political amnesty and a restoration of civil rights for dissident leader Kim Dae Jung, protection of human rights and the freedom of the press, and promotion of local autonomy and self-governance.

democracy, to be held in December 1987. To the surprise of most observers, Roh Tae Woo, the DJP candidate, won that historic election, taking advantage of the divided opposition. The two principal opposition leaders, Kim Dae Jung and Kim Young Sam, could not merge their tickets and ended up running independently, thus splitting the opposition votes. The first National Assembly election under the new constitution followed in April 1988, and this time the three opposition parties did better, winning enough votes to deny the ruling party a parliamentary majority and creating the first of many divided governments to come under democracy.

Since 1987 Korea has held five presidential elections without a constitutional crisis. In two of those elections, 1997 and 2007, an opposition candidate won the presidency, showing that the transition to democracy that began in 1987 has been smooth and durable.[3]

This successful democratic transition naturally begs the question, Why was it successful? How do we account for the timing and stability of Korea's democratic transition? Can the theory of double balance help explain it?

The Prelude to the 1987 Transition

The seeds of democracy were sown long before 1987 and as far back as at the very beginning of the Chun government. When Chun Doo Hwan became president in September 1980, he made two constitutional choices to boost the legitimacy of his government. First, whereas the Yushin constitution allowed an unlimited number of terms, Chun restricted the presidency to one term and vowed that he would retire after one term in February 1988. Second, whereas the Yushin system allowed the president to appoint one-third of the National Assembly, Chun abolished appointed seats, making all National Assembly members elected. Chun had two reasons for choosing a system more liberal than the Yushin system: his desire to differentiate himself from the unpopular rule of Park Chung Hee, and his attempt to improve the legitimacy of his government.[4]

---

3. Kim Dae Jung won the presidency in 1997 as the candidate of the opposition New Millennium Democratic Party, and Lee Myung Bak won the 2007 election as the candidate of the opposition Grand National Party.

4. These two features of the Chun Doo Hwan regime significantly influenced the subsequent dynamics between the ruling and opposition parties. The promise of the

Chun lacked legitimacy because he had seized power by force, rising to power through two coups, the first in December 1979, when he took over the military, and the second in May 1980, when he took control of the government. When President Park Chung Hee was assassinated in October 1979, Chun Doo Hwan, as chief of the Defense Security Command, headed the investigations of the Park assassination. That role gave him extraordinary power within the military and the government, allowing him, for example, to investigate almost every government official for a possible role in the assassination plot. In December 1979, General Chun arrested the army chief of staff, Chung Sŭng Hwa, on sedition charges; General Chung was implicated because he dined with the assassination leader on the evening that the assassination took place. Chun next purged most senior officers in the military and placed his supporters in top positions. Once Chun took control of the military, he became the most powerful man in Korea.

The power struggle within the military was not well understood by the public at that time. Politicians and political parties were instead busy preparing themselves for what they thought was coming soon: the restoration of democracy after the lifting of martial law. But as the military became more assertive and oppressive, the people began to realize that the military had little interest in democracy. Sensing that public pressure was necessary to discourage military leaders, prodemocracy groups and students organized a series of street demonstrations for democracy and against oppressive measures introduced by the military. Prodemocracy protests in the city of Kwangju became a full-scale riot in May 1980, which the military put down by brute force. Citing widespread demonstrations and violence, the military suspended constitutional rule altogether and began to rule the country through a new junta-like military-civilian committee on 31 May 1980. In August 1980, interim president Choi Kyu Ha was forced to resign and was succeeded by Chun Doo Hwan.

The manner in which Chun rose to power and attempted to strengthen his legitimacy had a significant impact on subsequent political developments.

---

single-term presidency set the broad timetable for political succession, and the elimination of appointed legislative seats increased electoral competition among political parties. Despite these features, the basic nature of the Chun regime was authoritarian, an extension of the Yushin system.

First, his suppression of the Kwangju uprising and the prodemocracy movement led to the radicalization of prodemocracy groups, especially the student activists. The prodemocracy movement against the Park government, which was led by student, church, and dissident groups, had been relatively moderate in that it did not reject liberal democracy or a market economy. The activists focused their demands on free and open elections and improved human rights.

After 1980, however, student activists began to embrace more radical ideologies, such as Marxism and even North Korea's *juche* ideology. At the same time, they became anti-American because they saw the United States as the key patron of the authoritarian Chun government. Student activists were angry that the leaders of American forces in South Korea, who had operational control over the Korean military, did not try to stop the Chun military from using force to crack down on protesters in Kwangju. With the radicalization of the prodemocracy movement, not a day went by on university campuses without prodemocracy demonstrations. At the same time, significant underground organizations made up of students, dissidents, farmers, and workers penetrated Korean society, undermining the grassroots foundation of authoritarian rule.

Second, party politics became another source of political instability as opposition parties became more influential under a more liberal parliamentary electoral system. In the first election under the Chun government, held in March 1981, the ruling Democratic Justice Party won only 35 percent of the popular vote, although a proportional-representation scheme allowed it to control 55 percent of the National Assembly seats. The electoral fortunes of the ruling party diminished over the next four years. In the February 1985 National Assembly election, the ruling party's position diminished while the new opposition party, the NKDP, vaulted to the position of the largest opposition party.

In the new political environment, the DJP could no longer muster a two-thirds majority for the passage of important legislation or constitutional amendments. Unlike the pre-1985 opposition parties, the NKDP was uncompromising in its commitment to restoring democracy. In fact the party began a nationwide campaign in 1986 for a constitutional revision and forced the Chun government to agree with the opposition demand to set up a special parliamentary committee to draft a constitutional amendment bill. The opposition's veto over policy through its influence in the National Assembly forced President Chun to negotiate.

Competitive party politics therefore played an important role in the movement toward democracy in the mid- to late 1980s.

The third factor in the growing pressure for democratization was Chun's choice of the single-term presidency. As Chun was set to retire in February 1988, succession politics began and gradually intensified within the ruling bloc after the 1985 parliamentary election. Prodemocracy activists kept pressuring President Chun to honor his promise to retire after one term.

These three factors coalesced in the summer of 1987. The ending of Chun's single-term presidency explains the timing of the crisis. NKDP's political strength after the 1985 elections provided the setting and context for the political negotiations; all prodemocracy groups accepted the National Assembly as the negotiation arena and the direct election of the president as their central objective. Prodemocracy groups mobilized ordinary citizens as well as activists to protest in the streets against the Chun government.

Explaining the Politics of Korean Democratization: An Elite Bargaining View

The historical narrative identifies the key trigger points in the history of Korean democratization, but it does not explain the factors contributing to the success of Korean democratization. For this, we begin by examining previous theoretical studies.

The transition to democracy in South Korea has been the subject of extensive research in the political science literature.[5] Most works tend to focus on pressures for democracy exerted by one group or another. One group of scholars, for example, emphasizes the strength of the civil society: that is, strong student, labor, and church groups that kept the democracy movement alive under harsh authoritarian rule (Kim 2000, Lee 1993). For others, political parties on both sides of the transition game that negotiated the terms of transition among them were the main forces for democratization (Shin 1995). Still others highlight the role of external factors, especially the influence of the United States (Fowler 1999, Gleysteen 1999).

---

5. See Kihl (2005) for an overview of the literature on Korean democratization.

Even though the structural variables identified by these scholars shaped the parameters of negotiation tactics and outcomes, they are limited in explaining the actual decisions of actors. As the narrative in the previous section demonstrates, the transition to democracy was the culmination of a series of important decisions made by both the authoritarian regime and the prodemocracy groups. The key question is why the authoritarian regime agreed to democratize. The decisions made by both the regime and prodemocracy groups were shaped by their relative bargaining power as well as their democratization strategy.

The large body of literature on the question of elite bargaining over democratization offers a parsimonious framework for analyzing the dynamics of negotiations between the authoritarian regime and the prodemocracy groups (Higley and Gunther 1992; Karl 1990; Linz 1978; O'Donnell, Schmitter, and Whitehead 1986; Przeworski 1991; Rustow 1970; Weingast 1997). Unfortunately, elite bargaining theory has received little attention in the literature on the Korean case.

To fill this gap in the literature, we offer an analysis of the 1987 negotiations based on an institutional, elite-focused, and incentive-based framework. The first step in understanding the negotiations is to identify the range of possible strategies and outcomes that existed at the time of the democratic opening, of which the successful and peaceful transition represents one possible outcome. In June of 1987, the peaceful transition to democracy was not at all certain.

In terms of the degree of democratization, we can place in order the potential outcomes of the negotiations from the least democratic, a coup, to the most democratic, the purging of authoritarian leaders:

- **Coup.** To prevent political and social chaos, military hard-liners could stage a coup to purge older military leaders, assert their own political power, and prevent democratization. If the coup succeeded, all of the national institutions would be under military control, similar to the situation on 16 May 1961.
- **Yushin-like constitution with martial law.** Chun could take a hard stance against his opponents and declare martial law to return to a Yushin regime like Park Chung Hee's.
- **Status quo.** Roh, as the ruling DJP candidate, could run for president under the current electoral system.

- **Parliamentary-style government.** The ruling party and the opposition parties could agree to a parliamentary system instead
  of a presidential system with a directly elected president. (The
  opposition, which did not want to share power with the ruling
  party after the democratic transition, supported a presidential
  system. The ruling party, which wanted to retain some power,
  favored a parliamentary system.)
- **Direct election of the president.** The ruling party could accede
  to opposition demands for the direct election of the president.
  The ruling party would receive some benefits from this conces-
  sion, such as gaining national and international legitimacy and
  credit for supporting democracy; concomitantly, this option also
  meant that the ruling party risked losing power.
- **Constitutional convention.** All parties could agree to establish
  a constitutional convention. Under this arrangement, all parties
  would give up their existing positions, giving great advantages to
  popular prodemocracy groups.
- **Purge authoritarian leaders.** Prodemocracy groups could attempt to drive authoritarian leaders out of office, either by force
  or through public pressure. If successful, the transition would be
  a complete break with the authoritarian establishment.

In a stunning reversal of policy, Roh Tae Woo, Chun's hand-picked
successor, announced on 29 June 1987 that the ruling party would agree
to key opposition demands, most notably the direct election of the
president. Roh's announcement ended the conflict over the terms of the
transition.

To understand the outcome of June 1987, we analyze President Chun
Doo Hwan's decision to democratize as a bargaining problem between
the authoritarian and the prodemocracy groups. To the extent that the
outcome was a result of the distribution of bargaining power, it reflected
the weakness of the ruling party's position in 1987 relative to that in
1980. At least three factors contributed to the weak position of the ruling
party. First, the ruling party was divided between the hard-liners and
the soft-liners. Second, the military option was no longer available to the
hard-liners. Third, unlike in 1980, the crisis in 1987 unfolded in what
Haggard and Kaufman (1995) call "economically good times," increasing

the electoral prospects of the ruling party in post-transition democratic elections.

Led by incumbent president Chun Doo Hwan, the hard-liners were willing to consider a parliamentary system, which would provide a legal channel for Chun to remain in power longer than his promised seven-year term. If the DJP maintained its majority status in this type of system, it would be possible for Chun to become the symbolic president and Roh to become the prime minister. This expectation was predicated on the two-member electoral system, which had historically allowed Chun's party to maintain a majority in the National Assembly (Brady and Mo 1992). But Chun was a hard-liner in the sense that, if he could have had his way, he would have preferred the status quo or even a reversion to the Yushin-type authoritarian system. Moreover, Chun was willing to use force if the opposition parties kept pressuring him through demonstrations. The hard-liners in the National Assembly, most of whom had military backgrounds, supported President Chun.

The soft-liners in the ruling party were more favorable to negotiating a transition with the opposition parties. They believed that the ruling party could negotiate a system under which they would retain power, including the two-member electoral districts. Moreover, the soft-liners held a less negative view on the direct election of the president than the hard-liners. Some soft-liners believed that the ruling party had a chance to win a plurality in a direct election if the opposition was divided.

In between the soft-liners and the hard-liners were the moderates, whose preferred position was closer to that of the hard-liners, but who were unwilling to consider using force to impose their preference. Roh Tae Woo was a typical moderate. As the DJP's hand-picked candidate for the presidency, he was more likely to gain the position through the traditional method of indirect election than through direct election. A direct election would put him at greater risk of losing power to one of the popular opposition candidates. In addition, he preferred to rule with the concentrated powers held by Chun. But he was opposed to martial law because of the possible negative effects on his image; he did not want to be perceived as an illegitimately elected president.

The hard-liners did not have a credible military option in 1987. Many military and police leaders were also reluctant to use force. Even though the military generally took a hard-line position, top generals did not want to see another incident like in Kwangju, where many civilians died in protests put down by the military. The police were also in a delicate position because of the intense scrutiny and criticism following the "accidental" killing of a student activist, Park Jong Chul, and their behavior in oppressing the demonstrators.[6] So this group likely favored a more democratic system, such as direct election. As the leader of the police, Ko Kun, a moderate career bureaucrat, added to the police force's reluctance to join the violent suppression of democratic demands.

The third factor that tipped the power balance in favor of the softliners within the ruling bloc was the economic performance of the authoritarian regime. After a brief recession in 1980, the Korean economy recovered its strong growth under Chun Doo Hwan. In 1986 and 1987, GDP growth reached 11 percent, making the three-year transition period of 1986 to 1988 the biggest boom years in modern Korean history. Citing this performance, the soft-liners could argue that the ruling party had a chance to maintain power even under democracy.

Overall, the bargaining conditions for the prodemocracy group were much more favorable in 1987 than in 1980. The resolve of the authoritarian regime to hold on to its authoritarian system was much weaker in 1987. The prodemocracy groups themselves became stronger, owing to increasing middle-class support for democracy and organizational skills that they had acquired in their struggles against the ruling regime in the 1980s. Nonetheless, the prodemocracy opposition did not have overwhelming advantages, partly because it was divided. The moderates were the established political parties led by the three Kims, Kim Dae Jung, Kim Young Sam, and Kim Jong Pil. Each Kim sought to win the direct election for the presidency; each also thought he had the best chance to win the direct election. Other issues, such as strengthening human rights and labor rights, were less important to the three Kims. Since the three Kims competed with each other as well as against the ruling party, a danger existed that they would split the opposition. In 1980, their divisiveness contributed to the return of the military rule.

The prodemocratic moderates also included the middle class and the United States. Economic development in the 1960s and '70s produced a large middle class in Korea whose interest in political freedom grew over

---

6. Park Jong Chul, who was a student activist at Seoul National University, died of torture in January 1987 during a police interrogation. His death became a rallying point for subsequent student demonstrations.

time. In 1987, a large number of middle-class citizens began to join prodemocracy demonstrations to show support for democracy, making the 1987 demonstrations more powerful than those in 1980. This group was also angered by the hard-handed tactics used against the demonstrators and prodemocracy activists, such as the tear gas employed so virulently by the police. But the middle class was moderate in the sense that it did not favor drastic change that would threaten its economic gains.

In the mid- to late 1980s, the United States held a similar position; while the United States supported the transition to democracy, it certainly did not want to threaten Korea's domestic stability. In the days before Roh's June 29 Declaration, President Ronald Reagan sent the U.S. assistant secretary of state to South Korea, where he met with all the key political figures. The assistant secretary's unequivocal public statements against military intervention and favoring political reform, together with his willingness to meet with opposition leaders, signaled to Chun and Roh that the United States was going to be less tolerant of strong-arm political interference by the South Korean army than it was in 1979 and 1980. Chun was sensitive to the U.S. position, especially after watching the Reagan administration stand aside as the Marcos regime collapsed in the Philippines.[7]

The prodemocracy side also had the radicals—that is, those who opposed compromise with the ruling party and favored complete or maximal democratization. The radicals were dissident groups, including student, labor, and religious groups, that had fought the authoritarian government for twenty years. These dissident groups had became radicalized during the 1980s; as noted, they had begun to support a socialist revolution and the North Korean regime, especially as the government suppression of the dissent movement became stronger. The turning point in their approach was the Kwangju uprising.

For two reasons, the divisions on the prodemocracy side were less damaging to the dissidents' cause than those on the government side hurt its cause. First, the prodemocracy groups were united behind the central demand for the direct election of the president. Democracy to

---

7. The difference in the American response to the Korean political crisis in 1987 and in 1980 is noteworthy. While the United States took a passive approach in 1980 and tried not to confront military leaders, it was more assertive and proactive in 1987 in promoting a smooth transition to democracy.

them was unequivocal and meant the direct election of the president. The different prodemocracy groups were therefore able to set aside many of their differences to fight for this common goal. Second, among the political leaders, Kim Dae Jung was the only one who commanded respect and loyalty from the dissident groups. Because the dissident groups had someone in the party system that they could trust, they were willing to moderate their demands and did not mobilize to undermine the transition process.

Two key sets of interest groups also had moderate preferences. Government bureaucrats favored a negotiated settlement because many of them had been educated to support democracy, at least in principle, and because they resented the dominance of the military in Chun's government. But they would also lose influence under democracy, owing to the deregulation and liberalization it entails. Bureaucrats therefore did not go so far as to support the drastic change favored by the opposition parties.

Understanding both the benefits and costs of democratization, the media and economic elites had similar interests. On the one hand, they would lose their privileged position under the authoritarian system, in which the mainstream media elites enjoyed certain privileges, such as restrictions on competition and access to political leaders. Business had also been able to use its position to win subsidies and privileges from the authoritarian government. On the other hand, both media and business would have greater freedom to pursue their interests under democracy. The freedom of the press was important to a majority of journalists. And the chaebol did not want the government to regulate their businesses and did not want to give money to the Blue House, disguised as political contributions.

To conclude, divisions in the ruling party weakened its bargaining position. For this reason, and because it lacked the ability to control the process through force, it could not preserve the status quo. Also an important factor in this outcome was the unity of the opposition parties, dissidents, and the middle class against authoritarian rule, under the common objective of winning the direct election of the president.[8]

---

8. Other factors were also relevant. The authoritarian government could neither afford bad international press nor risk domestic instability one year before the 1988 Olympics, which were to be held in Seoul. President Chun also cared about his historical

Economic Dimensions of the Korean Transition

Economic variables afford another set of insights into Korean democratization. At least four theories link economic conditions to the incidence and stability of democracy.

The first involves arguments based on classic modernization theory. Simply put, modernization theory postulates a correlation between economic growth and democracy (Lipset 1959). One direction of causality between the two is that economic growth promotes democracy. Between 1962 and 1987 the Korean economy grew at an average rate of 9.0 percent a year. As a result of this economic growth, by 1987 South Korea had become a major industrialized economy and an upper-middle-income country, with a per capita annual income of US$3,218. Modernization theory suggests that democratization came about in Korea at a point when the Korean economy reached a relatively high level of development.

Modernization theory also highlights the role of the middle class in promoting democracy. Economic development promotes the emergence of a middle class which, in turn, provides the foundation and chief cause of political democracy (Lipset 1959). With its basic economic needs satisfied by the initial successes of economic development, the middle class begins to press for more individual rights as well as for a political structure that can bring more economic benefits to them, including a wider range of public goods.

As the Korean economy grew rapidly in the two-decade period following 1963, the relative size of the South Korean middle class also grew. The proportion of professional, managerial, and clerical workers (not including sales employees) increased from 6.7 percent in 1963 to 16.6 percent in 1982 (Koo 1991). At the same time, economic growth also shifted the composition of the Korean labor force; 79 percent of the Korean workforce was engaged in the primary sector in 1961, but that percentage fell to 30 percent by 1988, with 70 percent working in the secondary and tertiary sectors (Johnson 1989).

---

legacy. With the coming end of his official term, Chun had a personal interest in how he would be perceived as ex-president. Lastly, some ruling members were confident about their chances under democracy; they were able to persuade Chun and Roh that they could take advantage of the opposition divisions that would be inevitable if the direct election were held.

Korean middle-class political orientations coincided with the suppositions of modernization theory. Koo (1991) presents data from a survey taken in the mid-1980s that showed the Korean middle class to be "extremely dissatisfied with the authoritarian political system and with the way in which the benefits of economic growth had been distributed, especially with the ways in which the rich have accumulated their wealth" (490). The middle class supported the labor movement and student activism and was sympathetic to the plights of farmers and the urban poor.

Middle-class support for democracy was more than moral support. Members of this group turned to actions in support of democracy at critical junctures. In June 1987, for example, a large number of white-collar workers joined students and prodemocracy activists on the streets, demanding the constitutional revision for a direct presidential system. Some say that the participation of the middle class in street protests in June 1987 marked a turning point in the bargaining game between the authoritarian regime and the prodemocracy movement; the government's resolve to resist the popular pressure for democracy began to falter when it realized that a violent crackdown on the demonstrators might result in another Kwangju-like tragedy—a risk it would not take.

Some scholars attribute the smoothness and stability of the Korean transition to the period of high economic growth. Haggard and Kaufman (1995) argue that a transition that begins during a period of high economic growth is more likely to be smooth and stable. During Korea's transition to democracy in 1986 and 1987, economic growth was especially high; the economy grew at 12.6 and 12.3 percent in 1986 and 1987, respectively. Johnson (1989) speculates that the economic boom at the time of the political crisis may have been a factor in the government's decision to accept democracy, because economically it could afford to experiment with it.[9]

---

9. In a related argument, comparative political scientists have long argued that "democracies may be established independently of economic development but may be more likely to survive in developed countries" than in developing countries (Przeworski and Limongi 1997). In fact, Przeworski and Limongi note that no democracy has failed in a country with a per capita income higher than approximately US$6,000 (1985 purchasing power parity). One reason for democratic stability in developed countries, they argue, is that wealth moderates the intensity of distributional conflicts so that distributional losers do not use violence to settle scores (Lipset 1959). South Korea reached a per

Others argue that the causality between economic development and democracy runs the other way. Many see democracy emerging as an economic imperative (Barro 1998). Advanced economic growth calls for extensive economic liberalization, public goods, and deregulation and the security of property rights, which are incompatible with authoritarian rule. Moreover, the idea of double balance asserts that economic growth cannot be sustained in the long run without relaxing political restrictions (see NWW).[10] Consistent with this argument, from the very beginning of his government Chun emphasized deregulation and liberalization as cornerstones of his economic policy. These reforms responded to the perceived policy failures of the 1970s (Haggard and Moon 1990). In the 1970s, the Park government launched the famed Heavy and Chemical Industry Drive in an effort to expand those industries. From 1977 to 1979, the heavy and chemical industries received 80 percent of the total investment in manufacturing. President Park took on this ambitious plan to advance and upgrade Korea's industrial structure, which labor-intensive manufacturing industries dominated at that time, and to develop a defense industry, which he felt was necessary to counter the deteriorating security environment on the Korean Peninsula following the collapse of South Vietnam in 1974.

These policies did not succeed, producing two main economic problems—inflationary pressure and moral hazard in the banking and corporate sectors. Inflation following the rapid expansion of credit for business investment was no surprise, rising to 26 percent in 1979, notably above the average rate of inflation of 16 percent between 1962 and 1978. With production over capacity and inflation high, the overall economic performance also took a dive. Economic growth rates, which had averaged close to 10 percent between 1962 and 1978, fell to just over 2 percent between 1979 and 1981, with 1979 registering a negative growth rate of minus 5 percent. Even exports fell to 7.5 percent between 1979 and

---

capita income of US$6,000 in 1990, suggesting that Korean democracy has reached an important threshold of democratic stability.

10. This argument differs from modernization theory. Modernization theory describes a situation in which authoritarian leaders reluctantly accept democracy because they see no other way to meet the demands of the middle class for political freedom or to control a society that has become too complex to control. Here, in contrast, democracy is viewed not as a compromise but as an engine for sustainable growth.

1982; the average rate of export growth between 1962 and 1978 had been 27 percent.

Moral hazard in the Korean economy also increased during this period, a departure from the early Park regime. The Park government's attempts to build a heavy and chemical industry sector in a short time involved two choices that led to the growing concentration of economic power in the hands of chaebol. First, the government limited the number of companies that could enter each heavy and chemical industry to a small number of chaebol, effectively sanctioning their monopoly positions. Second, the chosen companies benefited from a number of government incentives, such as heavily subsidized credit, protection from foreign competitors, fiscal incentives, and guaranteed sales. In 1973, the top fifty chaebol accounted for 32 percent of GDP. But by 1980, the top fifty chaebol dominated the economy, accounting for 49 percent of GDP. Given their size and importance in the economy, many chaebol had in practice become too big to fail. This change, in turn, had long-term political consequences, making it difficult to restructure overcapacity industries and forcing the government to provide even more credit to keep them afloat.

President Park himself recognized the excesses of his policy and directed the Economic Planning Board (EPB) to take corrective measures in early 1979. Haggard and Moon (1990) describe the outline of the new strategy that the EPB formulated as follows:

- an emphasis on comparative advantage rather than industrial targeting and import substitution;
- a transition to an economy led by the private sector;
- a general reduction of state intervention and wider play for market forces; and
- an emphasis on social development.

President Park's assassination on 26 October 1979 prevented him from implementing the new policies. President Chun faithfully and successfully carried out Park's new strategy. Inflation fell to 3.6 percent between 1982 and 1987, thanks to austerity measures as well as favorable international conditions—particularly, lower oil prices and interest rates. Structural reforms were not as successful, as the Chun government experienced difficulty reforming the entrenched chaebol and banks.

The chaebol, in particular, occupied a powerful position in the economy, and the government vacillated on chaebol reforms for fear that an economic slowdown might result from them.

The impact of President Chun's new economic strategy on democratization, however, should not be overemphasized. To date, no study has shown that either President Chun or any of his advisors seriously considered democratization out of economic necessity. His policies of economic liberalization therefore had the unintended effect of more power decentralization and diffusion in government, thus helping his opponents.

The four economic theories of democratization identify the economic conditions favorable to a democratic transition: a large middle class, a high level of economic development, a period of rapid economic growth, an elite consensus on the need for a more market-based economy, and an active labor movement. But economic theories of democratization face the same limitations as political theories. Both groups of theories offer structural conditions favorable to successful democratization, yet neither predicts and explains when and how democratization takes place or, indeed, whether it will take place at all. Another limitation is the lack of attention to the interaction between economic and political variables.

Synthesis: Double Balance in South Korea's Democratization

Each of the theories described in this chapter contains an insight into democratization, but none provides a sufficient explanation. Aspects of modernization and the civil society, with the growth of opposition groups under the authoritarian regime, were undoubtedly important. Reflecting its desire to counter the communist threat, the authoritarian regime's incremental economic openness also fostered significant—though incomplete—growth of a civil society. Institutions and party politics were also central, notably National Assembly elections that allowed the newly created opposition party to confront the regime with a strong and independent parliamentary opposition. The United States, always an important external actor for South Korea, also helped foster democratization through its explicit support for democratization and its unwillingness to support another military takeover in 1986 and 1987. And it was propitious that democratization took place during a strong period of economic growth, which Haggard and Kaufman (1995) associate with the likelihood of success; this idea is related to Przeworski and colleagues' (2000) finding that richer countries are more likely to remain democracies once established.

Our framework developed in Chapter 2 adds important aspects to the explanation of the transition, helping to explain how the different pieces fit together. First, in contrast to most natural states that democratize, South Korea began the transition from a limited- to an open-access order prior to democratization. Moving beyond most natural states, Korea attained most of the doorstep conditions by the mid-1980s. Early on, the Park regime had achieved a degree of rule of law for the economic elite, including property rights, contract rights, and various aspects of openness of opportunity (e.g., access to jobs in both the private and public sectors for their children; access to SMEs). Moreover, to counter the communist threat the regime expanded several dimensions of openness well beyond the elite, including education, economic opportunities, and various public goods. Again in contrast to most natural states, Korea widely shared the gains from its rapid and sustained economic growth, including a wide range of new economic opportunities, education, and new openness of jobs in both the private sector and the public sector. Both sectors relied on strong elements of meritocracy rather than personal relations, clientelistic connections, and privileges. Shared growth also helped foster the growth of the civil society. Both the Park and Chun regimes had achieved a degree of control over the military. Finally, the regime had created a degree of perpetuity for both state and economic organizations. As argued in Chapter 4, the state created various forms of credible commitments in the face of the communist threat. The authoritarian regime under Park successfully created aspects of the doorstep conditions.

Nonetheless, some backsliding toward natural-state institutions occurred at the end of Park's regime and during Chun's. The chaebol became more concentrated, gaining political power and privileges, especially associated with the late 1970s push toward heavy and chemical industries. At the same time, Chun imposed greater political repression.

Early economic openness, along with the growth from the mid-1960s through the mid-1980s, fostered new groups and new pressures for continued reform and for public goods and human rights. Other groups favoring greater political openness included church groups, the media, and much of the government bureaucracy, which resented the military presence. Widespread sharing of economic success led to increased demands for political openness, especially among the middle class. By the mid-1980s, strong opposition to military and authoritarian rule had arisen. The many different opposition groups united around the demand for presidential elections; this unity contrasted with the disunited regime, which was divided between hard-liners and soft-liners.[11]

Institutions also proved central to the democratic transition: reflecting structural trends, such as the growth of the opposition, the 1985 elections resulted in a substantial legislative voting bloc for the opposition, giving rise to competitive party politics. Divided government through power in the National Assembly gave the opposition strong bargaining leverage with the regime. On the eve of democratization, the opposition used the threat of greater dissent, protests, and civil unrest, raising the price for the regime for sticking with the status quo.

In combination, these factors forced the Chun regime to move toward democracy over the next two years. President Chun began by opening constitutional negotiations, but he broke off those negotiations when he saw that he could not win. This strategy backfired, unleashing unprecedented unrest and forcing Chun to give the opposition its main goal of an elected presidency.

All the while, in the background, the security threat lingered. The United States backed Chun's coup in 1980, but in 1987 it made clear that it would not tolerate another coup. It also publicly encouraged the opposition. Members of Korea's authoritarian regime watched as the United States allowed President Ferdinand Marcos's authoritarian regime in the Philippines to collapse.

Within this mix of institutions, structural forces, and possible outcomes, contending elites calculated their interests and strategies. The regime's inability to suppress the opposition, the lack of support from the United States for the military option, and party competition all combined to grant the opposition sufficient leverage to force the incumbents to compromise and give in to the opposition's most salient demand—

---

11. The opposition's unity on presidential elections helped create a constitutional focal point around which it could coordinate, allowing the opposition groups to act in unison and to protect the institutions established to create the elected presidency (see Mittal and Weingast 2013, Weingast 1997).

direct elections for the presidency. The result was a huge step toward new democratization, creating political openness very quickly.

This explanation reflects the idea of double balance. The authoritarian regime remained unbalanced: it maintained economic openness without political openness. And the popular pressure for greater political openness is consistent with the idea of double balance. As predicted by double balance, economic openness had several consequences that kicked off the corrective process toward more political openness. First, along with achieving the doorstep conditions, economic openness produced substantial growth. Second, widespread sharing of the gains, in part reflecting the security threat, meant that many Koreans shared in the growth. Third, this shared growth, in turn, fostered the growth of the middle class, the civil society, and a stronger opposition, resulting in demands for greater political openness. All three factors combined with the succession politics surrounding Chun's replacement in 1988 to yield democratization.

CHAPTER 6

Democratic Economic Management in Pre-crisis Korea: Democracy with Limited Pluralism, 1987–1997

Democratization in 1987 was a response to the lack of double balance under the authoritarian regime, and it did correct it by increasing the openness of the political system. Whether the new democratic system that emerged after 1987 reached a balance is another question. We argue that the democratic system suffered from another type of imbalance, one in which, paradoxically, the newly opened political system reversed some of the progress in economic openness.

The previous regime combined considerable economic openness with policies that fostered the formation and growth of powerful business organizations—the chaebol. Political suppression, meanwhile, prevented the parallel growth of political and social organizations. Democracy immediately opened the regime to pressures from the mass public, but the civil society's stunted growth meant that it had no organized means to counter the chaebol or to lead political officials to attend to interests other than the chaebol.

At the same time, the demands of political competition in mass electorates—campaigning, in particular—raised the importance of money in politics. As elected officials came to depend on large firms for funds to finance their campaigns, they lost considerable leverage over big business. The authoritarian regime had imposed considerable discipline on large businesses, especially under Park, forcing poor performers to restructure and keeping moral hazard in check. After democratization, the dependence of officials on campaign funds limited their ability to enforce this discipline.

The pre-1987 technocratic regime was severely tested as soon as democratization began. The new regime proved particularly vulnerable to special-interest politics involving groups already established at the time of democratization and, to a lesser extent, to populist appeals to the mass electorates. Economic performance also suffered under the new system; the economic crisis of 1997 may be the ultimate proof of the weakness of the new system.

In the sections that follow, we provide necessary background in a discussion of the new Korean democracy, and then address the lack of double balance during its first decade. A new imbalance in economic and political openness emerged, in which the economic system remained stagnant or moved backward, decreasing openness, while the political system experienced expanded participation. We examine the impact of this imbalance on macroeconomic policy and on business-government relations, leading, we argue, to the problem of business's capture of the state, as well as to broader implications for democracy.

Democratization and Political Economy

The impact of democratization on the political economy is not uniform across countries. It depends on, among other things, the nature of the regime that existed before democracy, including its degree of economic and political openness. In the case of Korea, the status quo ante was a developmental state characterized by a high degree of economic openness but limited political openness.

The Korean developmental state was a grand policy compromise among key stakeholders of the dominant coalition (Mo 2005). On the question of growth versus equity, the government chose a progrowth policy, against the opposition of labor, but it was not as growth oriented as business probably wanted. Even under an authoritarian system, the regime's interests were not identical to those of business because it had other constituents to include in the ruling coalition. As we discussed in Chapter 3, the ability to generate shared growth and various public goods was key to the success of the Korean developmental state (Campos and Root 1996).

The stakeholders held different interests regarding the level of competition in domestic markets. While business naturally favored a low level of competition, the government wanted more competition in order to build efficient, competitive industries. The government's preference for market competition was not unbounded, however, for in a perfectly competitive market the government would lose all its leverage against business. It therefore had incentives to protect the domestic market from international competition and prevent what it considered excessive domestic competition.

The government influenced the level of competition through its policies regarding trade, competition, and industry. Using a combination of incentives and discipline, the developmental state created competitive pressure on domestic firms. Government subsidies were distributed among firms according to their export performance. Furthermore, the government enforced periodic corporate restructurings to push the corporate laggards out of the market.

The developmental state was founded on authoritarianism, and many of its central aspects could not be sustained under democracy. First, to restrict political openness, the developmental state suppressed and excluded labor from the policymaking process. But the repressive exclusion of labor is not possible under democracy. In a democracy, labor will seek to increase its share of corporate income and social-welfare spending by the government, and so the democratic government must do more to accommodate labor's interests. Changes in the trade-off between growth and equity—specifically, increasing the degree of redistribution—are therefore unavoidable under democratization. An important question is whether demands for redistribution will go as far as radical populism, which can threaten long-term economic growth. Some democratizing countries have fallen prey to radical populism—many in Latin America, for example—while others have avoided it.

Business will also try to take advantage of democratization to shape government regulations according to its interests. For example, business will ask for deregulation and liberalization when those policies will create more business opportunities. But business will oppose policies that invite more competition from abroad or from new domestic entrants, and it will favor various subsidy programs and other privileges. Finally, business will oppose the developmental state's incentives and discipline on democratic grounds; the discipline it imposed was, after all, arbitrary and not based on the rule of law.

How successful business will be in obtaining its policy agenda is not predetermined. Unlike labor, business is one of the main beneficiaries of the developmental state, so democratization does not necessarily strengthen its political power. Yet business's considerable economic resources allow it to be a major player in a democracy, potentially dominating economic policymaking and even capturing the state.

While the developmental state is not sustainable under democracy, far less clear but more consequential is the question of which system will replace the developmental state (see Figure 6.1). Two types of natural states are possible. One possibility is a radical populism based on labor ascendancy; the other is a plutocracy, a natural state dominated by big business, providing it a range of rents. It is also possible for the developmental state to transit directly to an open-access order with democracy and competitive markets.

The natural-state systems are not mutually exclusive. For example, radical populism and plutocracy can exist in tandem, as they did in many of the natural states in Latin America in the 1970s and 1980s. In

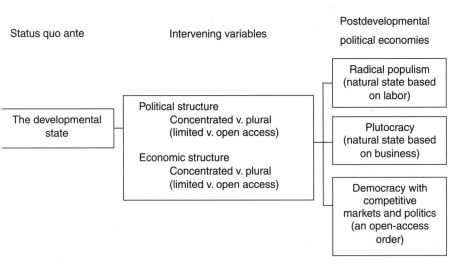

Figure 6.1. Political Economies That May Emerge after the Developmental State

the Latin American states, business elites dominated their domestic markets, obtaining policies that protected them from foreign competition, while populist governments won national elections by promising various types of redistributive expenditure programs (such as high wages for teachers, workers, and government employees).

In South Korea, the transition to democracy was smooth and stable. No significant violence marked the transfer of power to a democratically elected government. The lack of violence was not surprising, since the old ruling party under the authoritarian regime won the first presidential election held under democracy, in 1987. The ruling party went on to win the next presidential election as well, in 1992, this time on the basis of its 1991 merger with two other major parties. Therefore, no radical change of the political economy was expected, at least during the initial period of the transition to democracy. Given the traditional role of the bureaucracy in the policymaking system, policy continuity also persisted owing to the continuing bureaucratic influence. Policy change in Korea was therefore expected to be gradual.

One reason for Korea's smooth and conservative transition was the economic performance of the developmental state. As we emphasized in Chapter 3, elites did not capture all or even most of the benefits from the economic policy of the developmental state, thanks to the regime's policy of sharing the benefits of growth. The success of this shared-growth strategy meant that Korean economic groups were far more equal at the time of transition than groups in most other transition economies. Even though it might be vulnerable to bouts of populism, Korea was highly unlikely to embrace radical populism.

Instead, a plutocratic natural state represented a more realistic threat. The powerful chaebol, created by the developmental state, had evolved into a highly concentrated form of business organization, fostered by incentives from the state, such as subsidized credit. The conservative nature of the transition meant that labor and other newly formed groups were not sufficiently powerful to counterbalance the chaebol. The imbalance of forces left the government without sufficient support to control the chaebol. Because political repression under the developmental state had suppressed political openness, Korea began the transition to a democracy without a vibrant civil society—that is, with relatively few organizations to oppose the chaebol's interests.

A major question at the time of the transition was, would the democratic government be as successful as the developmental state in disciplining the chaebol, or would it come to be dominated by them? The conditions at the time of transition were unfavorable to the government's control of the chaebol. First, as we have seen, the old system of government-led corporate discipline was not viable under democracy. Second, the democratic government had come to depend on campaign contributions to stay in power, and in Korea, campaign contributions meant corporate donations. At the time of the transition, some of the old system of politics based on personal relationships and networks reemerged, and political parties competed for corporate money to finance their election campaigns. The absence of political openness prior to democratization meant that Korea began its democratization with an underdeveloped civil society and the absence of greater political pluralism. A wide range of social and political groups that would have formed and become politically active had been suppressed.

This setting had three implications for the initiation of democracy. First, economic organizations were far more powerful than political and social ones. Second, the influence of money was stronger than it would have been if the Korean political system had been more pluralistic, bringing previously unorganized interest groups to politics as counterforces against vested interests. The absence of these other organizations made it hard to mobilize and appeal to a range of potential constituencies that might have been active under a more substantial civil society. Third, the government could not ignore global trends toward deregulation and liberalization, which gave the chaebol more autonomy.

The third possible outcome to Korea's transition, an open-access economy, would have been ideal from the perspective of Korean development. But the history of development shows that the evolution toward an open-access market economy is a slow and often nonlinear process, even under democracy. As the idea of double balance suggests, an open-access economy requires not only procedural democracy, such as elections, but also substantial political openness: an underlying social structure that is plural, competitive, and supportive of a rich civil society. The rule of law and the protection of individual freedom are necessary to create and maintain a pluralistic social order, but they are the very values that are hardest to establish and sustain in new democracies.

Korean Democracy with Limited Pluralism

The political economy that emerged and persisted in the first ten years of Korea's democracy was a transitional system with characteristics of several alternative systems: the developmental state, populism, plutocracy, and even an open-access market economy. Even though the system made progress toward an open-access order, especially in the area of political participation and access, it did not satisfy all the conditions of an open-access order. From the point of view of regime change, the most salient structural change after 1987 was the emergence of an unbalanced structure vulnerable to populism and plutocracy. As argued in Chapter 2, this system of democracy with limited political and economic openness can lead to economic populism or plutocracy, or both.[1] The absence of a wider range of organized political and social interests prevented such groups from blunting the influence of or counterbalancing powerful, organized economic interests.

The most immediate impact of democratization is open political access and expanded participation. Democracy grants voters the right to vote in free and fair elections, and interest groups are allowed to organize and participate in policymaking. This large opening of political access forces the political system to respond to electoral interests, including increases in some rights. In Korea, the transition to democracy in 1987 led to an immediate improvement in the protection of political rights. Figure 6.2 shows that Korea's Freedom House score on political rights improved from 4 in 1987 to 2 in 1988 (with 1 being most free and 7 being least free).

Political participation by interest groups emerged as expected. A large number of interest groups were organized during this period. Table 6.1 shows that many industry associations, unions, and nongovernmental organizations (NGOs)—many of which are active today—originated during the first three years of democracy; democratization thus appears to have had a positive impact on the growth of the civil society. Democ-

---

1. This is not to deny that populist or plutocratic policies can afflict an open-access order or may even be a fact of life in a functioning democracy. But we are arguing that the particular pattern of populism and plutocracy seen in the first ten years of Korea's democracy represents the outcome of structural imbalances, not an occasional underperformance of democratic governance.

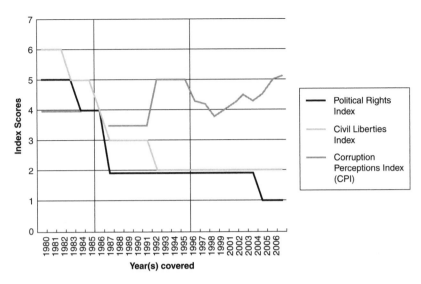

Figure 6.2. Trends in Korea's Political Development: Political Rights, Civil Liberties, and the Rule of Law

Political rights and civil liberties are measured on the Freedom House scale of 1 to 7, with 1 representing the highest degree of freedom and 7 the lowest. (1982* = January 1981 to August 1982; 1983* = August 1982 to November 1983; 1984* = November 1983 to November 1984; 1985* = November 1984 to November 1985; 1986* = November 1985 to November 1986; 1987* = November 1986 to November 1987; 1988* = November 1987 to November 1988; 1989* = November 1988 to December 1989.) The Corruption Perceptions Index (CPI) scores countries on a scale from 0 to 10, with 0 indicating high levels of perceived corruption and 10 indicating low levels of perceived corruption. CPI ratings for the years 1980–1985, 1988–1992, and 1993–1996 are average scores. *Source:* Freedom House, "Comparative Scores for All Countries from 1973 to 2006," *Freedom in the World,* www.freedomhouse.org/template.cfm?page=15; Transparency International, "TI Corruption Perceptions Index," www.transparency.org/policy_research/surveys_indices/cpi.

racy also brought more labor participation; strike activity surged as soon as the government agreed to the transition to democracy in June 1987 and continued for three years.

Expanded participation by itself does not produce a pluralistic political society. The absence of a wide range of groups to mobilize various interests means that elected officials will pursue fewer policies aimed at the broader constituency. The elections and participation that democratization introduces may expand, not restrain, the power of majority groups, making the political society more concentrated rather than less so.

While general conditions for political pluralism are not well understood and institutional requirements are hard to specify, the rule of law

Table 6.1. The Number of Interest Groups and NGOs by First Year of
Registration

Year of registration	Number of industry associations	Number of unions	Number of NGOs
Up to 1980	2,031	2,393	794
1981–1986	907	2,417	765
1987–1990	209	5,901	
1991–1999	1,401	6,647	2,058

Source: Sun-young Hong and Jae-cheol Jang, *20 Years of the Korean Economy Reexamined* (Samsung Economic Research Institute, 2006), 21.
Note: Numbers of NGOs are given for the 1980s and the 1990s; 765 is the number of NGOs originally registered in Korea in 1981–1990.

and the protection of individual rights do seem to be essential, as does
open access to organizations of all types. Political pluralism requires that
individuals are protected by the rule of law from the arbitrary exercising
of power by majorities, and that they have the ability to organize to protect their interests or to compete with the majorities. Thus, the rule of
law and the protection of individual rights can be indicators of the level
of political pluralism that exists in a political society.

The general trend in civil liberties from 1987 to 1997 was positive (see
Figure 6.2).[2] The Freedom House rating for Korea on civil liberties improved to 3 in 1988 as a result of the 1987 democratic reforms. But the
development of civil liberties in Korea has been slower than that of political rights, and Korea did not receive a "free" rating of 2 until 1993
(Freedom House considers a country with a score of 1 or 2 to be free).

The development of the rule of law has been even slower. Some question whether any significant progress has taken place. Transparency International's Corruption Perceptions Index shows that the perceived
level of corruption in Korea has not changed much since 1987 and remains in a range typical of very poor developing countries. Evidence on
the development of civil liberties and the rule of law confirms that politi-

---

2. As we remarked in Chapter 2, these indexes are intended as indicators of open
access and rule of law; they are not definitive scores designed specifically to measure
open access.

Table 6.2. Overall Concentration in Manufacturing,
1970–1998 (percent)

Year	Shipments		Employment	
	50 largest	100 largest	50 largest	100 largest
1970	17.8	28.7	15.4	22.8
1977	35.0	44.9	16.9	23.9
1982	36.9	46.2	16.4	22.2
1987	30.0	38.1	13.3	19.1
1992	31.9	39.2	13.8	18.3
1997	32.6	39.6	13.7	17.5
1998	40.2	47.8	17.4	21.0

Source: Shin 2003, 279.

cal pluralism did not keep up with the pace of political participation in the first ten years of democracy, creating a serious structural imbalance.

Nor did Korea's economic structure become more balanced. Many argue that the monopoly economic structure inherited from the developmental state remains intact to this day. Shin (2003) reports that industry-level competition remained constant from 1987 to 1997, suggesting that democracy did not make the industry structure more competitive or pluralistic (see Table 6.2).

In Korea, though, the quality of corporate governance in major chaebol, and their share of the economy, may be better indicators of the concentration of economic power than industry-level market concentration ratios. The chaebol, now leading firms in each industry, hold and exercise dominant market power in Korea. However, the quality of corporate governance at major chaebol deteriorated after 1987 as controlling families strove to maintain power in their groups with increasingly small numbers of directly owned shares (Lim and Morck 2010).

Macroeconomic Populism

With democratization, social welfare and redistribution became the most salient economic issues in politics. The removal of political repression unleashed many new demands. For example, the growing disparity in income and wealth had been one of the driving forces behind the prodemocracy movement. Although democracy caused many changes in economic policy, the most important was the redirection of policy toward redistribution and social welfare.

To understand the economic and political consequences of social insurance programs, we distinguish universalistic, impersonal programs that provide benefits to everyone based on an established set of objective criteria from particularistic ones, where benefits are passed out on the basis of patronage, clientelism, and political relationships. Social insurance policies are designed to be universalistic and impersonal, and their benefits are distributed among a wide range of groups in the society. Health insurance, unemployment insurance, and social security programs are examples of universalistic programs. In contrast, the government may redistribute income to benefit particular groups; these programs are personalistic because they are targeted to particular interest groups rather than to all citizens. Examples of specific, or particularistic, programs include subsidies earmarked for farmers and small and medium-size enterprises (SMEs), policies whose benefits are distributed based on corruption and bribes rather than impersonal criteria, and legally mandated above-market wages for special groups (e.g., teachers or government employees). Another difference between the two types of programs is that many universalistic programs provide public goods and services that complement markets, for example by reducing the individual risk of market participation. In most open-access orders, universalistic, impersonal programs reduce the crippling (and corrupt) demand for redistribution that often plagues natural states (NWW, ch. 4).

Pressures for both universalistic and particularistic redistribution existed in Korea at the time of democratization. General concern for social insurance and economic equity was, in a sense, a natural consequence of high economic growth. After two decades of such growth, most Koreans desired a better quality of life. As their income rose, their demand for social services, such as health insurance, increased. Moreover, the costs of the state's growth-oriented policy became apparent to them—including pollution, congestion, and rising property values. Thus the support for universalistic social insurance was widespread; it was not limited to political activists.

The idea of the welfare state had broad support among policymakers and the public. Democratization intensified the demand for social welfare because past authoritarian governments were perceived to have underresponded to these concerns. Social insurance programs may be considered the next step in shared growth: all open-access orders have big governments, and social welfare programs take up a large fraction of their spending (Lindert 2004; NWW, ch. 4).

The electorate did not limit its demands to universal policies, however. Particularistic demands, especially from groups that had been suppressed by the authoritarian regimes, were also strong. Such demands were based on perceptions of regional, class, and industrial discrimination. Economic development under authoritarian rule left some regions (Cholla, in particular, in southwestern Korea) underdeveloped. Emphasis on heavy industry and manufacturing led to serious sectoral imbalances between large enterprises and small and medium-size companies and between manufacturing and agriculture. And workers, for their part, sought to raise their wages as well as to reform labor laws, which they viewed as unfairly favorable to management. As soon as democratization began, these groups started wielding their political power.

Changed policy priorities under democracy are clearer if we look at the functional distribution of government expenditures (see Table 6.3). The share of social services increased substantially. Social services, as a share of central government expenditures, rose from 12.5 percent in 1986 to 20.0 percent in 1991. The surge in social service spending between 1987 and 1991 was mostly due to an increase in housing and community development expenditures; expenditure shares in health, social security, and welfare remained relatively unchanged during 1988 and 1989. The share of social services spending leveled off after dropping 2 percentage points in 1992 following completion of the government's Two-Million-Units Housing Project.[3]

The share of economic development in central government expenditures declined during the first half of the 1980s but rose again in the late

---

3. The government allocated fiscal resources to low-income, long-term rental housing units as part of a three-year (1989–1991) housing project. It exploited the program, called the Two-Million-Units Housing Project, as an economic stimulus to counteract the cyclical downturn of the economy. Although the project contributed to economic growth through aggregate demand expansion, it seriously eroded the price stability of the economy. Increases in construction employment, fueled by the project, accounted for 40 percent of total employment increases for 1989–1991. This employment expansion aggravated labor shortages in other sectors, particularly manufacturing, and accelerated wage increases.

Table 6.3a. Central Government Expenditures by Function (percent)

Year	Defense	Social services (see Table 6.3b)	Education	Economic development	General administration	Other
1982	27.3	13.7	17.0	21.6	9.2	11.1
1983	27.9	11.8	17.9	19.9	10.1	12.3
1984	26.6	15.0	16.8	19.1	9.0	13.6
1985	26.6	12.4	16.6	21.9	9.4	13.2
1986	27.5	12.5	17.0	18.1	10.0	14.9
1987	25.5	14.3	17.1	17.7	9.4	16.0
1988	25.2	14.1	17.7	19.4	9.0	14.5
1989	23.1	18.5	17.1	18.9	8.9	13.6
1990	20.0	20.4	17.0	20.4	8.5	13.7
1991	19.6	20.0	13.9	20.7	8.8	17.0
1992	19.3	17.9	14.4	18.7	9.8	19.8
1993	18.4	17.1	15.4	19.9	9.8	19.4
1994	17.2	17.8	13.9	25.4	11.1	15.6

Source: Public Finance Statistics, Ministry of Finance.

Table 6.3b. Breakdown of Social Services Expenditures (percent of total government expenditures)

Year	Health	Social security and welfare	Housing and local development	Other local development
1982	1.2	8.5	3.3	0.7
1983	1.5	4.7	4.8	0.8
1984	1.3	5.0	7.9	9.8
1985	1.3	5.2	4.8	1.0
1986	1.5	6.1	3.9	1.1
1987	2.2	6.2	3.6	2.2
1988	2.1	7.2	4.2	0.6
1989	1.9	8.0	8.0	0.7
1990	1.7	8.1	10.1	0.5
1991	1.8	8.5	9.2	0.5
1992	0.9	9.3	7.2	0.5
1993	0.9	9.3	6.2	0.6
1994	0.8	9.3	6.1	0.5

Source: Public Finance Statistics, Ministry of Finance.

1980s. Infrastructure investment was largely responsible for this rise, but government support for agricultural restructuring was also a factor.

The trends in fiscal operations show that redistributive pressures led to increased spending on social services. This rise did not strain fiscal management, however. The size of social services expenditures as a share of GDP remained moderate, at around 20 percent. Importantly—and in contrast to particularistic policies in natural states in Latin America and Africa, for example—Korea maintained fiscal discipline; its increases in social welfare spending were financed by raising taxes and lowering expenditures elsewhere.

Nor did increases in social service spending crowd out productive investment, as evidenced by the consistent levels of spending on education and economic development. The rise of social service spending instead came at the expense of national defense. The share of defense spending in total outlays was drastically reduced. Whether this trade-off can be justified remains to be seen and is beyond the scope of this chapter.[4]

In parallel with the rise of expenditures in social services, benefits to specific interest groups, such as farmers and small and medium-size enterprises, also increased. After 1987 the government designated agriculture and SMEs as two of the top three investment priorities, along with social overhead capital (SOC) investment (investments in schools and physical infrastructure). Most expenditure items benefiting farmers and SMEs do not count as social service spending; they are particularistic benefits.

Agriculture, SMEs, and social welfare were three of the top four major expenditure items in 1993 and 1994, and they were all rising at a rapid rate (see Table 6.4). Government financial support for SMEs almost doubled in 1994, to 2.1 trillion won from 1.1 trillion won in 1993.

To see the long-term pattern, we look at the growth trends of five individual programs with clear target groups (see Table 6.4).[5] The budget for the Agricultural and Fishery Development Program jumped 112 percent in 1987, the first year of democracy. Expenditures on behalf of

---

4. The six-category functional classification of government expenditures in Table 6.3 does not paint a complete picture of the redistribution. Expenditures in social services (e.g., health care, social security and welfare, and housing and community development) are mostly universalistic, in that they benefit the middle class as well as the poor.

5. These trends do not, of course, measure the total amount of budgetary benefits that each group receives.

Table 6.4a. Major Expenditure Items in General Account Budgets (billion won)

Expenditure item	1993 budget	1994 budget	Change (%)
Social overhead capital expansion	4,680	6,077	29.9
Agriculture and fisheries	4,484	5,320	18.6
Small and medium-size enterprises (SMEs)	1,101	2,100	90.8
Science and technology	862	1,138	32.1
Education	748	1,004	34.1
Social welfare	2,766	3,352	21.2
Environment	307	413	34.5

Source: Economic Planning Board, 1994 *Government Budget Draft.*

Table 6.4b. Growth Trends in Particular Expenditure Items (percentage rate of growth)

Year	Agricultural and fishery development	SME support	Job training	Job stability	Worker welfare
1985	5.8	23.7	0.2	15.9	58.3
1986	22.4	27.9	7.7	130.9	−22.7
1987	112.0	−19.5	23.3	28.9	33.4
1988	−30.7	−78.2	28.4	51.4	13.3
1989	22.3	28.8	22.2	5.9	45.9
1990	37.1	2.0	3.6	4.3	1.1
1991	11.1	−29.5	−11.0	−13.0	12.8
1992	35.7	38.9	11.5	−8.3	26.7
1993	15.7	−13.7	5.2	149.7	6.1
1994	23.2	76.1	13.9	20.4	14.8
1995	9.3	19.8	21.8	−20.9	16.6
Program size in billion won (1995)	3,242	29	114	16	77

Source: Economic Planning Board, *Government Budget Draft,* various issues.
Note: SME = small and medium-size enterprise.

workers (job training, job stability, and worker welfare) steadily increased after 1987. No clear pattern emerges in the SME support program, which constituted only a small part of the overall government program for SMEs.

Monetary policy provides another set of policy instruments that the government can employ to meet demands for redistribution, especially control of bank credit. Korean monetary policy had long been characterized by government intervention in the credit market. In Chapter 4 we saw that, after shifting its policy stance from stabilization to export-led growth in the early 1960s, the government used selective credit policies to marshal financial resources for favored strategic sectors. Selective credit policies in the form of policy loans were used for export promotion in the 1960s and the Heavy and Chemical Industry Drive in the 1970s. By the end of the 1970s, government policies in favor of targeted industries created overcapacity in heavy and chemical industries, unbalanced growth between large and small firms, and chronic inflation. Recognizing the seriousness of the problem, the government reduced the scope of its credit controls. During the early 1980s, selective credit provision to targeted industries gave way to financial liberalization and functional support, such as research and development subsidies.

In the mid-1980s, however, the government's intervention in the credit market increased because of the large-scale restructuring of industrial firms. As a worldwide recession continued after the second oil crisis, which began in 1979, many debt-ridden firms became insolvent, particularly in the overseas construction, shipbuilding, textile, and machinery industries. This situation set the stage for moral hazard, with disastrous economic consequences.

During this period, the Korean government began promoting balanced economic growth and gave SMEs a high priority in credit allocations. For example, the government tightened monitoring of the required ratio of SME loans to total loans. The SME lending requirements were later strengthened to increase financial support for SMEs. The required lending ratio for local banks was raised in 1980 and 1986, and foreign bank branches and nonbank financial institutions, such as short-term investment and finance companies, merchant banking corporations, lease companies, and life insurance firms, were also made subject to this lending requirement.

After 1986 the economy began to run a large current account surplus while enjoying a strong growth rate of more than 10 percent a year. The strength of the economy spurred further attempts to liberalize the financial sector and reduce policy-based loans, especially export credits. In reducing policy loans, the Bank of Korea (BOK) cut loans to large corporations first. For instance, per-dollar export credits to large firms fell from 740 won at the end of 1985 to 170 won by the end of 1987. Large corporations were completely excluded from export credit programs after 1988, and their commercial bills were not eligible for BOK rediscounting after 1989.

After 1987 the government placed greater emphasis on social equity (i.e., support for SMEs) in response to increasing public concern over the concentration of economic power among a few large business groups. Preferences were given to previously disadvantaged sectors, such as SMEs, agriculture, and housing. Consequently, small and medium-size enterprises drew a growing share of bank loans (see Table 6.5).

At the same time, the government employed credit controls over large business groups to reduce the concentration of bank loans to chaebol. In 1987 the government introduced credit ceilings to limit the shares of bank loans to the nation's thirty largest business groups. Furthermore, to prevent corporate capital structures from deteriorating through excessive borrowing and to increase credit to SMEs, the Bank Supervisory Board directed the thirty largest conglomerates to self-finance a certain proportion of their new investments by liquidating their shareholdings in affiliates or real estate holdings, and to repay their debts by raising new capital in the stock market. This step led to a gradual reduction in

Table 6.5. Share of Bank Loans to Small and Medium-Size Companies and Conglomerates (percent)

	1983	1985	1988	1989	1990	1991	1997	1998	1999
Small and medium-size companies	33.1	31.5	48.1	50.1	55.5	56.8	75.0	73.7	75.9
30 largest chaebol	—	—	23.7	20.7	19.8	20.4	25.0	26.3	24.1

Source: Bank of Korea.

Table 6.6. Composition of Policy Loans (percent)

	1980	1985	1988	1990	1991	1992
Industrial policy funds	74.2	72.1	68.5	62.4	61.4	56.4
Income subsidy funds	25.9	27.9	31.5	37.5	38.6	43.6
Small and medium-size company funds	4.7	3.8	3.6	6.4	6.6	6.9
Agriculture funds	4.8	5.3	7.4	7.2	7.2	6.7
Housing funds	10.7	11.2	12.8	15.7	16.4	17.1

Source: Bank of Korea.

the share of bank loans to the thirty largest conglomerates—from 24 percent in 1988 to 20 percent by the end of 1991. In addition to the rapid expansion of credit for SMEs, increasingly large proportions of policy loans were income subsidies rather than industrial policy funds. The share of income subsidies among policy loans jumped to 43.6 percent in 1992 from 27.9 percent in 1985 (see Table 6.6). The main beneficiaries of income subsidy loans were SMEs, agriculture, and housing.

The evidence presented suggests the following tentative conclusions about the effects of democratization on Korean macroeconomic policy. First, particularistic programs for small and medium-size enterprises and farmers became more extensive even as the government responded to redistributive pressure with a steady increase of universalistic programs, such as social services. Second, the government raised tax revenue, especially from high-income taxpayers, to finance many redistributive programs. The cost of credit subsidies for SMEs, however, was borne by borrowers, who had to pay higher interest rates, and by the whole economy, which suffered the resulting inflation. Lastly, SMEs and farmers, among the disadvantaged groups, were much more successful than the urban poor, underdeveloped regions, and workers generally in the political competition for government-led redistribution.

Strong interest groups, such as labor unions, pressed for higher benefits not only through government fiscal and monetary policies but also through their bargaining power in the market. The pattern of wage growth since 1987, for example, shows that the redistribution of income toward workers took place through rapid increases in nominal wages, which consistently outpaced productivity gains after 1987 (see Table 6.7).

Table 6.7. Wages and Strike Activity

	1987	1988	1989	1990	1991	1992	1993	1994	1995	1996	1997	1998	1999
Growth rates (%)													
Manufacturing													
Nominal wage	11.6	19.6	25.1	20.2	16.9	15.7	10.9	15.5	9.9	12.2	5.2	-3.1	14.9
Labor productivity	6.1	14.6	2.6	12.0	16.7	14.5	20.2	17.4	17.6	10.2	12.0	20.3	7.9
All industries													
Nominal wage	10.1	15.5	21.1	18.8	17.5	15.2	12.2	—	11.2	11.9	7.0	-2.5	12.1
Labor productivity[a]	10.0	14.6	7.2	15.0	16.8	9.1	7.4	12.7	13.5	9.2	7.3	8.3	4.9
Real wage	6.9	7.8	14.5	9.4	7.5	8.4	7.0	6.1	6.4	6.7	2.4	-9.3	11.1
Labor market conditions													
Unemployment rate (%)	3.8	3.0	3.1	2.9	2.6	2.7	3.1	2.7	2.0	2.0	2.6	6.8	6.3
Strike activity													
Number of labor disputes	3,749	1,873	1,616	322	234	235	144	121	88	85	78	129	198
Volume[b]	1,628	1,191	1,365	950	678	307	267	302	—	—	—	—	—

Source: Ministry of Labor, *Monthly Labor Statistics*, various issues.

[a]Nominal GDP/number of employed workers.

[b]Volume of strike activity is defined as days not worked due to industrial action.

In both real and nominal terms, the rates of wage increase were most rapid during the five-year period from 1988 through 1992. The ratio of employee compensation to GNP steadily increased after 1987; by 1992, the ratio reached 61.0 percent, from 51.2 percent in 1986. In contrast, the ratio remained in the low 50s from 1980 to 1986.

This increase in labor's relative and absolute income speaks to the change in industrial relations brought about by democratization. Because the basic structure of labor laws and institutions—the official rules—did not change, it seems that removing the informal authoritarian mechanisms of labor control, such as police surveillance and interference, were instrumental in enhancing the workers' capacity to negotiate. For example, the rate of increase in wages peaked in 1989 and 1990, even as the government moved to rein in the labor movement.

Democratization also had a direct effect on strike activity, with the number of labor disputes rising rapidly soon after democratization. After the government began to crack down on illegal labor disputes and reversed its hands-off policy in 1989, the number of disputes fell. The number of disputes continued to fall in 1993 and 1994 under Kim Young Sam (see Table 6.8), but in terms of the number of workers involved and the number of work days lost, the downward trend in strike activity beginning in 1990 was reversed in 1993 and 1994. In the face of this conflicting evidence, we employ the concept of strike volume to measure overall strike activity (Hibbs 1976).[6] In terms of volume, strike activity actually rose in 1989. Although fewer disputes arose in 1989 than in 1988, the disputes involved more workers; the number of strikers per dispute was 253 in 1989, compared with 157 in 1988.[7] After 1989, strike volume continued to fall until 1994, when it rose again.

Democratization empowers voters and interest groups, especially those subject to political oppression by the authoritarian regime. As we have seen, the direct economic consequences of this change were increased government spending on social welfare and redistribution and higher wages for workers. But judgment on the costs of economic populism is

---

6. Following Hibbs (1976), we derive strike volume by multiplying three measures of strike activity: size, duration, and frequency. *Size* is defined as strikers per dispute, *duration* as work days lost per striker, and *frequency* as strikers per 1,000 permanent workers, in nonagricultural firms with more than 10 employees.

7. This increase in strike activity explains why the government took action in 1989.

Table 6.8. Strike Activity and Government Policy

	1987	1988	1989	1990	1991	1992	1993	1994	1995	1996	1997	1998	1999
Strike activity													
Number of disputes	3,749	1,873	1,616	322	234	235	144	121	88	85	78	129	198
Number of workers involved	1,262,285	293,455	409,134	133,916	175,089	105,034	108,577	104,339	49,717	79,495	43,991	146,065	92,026
Number of work days lost	6,946,935	5,400,837	6,351,443	4,487,151	3,271,334	1,527,612	1,308,326	1,484,368	392,581	892,987	444,720	1,452,096	1,366,281
Size (strikers per dispute)	337	157	253	416	748	447	754	862					
Duration (work days lost per striker)	5.5	18.4	15.5	33.5	18.7	14.5	12.0	14.2	—	—	22.7	26.1	19.2
Frequency (strikers per 1,000 workers)[a]	0.879	0.413	0.347	0.068	0.048	0.047	0.029	0.025					

Strike volume	1,628	1,191	1,365	950	678	307	267	302					
Government policy													
Number of workers arrested	—	79	602	485	486	—	—	—					
Number of police interventions	—	—	—	31	10	7	1/2[b]	5					
Economic conditions													
GDP growth rate (%)	11.5	11.3	6.4	9.5	9.1	5.1	5.8	8.4	8.9	6.8	5.0	−6.7	10.9
Unemployment rate (%)	3.8	3.0	3.1	2.9	2.6	2.7	3.1	2.7	2.0	2.0	2.6	6.8	6.3
Electoral cycle													
Election year?	yes	yes	no	no	yes	yes	no	no	no	yes	yes	no	no

Source: Ministry of Labor, Korea Labor Institute, Korea Trade Union Congress.

[a] Frequency equals the number of strikers per 1,000 permanent workers in nonagricultural firms with more than 10 employees (see Hibbs 1976).

[b] One arrest before policy shift in July and two afterward, for a total of three arrests in 1993

controversial. Higher wages, higher cost of capital, and higher taxes added significant costs to Korean companies, reducing their international competitiveness. At the same time, the government maintained strong discipline in fiscal and monetary policy. Strike activity and wage growth also receded after three years of democracy. Thus, macroeconomic management hardly failed.

Business's Capture of the State

Although Korea did not fall victim to radical populism during its democratic transition, it did experience a substantial shift in the government-business relationship, a shift that we directly link to the economic crisis of 1997 (see Chapter 7).

Business and government certainly had a close relationship under the developmental state (McIntyre 2001). Some even argue that the relationship was more of a partnership than a hierarchy (Kim 1997). As detailed in Chapter 4, state and business leaders had an exchange relationship in which the government rewarded the business for good performance, and business delivered a good performance (and campaign contributions and votes) in return for government support. Records of frequent meetings, consultations, and exchanges of information between corporate managers and government officials provide further evidence for the business-government partnership. It has also been argued that, in East Asia, business-government interactions are facilitated by the common social backgrounds of government officials and businessmen, cross-penetration (referring to the "descent" of bureaucrats into private-sector jobs after retirement), and state leadership in creating public-private cooperation.

But the literature on the developmental state also identifies the government as the key provider of corporate discipline (Amsden 1989, Wade 1990). The government employed a combination of rewards and sanctions, sometimes as a principal and sometimes as a partner, in order to align corporate interests with its development goals. As some had feared, democratization brought an end to the government-led system of corporate discipline without creating an alternative system of discipline.

Campaign contributions dramatically changed the balance of power in government-business relations. Under the developmental state, the ruling party (and the government) had the upper hand over business.

Shared growth combined with repression to allow the regime to stay in power without recourse to electoral campaigns.

Under democracy, however, the ruling party became more fragmented and faced serious electoral challenges from the opposition parties. Political competition forced parties to generate political support and to bring their messages to voters. In this setting, campaign contributions became more important to the ruling party, affording new leverage to business.[8]

To understand the logic of campaign contributions in Korea, we draw on Mo (2009a) to provide an analytical framework. The two main parties to exchanges of contributions and political favors in Korea are the ruling party and the business sector. We focus on the ruling party because it has been more prone to corruption than any opposition party, accounting for most of the corruption in Korea.

The ruling party's bargaining power relative to corporate donors depends in part on the benefits it can potentially deliver to donors after the election. When the party candidate makes promises to the donors, he will be much more credible if, first, he has the support of the incumbent president, who has the power to grant favors before and after the campaign, but before he leaves office, and second, if he has a high probability of winning. Thus, the bargaining power of the ruling party will be strong when the ruling party is cohesive; that is, in the absence of conflict between the incumbent president and his candidate, and when the candidate is expected to win. In contrast, the incumbent party's bargaining power is weak if the opposite scenario holds: that is, its candidate is an underdog or long shot in the polls and has a strained relationship with the incumbent president.

How much benefit a corporate donor expects from his contributions also depends on how dependent his business is on the government. If government intervention in the economy is extensive, a good business-government relationship is an important determinant of corporate success, and the benefit of a given contribution, made in exchange for political favors, will be large. The opposite is true when the economy is

---

8. Ironically, while campaign contributions became more important politically, the total amount of campaign contributions from corporations may have declined, at least at the presidential level, as business may have used its new bargaining power to drive down the price of political favors.

Ruling party

		Coherent/ high probability of winning	Fractured/ low probability of winning
Business	Market-dependent	Type I: *Bargaining* Medium amount of money	Type II: *Arm's length* Small amount of money
	Government-dependent	Type III: *Predation* Large amount of money	Type IV: *Capture* Medium amount of money

Figure 6.3. Corporate Contributions under Different Types of Political Exchange

market oriented. Since corporate success in a competitive market is determined largely by market factors, the benefit of the same contribution–political favor exchange in a market-driven economy is likely to be smaller. As the economy becomes more dependent on the government, the value of a political favor will increase, forcing donors to make more contributions for the same favor. Thus, the donors' bargaining power is larger when the economy is more market oriented.[9]

The values of these two variables—the political strength of the ruling party and the economic orientation of the business sector—create four analytically distinct types of political exchange (Figure 6.3). In the first case, when business is politically vulnerable but economically independent, the ruling party and business are expected to bargain, and on a relatively equal footing. By contributing to a strong ruling party, business seeks to ensure that the party will create or maintain a favorable business environment.

When the ruling party is weak in a market-oriented economy, business interests are cautious about contributing to the ruling party. If they

---

9. Empirical research shows that there is a negative relationship between economic freedom and corruption (Chafuen and Guzman 2000).

do contribute, they will not offer the ruling party much more than what they give to the leading opposition party. In this uncertain environment, business will try to remain at arm's length from every contending political party and hedge its bets by distributing funds thinly across parties.[10]

The third type of political exchange occurs when a strong ruling party meets a government-dependent business sector. In this case, the ruling party holds a preponderant amount of bargaining power and can dictate the terms of exchange to the business. If the ruling party has authoritarian tendencies, it can take the practice to an extreme form of predation. The level of illegal contributions will also be high. Not only can the ruling party demand more money but it can also raise money separately through the incumbent president and the candidate.

Finally, when a government-dependent business sector faces a fractured or weak ruling party, the business sector has a chance to manage the government-business relationship on its terms. If, on the basis of campaign contributions, business succeeds in capturing the government after the election, it can reap large economic benefits, so it will be willing to donate relatively large amounts of money to the ruling party. But since the ruling party is weak, it may not take much for the business sector to win the desired concessions. Thus, the size of contributions under this type of political exchange will stay in the medium range.

Implications for Democratization

When democratization began in 1987, the market for campaign contributions clearly favored the ruling party; further, predation characterized the exchange relationship between the ruling party and business. Over time, however, the bargaining power of the business sector grew. The ruling party became weaker politically, and the corporate sector became more independent of the government. By 1992, the exchange relationship between the ruling party and business approximated that of capture. The absence of a strong civil society with its deep, long-term organization of society's pluralistic interests meant an absence of political and social groups that could mobilize voters and counterbalance business's influence.

---

10. This argument assumes that donors want to buy access or seek political benefits when making political contributions. If, instead, they are ideologically motivated, they may contribute more money to their favored candidates in close elections.

In the 1987 presidential election, both the incumbent president and the ruling-party candidate solicited—and received—unprecedented levels of illegal donations, with a combined total in the range of 300 billion won. The 1992 election differed from 1987 in three important ways. First, the role of the incumbent president in campaign finance was significantly diminished. The relationship between the incumbent president and the ruling-party candidate became so estranged before and after the election that the incumbent president not only abstained from fund-raising but also left office without transferring parts of his secret fund to his successor.

The incumbent president's inactivity was significant because it showed that the balance of power between campaign contributors and political officials had changed in 1992 in favor of the former. In 1987, firms were forced to respond to pressure from the incumbent president, who still wielded considerable power; at that time, no one was sure if Chun Doo Hwan was going to keep his promise to retire peacefully after the election. In 1992, companies responded mainly to the electoral prospects of individual candidates. Therefore, campaign contributions appear to have been supply driven in 1992, whereas they were demand driven in 1987. In terms of the analytic framework of Figure 6.3, this moved South Korea from a Type III (predation) exchange relationship toward Type IV (capture).

REFORMS DEFEATED AS CHAEBOL CONTINUE TO EXPAND

The political consequences of the chaebol's power were significant. First, the chaebol were able to defeat a series of corporate reform attempts, such as moves to strengthen fair-trade laws and impose new entry and borrowing restrictions (Mo 2001). Second, they avoided government-led corporate restructurings. Third, the new dependence of political officials on campaign finance severely diminished the government's ability to continue its successful if informal means of controlling chaebol, including forms of moral hazard.

The politics of chaebol reform did not favor success. While the chaebol were organized and united, the support for chaebol reform was diffuse and unorganized. Here again, the absence of political pluralism and long-standing institutions of civil society meant fewer organizations and less political influence to counter the chaebol. Supporters of chaebol reform consisted of a wide range of groups, including activists, intellectuals, and bureaucratic agencies that had a reform mandate, such as the Fair Trade Commission. Given the unorganized nature of their opposition, the chaebol continued to exert a strong influence on those who depended on them for political contributions. This political environment prevented comprehensive reform. Even though the government attempted to restrain the power of the chaebol using credit controls, fair trade regulations, and specialization policy, it failed to address the fundamental problems of Korea's industrial structure: the absence of an exit market and nontransparent business practices. Many government actions designed to reform the chaebol, such as controlling credit and measures to force the chaebol to specialize in core business areas, were based on dubious economic logic. In taking such actions, the government seems to have been guided by bureaucratic expediency ("regulate what you observe") and the desire to maintain or expand its power. As a result, the government's chaebol policy lacked coherence and sound principles.[11] In sum, chaebol reform efforts failed largely because the organized chaebol were able to keep the unorganized reform pressures under control.

MORAL HAZARD WORSENS

Because of the underdevelopment of Korea's financial markets (e.g., no market for corporate control) and the weakness of internal discipline (such as weak minority shareholders and workers), the government was the only potential mechanism for enforcing corporate discipline in Korea's developmental state prior to democratization. Indeed, the Korean government did periodically intervene to force insolvent firms out of the market during the period of rapid growth.

Before 1985, there were three major episodes of government-enforced corporate restructuring: notably, from 1969 to 1971–1972, from 1980 to 1982 and from 1985 to 1989. The first round, which lasted for three years after it began in 1969, targeted companies having difficulty repaying

---

11. The government did sometimes take strong measures against chaebol leaders. Hyundai, for example, had to endure several years of government sanctions after its owner-manager, Chung Ju Young, ran for president in 1992. But the Hyundai case was an exception that proves the rule. So long as the chaebol did not participate directly in politics, they were able to keep their ways of doing business.

foreign-exchange debts. The second round began in 1980, in the aftermath of the second international oil crisis and in the midst of the political turbulence following President Park Chung Hee's assassination in 1979. Its main objective was to restructure the overinvested heavy and chemical industries. And in the third episode (1985 to 1989), the government attempted to institutionalize corporate restructuring with the passage of the 1986 Industry Rationalization Support Act.

What determined the timing of these government policies? It appears that in each case the government reacted to the deterioration of the financial conditions in problem sectors, but not until the problems had become so serious that the government could no longer delay action. In the first round, many foreign-exchange borrowers had become effectively insolvent. In the second round, the government had known as early as 1978 that something had to be done about the heavy and chemical industries.

As political officials became more dependent on chaebol for their election campaign funds—and lacking support constituencies to oppose the chaebol—democratization broke down the long-standing system of controlling for moral hazard (Haggard and Mo 2000). The chaebol sought to block liberalization policies that would allow greater entry and competition from new firms or from SMEs (Jesse, Heo, and DeRouen 2002). The government simply could not enforce a range of business regulations, including rules concerning prudential decision making with respect to investments and the running up of debt. With economic liberalization further easing the controls on the chaebol, moral hazard gave them the incentive to greatly increase their risk.

Another reason why we think that government intervention was reactive and piecemeal is that no clear correlation existed between the timing of corporate restructuring and macroeconomic variables (see Table 6.9).[12] One macroeconomic variable with predictive power seems

---

12. One hypothesis for the timing of the government's policies is that the government initiated restructuring when economic growth slowed, current account deficits worsened, or the rate of commercial bill defaults rose. But the Korean government has intervened when economic growth was robust (as in 1969) and failed to intervene in a recession (in 1965). Nor are current account deficits a good indicator; the government took no action after the first oil crisis, for example. Default rates did rise during the first two rounds of corporate restructuring, but a rise in default rates did not generally precipitate government intervention, for example, in 1965–1966.

Table 6.9. Business Cycles and the Timing of Corporate Restructuring

Year	GDP growth (%)	Current account balance (million dollars)	Total borrowings to total assets (manufacturing)	Default rate for commercial bills	Periods of major corporate restructuring
1962	2.1	−55.5	—	0.44	
1963	9.1	−143.5	—	0.46	
1964	9.7	−26.1	—	0.41	
1965	5.7	9.1	—	0.51	
1966	12.2	−103.4	—	0.55	
1967	5.9	−191.9	—	0.37	
1968	11.3	−440.3	—	0.38	
1969	13.8 ⎫	−548.6	—	0.43	Insolvent
1970	8.8 ⎬	−622.5	—	0.53	foreign- exchange
1971	8.5 ⎭	−847.5	55.9	0.44	borrowers
1972	4.8	−371.2	51.4	0.31	
1973	12.8	−308.8	38.5	0.16	
1974	8.1	−2,022.7	49.7	0.11	
1975	6.6	−1,886.9	47.0	0.14	
1976	11.8	−313.6	46.8	0.15	
1977	10.3	12.3	47.0	0.13	
1978	9.4	−1,085.2	48.0	0.08	
1979	7.1	−4,151.1	48.4	0.10	
1980	−2.7 ⎫	−5,320.8	49.3	0.17	Heavy and
1981	6.2 ⎬	−4,646.0	49.4	0.14	chemical industries
1982	7.6 ⎭	−2,649.6	45.9	0.12	
1983	11.5	−1,606.0	43.7	0.11	
1984	8.7	−1,372.6	41.5	0.09	
1985	6.5	−887.4	46.7	0.07	
1986	11.6 ⎫	4,617.0	46.0	0.10	Case-by-case
1987	11.5 ⎬	9,853.9	42.9	0.09	review and restructuring
1988	11.3 ⎭	14,160.7	39.5	0.04	
1989	6.4	5054.6	38.5	0.04	
1990	9.5	−2,179.4	44.6	0.04	
1991	9.7	−8,417.4	44.5	0.06	
1992	5.8	−4,095.2	47.2	0.12	

(*continued*)

Table 6.9. (continued)

Year	GDP growth (%)	Current account balance (million dollars)	Total borrowings to total assets (manufacturing)	Default rate for commercial bills	Periods of major corporate restructuring
1993	6.3	821.1	46.8	0.13	
1994	8.3	−4,024.2	44.5	0.17	
1995	8.9	−8,665.1	44.8	0.20	
1996	6.8	−23,120.2	47.7	0.17	
1997	5.0	−8,287.4	54.2	0.52	
1998	−6.7	40,371.2	50.9	0.52	
1999	10.9	24,521.9	42.8	0.43	

Source: Bank of Korea.

to have been the ratio of total borrowings to total assets in manufacturing. This variable was above 50 percent in 1971 and 1972, during the first round of corporate restructurings. By the later 1970s, it had climbed back up close to 50 percent, which may have led to the second round, in 1980–1982. The ratio did not exceed 50 percent until 1997, when it was 54.2 percent. But it was widely understood that the government played politics in selecting target firms and awarding assets to third parties. Even after the passage of the Industry Rationalization Support Act of 1986, every case of corporate restructuring came with political controversies.

During these restructuring episodes, the authoritarian developmental state forced many firms out of the market, although it may not have been systematic or objective in the process. The possibility of government-imposed corporate restructuring must have had a huge psychological impact on market participants, including the largest firms. Lacking in the literature are solid, firm-level empirical studies demonstrating the effect of corporate restructurings on corporate finance and management.

After democratization in the late 1980s, however, the government no longer possessed the power to control moral hazard. Moreover, no major chaebol failed between 1989 and the economic crisis of 1997. The government did not intervene because it did not want to pay the political costs associated with forced corporate restructuring and because such actions would have been incompatible with the policy of deregulation that it was trying to promote.

Conclusions

The first ten years of democracy saw the expansion of special-interest politics. With the power of the government weakening, interest groups (such as chaebol, labor unions, farmers, and entrenched bureaucracies) grew more powerful and wielded effective veto power in their policy areas. Consequently the Korean government failed to act on many important reform agendas, increasing its vulnerability to outside economic shocks.

The central implication of our approach for the first decade of democratization, 1987 to 1997, is that the lack of double balance during the authoritarian era—considerable economic openness without corresponding political openness—left a legacy inherited by the new democracy: powerful economic organizations that could advocate for their own interests, faced by a weak civil society that could not counteract them.

As we will see in the next chapter, the system of moral hazard served as the direct mechanism linking democratization to the 1997 financial crisis. As political officials became more dependent on chaebol for their election, democratization broke down the long-standing system controlling against moral hazard. The NWW framework suggests that this outcome is characteristic of a lack of double balance: new political openness but not enough new economic openness, in the sense of more access to new organizations, firms, and financing. What is seen as significant economic liberalization occurred in the form of eased regulatory restrictions on firms, especially the chaebol. Liberalization also allowed the chaebol to make more risky investments, setting the stage for the financial crisis of 1997. If successful, these investments promised large profits. But if unsuccessful, they implied large losses, the threat of bankruptcies and economic dislocations, and the possibility of government bailouts.

Opposition to the chaebol remained unorganized, and their dominant role in campaign finance made it hard for elected officials to oppose chaebol interests. Hence efforts to reform the chaebol failed. In particular, the government was unable to react to impending signs of corporate and financial difficulties once they became apparent.

Two results of economic liberalization during the first decade of democracy were especially important. First, the chaebol sought to lift restrictive regulations that hindered their operation. One effect of these regulations had been to control moral hazard and thus restrict insolvent firms from taking on greater risk in the hope of recovering. Under democracy, the government had a much more difficult time controlling moral hazard (Haggard and Mo 2000). Second, the chaebol sought to block liberalization policies that would allow greater entry and competition from new firms, including small and medium-size firms (Jesse, Heo, and DeRouen 2002).

CHAPTER 7

The 1997 Financial Crisis: Causes and Subsequent Reform

Democratization, built on an inadequate foundation for political pluralism, expanded the power of organized interests with respect to the government. Economic openness prior to democratization at once fostered the growth of the South Korean economy and of a politically powerful set of organized economic and business interests. The absence of political openness before democratization, however, meant a relative absence of political and social organizations that could counterbalance the powerful economic ones. Although democracy forced political officials to attend to the interests of the electorate, the weak civil society allowed economic groups to dominate politics and influence policy. Thus, South Korea failed the criterion of double balance: although it had created a competitive electoral democracy, it had failed to produce a competitive market economy.

Business-government relations were central to this pattern, and business saw its power grow rapidly in the first decade under democracy. The institution of electoral politics forced the government to give up many of the discretionary policy tools that the previous authoritarian regime had used to contain the influence of special interest groups. Those political forces meant that the political economy once again lacked double balance, precipitating another corrective process that this time took the form of the 1997 financial crisis. The crisis was then followed by substantial economic reforms, reducing the gap between political and economic openness, and moving Korea toward double balance.

Also important at this point in Korea's development was the diminishing security threat from the North. As South Korea grew rich—far richer than in 1960—and improved its national security, and as Cold War politics waned, especially China and Russia's support for North Korea, the security threat diminished from its earlier high levels. As we saw in Chapter 5, the diminishing security threat, combined with removing constraints of the authoritarian regime and the growth of the middle class, unleashed demand for a wide range of economic and social programs.

Following democratization, the chaebol used their new power to expand their business and turned to bank loans to fuel that expansion. When the chaebol, which had already been heavily leveraged, increased their borrowing significantly, a classic problem of moral hazard developed. Knowing that they had become too big to fail, the chaebol demanded and received even more credit. They understood that the dislocations following the failure of one or more chaebol would be so large that the threat of failure would force the government to help keep them solvent. Moral hazard induced the firms to take larger and larger risks, making them—and the Korean economy more generally—vulnerable to a major economic downturn. These business groups were in essence gambling with public money. If the risky ventures succeeded, they would keep the returns, but if the ventures failed and the chaebol became insolvent, the government would pick up the losses. This asymmetry of returns gave the chaebol incentive to expand their gambling through much greater leverage. The chaebol expansion reached its peak in 1994 to 1996, and their excesses set the stage for the financial crisis in 1997.

Our explanation for the role of economic openness, or lack thereof, in the 1997 financial crisis is not inconsistent with a standard interpretation of the crisis, that premature financial liberalization and deregulation without a strong regulatory system contributed to overborrowing by the chaebol. Even though financial liberation is widely understood as increasing economic access, the Korean crisis shows that it does not lead to genuine economic openness unless it is accompanied by prudential regulations that in turn require an expansion of political openness. In the absence of double balance, economic liberalization may expand social risk or moral hazard.

In this chapter, we explain the critical role of business-government relations in the investment boom of 1994 to 1996, focusing on how the government failed to contain the chaebol's moral hazard incentives. In short: the moral hazard underlying the chaebol's becoming too big to fail was endogenous to the political system. In the sections that follow, we discuss the investment boom prior to the crisis, the post-crisis economic reforms, and the impact of those reforms on business-government relations.

During the 1997 crisis, the Korean government reacted quickly, negotiating a reform agreement with the International Monetary Fund (IMF). The government recognized the importance of corporate discipline and undertook extensive economic reforms to reduce the problem of moral hazard in the corporate sector.

An important, open question is whether such reforms have continued to make the Korean political economy less vulnerable to the problem of moral hazard. We argue that while the chaebol remain dominant business organizations, they are less likely now and in the future to cause a financial crisis through excessive borrowing. Economic reforms have created a number of new actors in the economy, such as capital markets, more independent banks, and active minority shareholders who act as nongovernment sources of corporate discipline.

The Investment Boom of 1994–1996

The roots of Korean firms' heavy indebtedness and subsequent insolvency lie in the boom in business investing from 1994 to 1996.[1] During those three years, facility investment in manufacturing rose by an average of 38.5 percent per year. Investment was particularly robust in 1994 and 1995, when it grew at rates of 56.2 and 43.5 percent, respectively. Korea had not seen this kind of expansion since the famed Heavy and Chemical Industry Drive of the 1970s.

The investment boom was not uniform across business sectors, however. In contrast to Thailand, where property investments played an important role in the subsequent crisis, manufacturing led Korea's investment boom. Within manufacturing, surveys show that the bulk of the investments (65.7 percent) were made to expand existing production lines (see Table 7.1); relatively small percentages of manufacturing investments went to corporate restructuring and rationalization (15.5 percent),

---

1. This section borrows from Haggard and Mo (2000).

Table 7.1. Cycles of Facility Investments

	1st expansion (1972–1979)	1st adjustment (1980–1982)	2nd expansion (1983–1991)	2nd adjustment (1992–1993)	3rd expansion (1994–1996)	3rd adjustment (1997–1998)
Average growth rate (%)						
All industries	41.8	1.3	20.0	–1.0	30.1	–18.8
Manufacturing	41.3	–11.3	29.6	–8.9	38.5	–29.0
Heavy and chemical industries	39.9	–11.2	32.0	–10.8	43.1	–28.6
Light industries	46.8	–8.2	22.5	0.9	15.0	–32.0
Large enterprises	39.6	0.3	28.7	–7.6	45.7	–11.6
SMEs	53.2	–22.0	24.0	–10.5	17.7	10.5
Nonmanufacturing	42.7	21.8	10.0	15.5	17.3	1.1
Reason for investment (manufacturing) (%)						
Capacity expansion	62.9	62.9	69.6	61.2	65.7	66.5

Rationalization	20.7	20.7	17.3	20.1	15.5	14.7
Pollution control	4.1	4.1	1.1	2.5	2.5	1.7
R&D facilities	3.6	3.6	4.3	6.6	6.2	8.4
Other	8.6	8.6	8.5	9.7	10.1	8.9
Sources of funds (manufacturing) (%)						
External financing	76.4	76.4	65.8	68.7	71.7	72.7
Bank loans	20.1	20.1	31.0	31.5	29.5	32.6
Foreign currency borrowing	12.9	12.9	12.1	10.3	20.4	11.4
Internal financing	23.6	23.6	34.3	31.3	28.3	27.4

Source: Korea Development Bank, *Survey of Facility Investment Plans* (Seoul), various issues.

Note: SMEs = small and medium-size enterprises.

pollution abatement (2.5 percent), and research and development (6.2 percent). Moreover, investments in heavy and chemical industries grew at an annual rate of 43.1 percent while the rate of growth for light industries was only 15 percent. In terms of firm size, large firms rather than small and medium-size businesses set the pace: investments by large enterprises grew 45.7 percent while small and medium-size enterprises increased their investments by 17.7 percent. In sum, real manufacturing investment by the large chaebol in heavy industries dominated this boom, notably in the production of automobiles, petrochemicals, steel, and electronics.

For students of Korea, this pattern sounds familiar. Compared with the two previous episodes of rapid investment growth (1972–1979 and 1983–1991), however, the 1994–1996 period displayed two distinguishing features. First, the emphasis on manufacturing and large enterprises was even more marked than in the past. Second, dependence on foreign currency borrowings was substantially higher in 1994–1996 (20.4 percent) than it had been during 1972–1979, when it accounted for only 12.9 percent of the total investment, or 1983–1991, when it represented 12.1 percent (see Table 7.1).

Both long-term structural needs and short-term economic factors help explain the increase in facility investments by Korean firms in the mid-1990s. Increased investment was in part a response to the decline of Korean firms' competitiveness, associated with rapid increases in labor costs in the late 1980s, which was in turn a function of the country's democratization (Mo and Moon 1999). As in the past, a declining ability to compete in labor-intensive industries contributed to increased purchases of capital equipment, much of it from abroad (Cha 1998). Cyclical factors were also relevant. The country was coming out of two years of negative investment growth (1992–1993), the first time investment had fallen since 1980, and particular industry sectors, such as semiconductors, had begun to enjoy unprecedented growth. Additionally, the yen began to appreciate against the dollar in 1993. This development appeared to provide an opportunity for Korean exporters to take market share from their Japanese competitors. In fact, although the yen continued to rise against the dollar until the second quarter of 1995, it then started an equally rapid descent.

Along with these economic factors, government policy also proved central in igniting the boom. Consider macroeconomic policy: when

President Kim Young Sam took office in 1993, his advisors were concerned that his ambitious economic and political programs would not succeed without a robust economy. Growth was sluggish by Korean standards, and the government put a priority on "recovery" with an economic stimulus package (the so-called New Economy 100-Day Plan), which it announced on March 22, 1993. The package consisted of interest rate cuts, an increased supply of facility investment funds, and early

Table 7.2. Macroeconomic Management, 1993–1996

			Interest rates				
	Quarter	Yen-dollar exchange rate[a]	Money supply[b] (%)	Overnight call rate[c] (%)	Yield on 3-year corporate bonds[c] (%)	GDP growth rate (%)	Equipment investment growth rate (%)
1993	1	117.01	16.7	10.86[a]	11.44[a]	4.1	−11.8
	2	107.34	18.9	13.02[a]	12.37[a]	4.9	−1.1
	3	105.28	21.5	12.41[a]	14.04[a]	6.9	5.0
	4	109.70	17.3	11.50[a]	12.21[a]	6.7	8.7
1994	1	105.14	15.8	11.29	12.16	8.9[d]	20.9
	2	102.72	15.8	12.12	12.39	7.9	16.8
	3	98.81	14.8	13.34	13.18	7.8	24.3
	4	100.12	17.6	12.92	13.39	9.4	30.6
1995	1	90.79	16.5	14.17	15.06	10.0	24.9
	2	84.53	15.9	13.03	14.75	9.8	18.5
	3	100.49	13.9	11.50	13.43	9.8	22.1
	4	101.81	13.7	11.20	11.93	6.7	1.0
1996	1	105.82	14.6	10.52	11.88	7.8	4.9
	2	108.86	16.2	11.12	11.18	6.9	4.6
	3	109.75	17.4	13.97	12.14	6.6	9.3
	4	113.76	17.8	13.84	12.27	7.2	13.7

Source: Economic Planning Board, Ministry of Finance and Economy, *Economic White Paper* (Seoul), various years; National Statistics Office, *Major Statistics of Korean Economy* (Seoul), various issues.

[a]End of quarter.

[b]Annual increase in end-of-quarter average balance.

[c]Average over the period.

[d]Estimated.

implementation of government projects. As Table 7.2 shows, the money supply increased rapidly in 1993 after the stimulus package was announced. But investment activity was also affected by a more complex array of liberalization initiatives, supported by market reformers at the Economic Planning Board and the Korea Development Institute. These policies included deregulation of both corporate entry and the financial system. In 1993, the Kim Young Sam government introduced its "business specialization policy," under which the chaebol were asked to designate core industries and phase out their noncore businesses.

This policy was designed to curb the increasing concentration of chaebol power and influence; in return, the government offered the conglomerates exemptions from credit and equity-investment controls. First introduced in 1974 and strengthened in subsequent years, the credit control system was designed to control chaebol expansion through credit control, regulations on entry into the market, investments, acquisition of assets and real estate holdings, and the capital requirements in investment projects. Because the government had limited entry into a number of business sectors in the past, deregulation led to rapid increases in facility investment in some key industries.

In 1995–1996 the government struggled to deal with the overcapacity in petrochemicals brought about by the temporary end of investment controls in 1990. In 1994, the government had been pressured to relax entry and investment restrictions in the steel and semiconductor industries. After a long controversy, it granted Samsung a permit in December 1994 to build a passenger car factory. Samsung had made many attempts to enter the passenger vehicle industry, against strong opposition by both incumbent firms and bureaucrats at the Ministry of Trade and Industry. Politics appeared to break the stalemate in favor of Samsung: the company decided to locate the plant in Busan, the economically struggling hometown of President Kim Young Sam.

The chaebol's motivations for capacity expansion represent the demand side of increased corporate borrowing; we also need to understand the supply side: why banks made the loans. As Table 7.3 shows, the expansion of investment between 1994 and 1996 relied heavily on borrowing, especially short-term debt. Again, domestic and international liberalization factor into the story. On the domestic front, the government deregulated the commercial paper market in 1994 by lifting administrative controls on the yields and supply of commercial

Table 7.3. Funds Raised by the Corporate Sector

	1994		1995		1996		1st half of 1997	
	Amount (billion won)	%	Amount (billion won)	%	Amount (billion won)	%	Amount (billion won)	%
Total funds raised	89,045.5	100.0	100,016.2	100.0	118,201.0	100.0	61,102	100.0
Borrowings from banks and NBFIs	39,649.6	44.5	31,854.8	31.8	36,995.3	31.3	29,755	47.9
Direct finance	33,939.9	38.1	48,070.6	48.1	55,600.6	47.0	19,161	30.9
Commercial paper	4,405.0	4.9	16,096.2	16.1	20,690.6	17.5	5,277	8.5
Borrowings from abroad	4,407.3	4.9	8,392.3	8.4	12,062.9	10.2	5,732	9.2
Others	11,043.6	12.4	11,698.5	11.7	13,542.2	1.5	7,453	12.0

Source: Cho 1998.

Note: NBFIs = nonbank financial institutions.

paper (CP), offering an attractive financing instrument for companies and a profitable market for the CP-discounting merchant banks. Liberalization of the CP market led to the rapid expansion of short-term financing (Cho 1998).

The Korean government also tried to solve the problem of weak short-term finance companies by offering them new business opportunities instead of forcing them to restructure or close. The government converted twenty-four financially weak short-term financing companies into merchant banks in two separate rounds, converting nine in 1994 and fifteen in 1996. Most of the new merchant banks aggressively pursued new businesses, including risky foreign-exchange transactions. Of the sixteen merchant banks whose licenses were revoked in 1998 by the government following the financial crisis, fifteen were new entrants in 1994–1996.

Liberalization of the financial market was not limited to the domestic arena. In the name of globalization, the Korean government eliminated many restrictions on the movement of capital, allowing Korean banks and firms to borrow from abroad and international investors to invest in Korean assets. The foreign supply of capital was plentiful, and foreign banks were happy to lend to Korean banks and firms in 1995 and 1996. After Korea joined the Organization for Economic Cooperation and Development (OECD) in February 1996, Korean banks were able to borrow even more easily because of the confidence that its OECD membership inspired. Between 1994, when Korea's application passed its first test, and 1996, when it officially joined the OECD, foreign banks more than doubled their lending to South Korea, from $52 billion to $108 billion.

Korean banks also invested in the range of $23 billion in foreign assets, using funds borrowed from foreign banks. The idea that Korea's financial market liberalization was misguided because of the lack of appropriate regulation has become a leitmotif in the literature on the crisis (Goldstein 1998, World Bank 1998). Merchant banks have come in for particular scrutiny because their inability to roll over short-term foreign borrowing was an important trigger to the crisis. However, the claim of inadequate regulation begs the deeper issue of whether, despite the apparent deregulation of both corporate activity and the banking sector, lending was effectively encouraged and supported by government policy, which in turn generated moral hazard.[2]

We suggest four reasons why the nature of business-government relations contributed to problems of moral hazard during the investment boom of the mid-1990s. First, as we argued in Chapter 6, democratic politics exacerbated the moral hazard problem with respect to corporate failure. During Korea's developmental-state period prior to democratization, the government had served as the sole effective mechanism of corporate discipline because of the underdevelopment of financial markets, including the market for corporate control, and the weakness

---

2. An argument in the popular press held that industrial policy was the culprit. Certainly the government had allocated credit to favored sectors through policy loans and administrative guidance in the past (Cho and Kim 1995). However, one has to be careful about linking the economic crisis to the moral hazard problem through the route of industrial policy (Chang 1999). First, the problem of moral hazard in the banking sector had always existed, so we have to ask why it became particularly problematic in the mid-1990s. Second, explicit industrial policy had been abandoned beginning in 1986 and, as we have noted, the government's push in the direction of deregulation was a theme of the Kim Young Sam administration.

of internal discipline (such as minority shareholders). During the periods of rapid growth, the Korean government periodically intervened to force insolvent firms out of the market—including 1969 to 1971–1972, 1980 to 1982, and 1985 to 1989.

Following democratization, however, the government no longer intervened to force out the weak firms. The cessation of intervention occurred for several reasons. First, the chaebol gained significant political influence under democracy through the importance of campaign financing, and this weakened the ability of political officials to oppose their interests. Also, the lack of balance under the developmental state led to an asymmetry of political influence in the democratic period, with far stronger economic interest groups than political and social ones. As a consequence, the government lacked the political support to pay the political costs associated with forced corporate restructuring.

Second, despite the nominal abandonment of targeted industrial policies, the government continued to act directly in the financial markets through the Korea Development Bank (KDB), whose main function was to provide long-term investment funds to companies. Since corporate borrowing in 1994–1996 was driven by facility investment, and since the KDB provided a large percentage of facility-investment funds, private financial institutions may have seen KDB lending decisions as signaling either government support or government displeasure. KDB was one of the lead banks involved with Hanbo Steel, the first Korean chaebol to go bankrupt in the crisis of 1997, and investigations of that company's bankruptcy case revealed that commercial banks had followed KDB's lead in increasing their lending to Hanbo in 1993. Hanbo is arguably a special case of corruption, an issue we will return to later. But the evidence suggests that banks interpreted KDB's substantial lending as indicating government policy and commitment.[3]

---

3. During the 1994–1996 period, the KDB increased its credit supply at rapid rates: 26.1 percent in 1994, 24 percent in 1995, and 18.3 percent in 1996. This rate of increase in KDB lending surpassed that of facility investment in manufacturing in 1996. At the time, the KDB supported the government's investment promotion policy. Certainly the KDB had the capacity to influence private financing of investment projects. KDB loans accounted for 11 percent of total financial credit in 1995. More tellingly, the KDB's equipment investment loans outstanding as of the end of 1994 (18.2 trillion won) were 45.7 percent of the total outstanding loans of the KDB and all deposit banks (39.9 trillion

The third political source of moral hazard resides in the incentives for monitoring corporate behavior on the part of banks. The government, which exercised control over the banks, reduced incentives to monitor lending, particularly when macroeconomic policy was accommodative. With the risk of lending minimized, the banks became inefficient, backward, and dependent. Korean banks are notorious for maintaining an excess number of workers and branches. They also lagged behind in using modern financial techniques, emphasizing collateral rather than the merits of investment proposals and cash flow.

Moreover, liberalization created additional incentive problems with respect to Korea's nonbank financial institutions. The chaebol's hold on nonbank financial institutions (such as merchant banks) increased following the move toward greater financial deregulation. Because many of these nonbank financial institutions were controlled by the chaebol, these lending institutions did not carefully monitor their loans to their chaebol parents. This problem worsened during the 1990s because financial deregulation allowed the nonbanking financial sector to expand its market share rapidly. With the nonbank financial institutions' questionable governance, the banking sector as a whole became more vulnerable to moral hazard.

Finally, influence peddling in the banking sector may have increased, or at least continued, in the mid-1990s. Because of the political relationships between politicians, the banks, and their clients, the banks had fewer incentives to monitor loans carefully and weakened information for managing their loan portfolios.

The investigation of the Hanbo bankruptcy revealed the presence of an influence-peddling network in which the firm lobbied not only bank officials but also government officials and legislators to maintain its credit lines. All principal actors in the Hanbo lending scandal were members of Kim Young Sam's political faction, including the president of Korea First Bank (Hanbo's main creditor), key officials in the Ministry of Finance and Economy and the Blue House, and the superintendent of the Bank Supervisory Board (the agency responsible for banking regulations). As we will see, the effects of corruption were not limited to

---

won). In 1994, the KDB accounted for 44.2 percent of the increase in equipment investment financing by the KDB and all deposit money banks.

the moral hazard it engendered; corruption also affects the credibility of government policy more generally.[4]

Explaining the pattern of investment during a short time frame is necessarily difficult, since many market forces and government policies come into play. A combination of politically motivated macroeconomic policy and, particularly, deregulation contributed to the burst of manufacturing-facility investment in the mid-1990s. However, the nature of the government's regulation of the economy and, more profoundly, ongoing characteristics of business-bank-chaebol relations also contributed to the moral hazard problem in the banking sector. Those characteristics included direct government involvement in lending, weak incentives for banks to conduct due-diligence and monitoring functions, expansion of the chaebol into the nonbank financial sector, the unwillingness of the government to force corporate bankruptcies, and outright corruption. These distorted incentives in the financial sector allowed the chaebol to raise and invest unprecedented amounts of capital in 1994–1996.

This argument shows that the genesis of the financial crisis was not simply economic and financial; nor was it simply a regulatory failure. In fact, profound political forces underlay the crisis. The political influence of the chaebol stemmed from three factors: their growth during the pre-democracy phase, without a counterbalancing civil society; the central role of campaign finance, which forced elected officials to stop imposing discipline on the chaebol; and the incentive problems associated with the chaebol being too big to fail. In combination, these factors allowed the chaebol to gain favorable treatment—including lax enforcement of regulations and ever-larger loans—so they could take greater risks. These risks made them and the larger Korean economy more vulnerable to a crisis.

Post-Crisis Economic Reforms

In November 1997, when the Korean government could no longer meet its foreign liabilities, it turned to the IMF for help. Tough negotiations led to the agreement in December 1997 under which the South Korean

---

4. Chang (1999) dismisses the role of corruption on the grounds that it was limited to a few cases, but Hanbo's significance to the banking sector should not be underestimated.

government pledged to restructure its troubled banking sector and place many weak companies under bank-led restructuring programs. The government also promised to carry out extensive institutional reforms aimed at strengthening the long-term competitiveness of Korean banks and companies. The reforms sought to replace the system of "governed" markets with a system that was more market oriented. "Good governance," "liberalization," and "deregulation" became catchphrases in post-crisis policy debates and pronouncements.

After the IMF bailout agreement, the task of implementation fell squarely on the new president-elect, Kim Dae Jung, who won the election on 18 December 1997. On taking office in February 1998, President Kim quickly moved to stabilize the devastated financial markets. This involved multiple tasks. First, the government had to close or merge insolvent financial institutions and strengthen the capital base of those that remained viable. This required disposing of nonperforming loans and recapitalizing financial institutions through public funds or foreign investment. Second, the regulatory system needed to be reformed to ensure transparency, accountability, and sound management in financial institutions. Third, the government needed to engineer further deregulation and liberalization of the financial markets to induce foreign investment as well as to demonstrate its commitment to financial reform. Lastly, the government had to develop the institutional capacity to carry out these reforms.

Fortunately for Kim Dae Jung, the institutional and legal foundations for financial reform had already been laid by the time he came to power. In December 1997, the National Assembly passed the thirteen financial reform bills that the preceding president, Kim Young Sam, had wanted so desperately during the months preceding the IMF bailouts. These reforms consolidated the fragmented regulatory agencies into one agency with streamlined responsibilities (to become the Financial Supervisory Commission), reformed the deposit insurance system, and created the legal foundations for raising bank bailout funds and reorganizing troubled financial institutions. After several months of adjustment and preparation, the new institutional arrangement became fully operational in April 1998.

With the necessary institutions in place, the Kim Dae Jung government moved to force out insolvent financial institutions. In January 1998, the government effectively nationalized 2 commercial banks (Korea

First Bank and Seoul Bank) by reducing existing shareholder equity to one-eighth and injecting 1.5 trillion won (US$1.5 billion at the exchange rate of 1,000 won per dollar) of new equity into each. It then proceeded to sell those two banks to foreign investors. In April, the government listed twelve banks that failed to meet the capital-adequacy requirement of the Bank for International Settlements and asked them to submit restructuring plans for further review. Government actions against troubled nonbank financial institutions were also swift. By April, thirteen out of thirty merchant banks had had their licenses revoked, one merchant bank had been suspended, one trust company had been closed, and two securities firms had been suspended. At the same time, the government, through the Korea Asset Management Company, purchased nonperforming assets from financial institutions and sought to reduce their debt burden by purchasing the bonds that they issued.

In the following months, the government committed additional public funds, totaling 50 trillion won, to purchase nonperforming assets, recapitalize financial firms, and protect deposits. On 29 June 1998 the government finally decided the fate of those twelve banks without adequate capital provisions. It suspended five (Donghwa, Dongnam, Daedong, Kyunggi, and Chungchung), ordering them to merge with stronger banks. The rest survived, but with strong restructuring conditions, such as changes of management, reductions in manpower, and new equity financing. As a result of these measures, financial market stability returned. Banks again began to lend, and interest rates began to fall.

Financial reforms continued after 1998. Subsequent reforms have continued to emphasize the strengthening of central banking and financial supervision systems, financial sector restructuring, prudential regulations, capital account liberalization, governance of financial institutions, and capital market reforms (Hahm and Lim 2006).[5]

Hand in hand with financial restructuring, the Kim Dae Jung government also pursued corporate restructuring. Corporate and financial restructurings were inseparable because corporate-sector insolvency, in

---

5. Important reform measures include the introduction of financial holding companies (FHCs), including the incorporation of Woori FHC and Shinhan FHC in 2001, and a new set of prudential regulations in 2002 that limited bank lending to one borrower and to large shareholders and that raised the bank ownership limit on domestic residents to 10 percent.

turn, had driven Korean banks into insolvency. Since the 1980s, Korean companies had seen their profitability decline even as they increased their borrowings. By the time of the crisis, most large Korean firms had difficulty servicing their debts.

On 13 January 1998, Kim Dae Jung reached an agreement with corporate leaders on five principles of corporate restructuring: enhancing transparency in accounting and management, limiting mutual payment guarantees among chaebol members, improving firms' financial structure, streamlining business activities, and strengthening managerial accountability. By February, the government was ready to implement these principles, after revising ten relevant laws.

The reliability of Korean firms' accounting data also became a reform issue. Murky accounting practices had allowed firms to bypass restrictions on investment and transfer pricing; they had also discouraged foreign investment. In response, the Kim Dae Jung administration pushed the revision of the Outside Auditor Law to accelerate the adoption of consolidated financial statements and to require listed firms to establish an outside auditor selection committee. The National Assembly passed these revisions on 14 February 1998. Consolidated financial statements would provide more accurate information about the chaebol's financial conditions by showing internal transactions among their subsidiaries, including their cross-shareholdings and mutual payment guarantees. The government also strengthened the role of outside auditors by requiring that they be selected by a committee of shareholders and creditor banks rather than by controlling shareholders alone, and by increasing the penalties on outside auditors for wrongdoing.

The government also moved to resolve the issue of mutual payment guarantees among different firms within the same chaebol. Among other problems, these guarantees made it more likely that if one component of a chaebol became financially distressed, so too would the others (Lim and Morck 2010). The government prohibited the new issuance of such guarantees among chaebol subsidiaries, beginning 1 April 1998, and required the chaebol to phase out existing guarantees by March 2000.

To induce corporations to reduce their bank debt, the government directed banks to negotiate financial restructuring agreements with their debtor companies by April. A total of 64 conglomerates or debtor groups were directed to this program, and the 5 largest chaebol in particular were asked to reduce their debt ratios below 200 percent by the end of 1999. Officially, these agreements between banks and chaebol were voluntary, but there was no doubt that the government was deeply involved. To discourage future corporate borrowings, the government revised the corporate tax law on 14 February so that beginning in the year 2000 it would disallow tax deductions for interest payments on "excessive" borrowings.

The government also relied on the banks to close insolvent firms and force the chaebol to streamline their business activities through liquidating and consolidating subsidiaries. This included exchanges of subsidiaries among the chaebol (so-called big deals) and other restructuring measures. On 18 June the banks announced a list of fifty-five insolvent firms, including twenty chaebol subsidiaries, that were to close. Other firms judged to be troubled, if not insolvent, were required to enter into "workout" a plan with their main creditor bank under which the troubled firms would receive additional financial support in return for restructuring efforts. The workout plan has been applied to the smaller chaebol, those ranked sixth or below in total sales.

The fifth and last principle of corporate restructuring sought to hold owner-managers accountable for their decisions. Although the chaebol's owner-managers had effectively exercised control over their subsidiaries, they held positions of questionable legal status, such as "group chairman." These positions gave owners control of the chaebol while allowing them to legally avoid liability for the damage their actions may have caused. To address this problem, the government changed the regulations to force the chaebol to abolish the position of group chairman and to appoint owner-managers to the board of at least one of the member firms. To enhance monitoring of corporate decision making, the government in February 1999 revised the regulations for companies listed on the stock market, requiring listed firms to appoint outside directors.

At the same time, the government further strengthened minority shareholders' rights in May 1999 by lowering the minimum share requirement (from 1 to 0.01 percent) for filing a derivative suit, a suit of personal liability against management for an illegal activity or a serious breach of due diligence. Efforts to enhance the rights of minority shareholders had begun with the Kim Young Sam administration, and subsequently a popular grassroots movement had developed, led by a citizens' group called People's Solidarity for Participatory Democracy (Jang 2000). These changes in corporate governance have allowed citizens' groups, acting as representatives of minority shareholders and sometimes foreign investors, to uncover questionable transactions in several prominent chaebol firms, including SK Telecom and Samsung Electronics. Many predicted that the new corporate governance system, more than any other reform, would bring about fundamental changes in the way companies are run in Korea when foreign shareholders, whose number increased rapidly as a result of financial liberalization, started demanding accountability and board representation (Jang 2000).[6]

The ability of the Kim Dae Jung government to carry out politically difficult post-crisis reforms is attributed to the following factors: the crisis conditions, external pressures and leadership, and coalitional dynamics (Mo and Moon 1999; 2003). The crisis conditions effectively neutralized political opposition to economic reforms. Having been singled out as the main culprits in the crisis, the chaebol's voice lost credibility. Nor did labor mount significant opposition; labor unions had played an unconstructive role in the persistence of policy gridlock in the pre-crisis period. Perhaps the Korean government had no choice but to implement a comprehensive reform program because the IMF demanded such a program. But the preferences of domestic actors also mattered. Even before the crisis, President Kim had cultivated a reputation as a market-friendly economic reformer, so his favored policies did not depart significantly from the IMF recommendations. Even if he had wanted more radical reforms, he would have been constrained by his conservative coalition partners in the government. In the 1997 election President Kim formed a coalition with the United Liberal Democrats, holdovers from the Park Chung Hee era, who dominated the initial formulation of the Kim Dae Jung government's reform policy through their presence on the Emergency Economic Committee.

---

6. After 1998 the focus of corporate reform moved on to competition policy and corporate corruption. The chaebol's post-crisis expansion made the shift in emphasis necessary. In August 1999 the government added three new principles of corporate reform: improved management structure of secondary financial institutions, limits on equity investments by the chaebol, and prevention of irregular inheritance and gift giving. The government also restored the thirty-group designation system under which the investment decisions of the thirty largest business conglomerates are closely monitored.

The Impact of Economic Reforms on Business-Government Relations

The corporate reforms of the Kim Dae Jung government reversed the privileged position of big business. Arguing that the chaebol were responsible for the 1997 economic crisis, the government began to favor an arms-length relationship with business, if not an outright adversarial one. In the process of corporate and financial restructurings, the government reversed its weak position relative to big business and ended up gaining dominance over it.

Government dominance turned out to be short-lived, however. Once the government completed the corporate and financial restructurings, it found its power limited in a newly reformed market economy.

Lasting legacies of economic reforms in business-government relations can be found elsewhere instead, especially in financial markets. The most striking change has been the rise of foreign ownership and control in the banking sector (Mo 2009b). Among the seven nationwide commercial banks operating now, only Woori FH is still owned by the Korean government (almost all commercial banks had been effectively nationalized in the wake of the financial crisis). Foreign investors now have majority stakes in six out of the seven commercial banks and have gained control of three of them (KEB, Citibank, and Standard Chartered Bank). It has been estimated that foreign-controlled banks account for 33.3 to 50.0 percent of bank assets in Korea. The other three banks in which foreign investors hold the majority of shares but lack a controlling interest, Kookmin, Hana, and Shinhan, have at least one foreign director on their board, indicating that foreign investors have gained some influence over the direction of management in those banks. This suggests that since the crisis began, the ownership of Korean commercial banks has been effectively transferred from the government to foreign capital rather than to domestic capital.

Foreign investors have also been the main source of investment funds in the equity market. The share of equity market capitalization by foreign investors has been rising steadily, reaching 43.3 percent in 2005.

Shareholder activism is another change with significant implications for corporate discipline. Civil society groups, such as People's Solidarity for Participatory Democracy, have brought minority shareholder rights to the forefront of public debate. They often align with foreign investors to demand more accountability from the chaebol. Institutional investors such as pensions and mutual funds have also been active in asserting their shareholder rights.

It is too early, however, to conclude that financial reform, transparency, foreign-investor monitoring, and more competitive and open financial markets now act as strong counterbalances against the chaebol. We can, for example, point to the persistent family control of the chaebol as evidence that the impact of financial reform on corporate discipline is limited. Although the proportion of shares that they directly own has declined, owner-families have been able to maintain control through extensive intersubsidiary shareholdings. The average in-group share for the top 30 chaebol controlled by the family—directly owned and owned by subsidiaries—was 43.4 percent in 2000. This proportion is almost equal to 1995 and 1996 levels, even though the proportion of the directly owned shares fell to 4.5 percent in 2000, down from 10.5 percent in 1995 and 10.3 percent in 1996. This growing gap between the shares directly owned and the shares actually controlled by owner-families shows that the chaebol are more vulnerable now than they were before to the expropriation of minority shareholders by controlling shareholders.[7]

Nevertheless, the post-crisis economic reforms have built the basic institutional structure for market-based corporate discipline in Korea. Even more significantly, they have brought in many new economic players—such as banks, foreign investors, and institutional investors—who are independent of both the government and the chaebol. In this sense, the levels of economic openness and pluralism have significantly improved in the post-crisis period.

Conclusions

The idea of double balance helps explain the political genesis of the 1997 financial crisis and its aftermath. Korea could not have avoided a crisis in 1997, but political factors greatly exacerbated the magnitude of the crisis. Under the predemocratic regime, economic openness and favorable policies allowed the growth of powerful economic organizations. In contrast, the regime suppressed political openness, precluding the parallel

---

7. Samsung is a typical case. In 2005, the founder's family controlled 31.13 percent of shares while their direct ownership share fell to 4.41 percent. Before the crisis, the founder's family controlled close to 50 percent of shares.

growth of the kinds of powerful political and social organizations that could counterbalance the influence of economic organizations. This lack of balance manifested itself in the new Korean democratic politics mainly through campaign finance. Elected officials needed funds to run their campaigns, which the chaebol willingly provided. This promoted a dependence that, in turn, made it difficult for the government to impose controls on the chaebol, allowing the unconstrained conglomerates to take on much new debt and riskier investments, and in some cases doing so while in financial difficulties. The relative dearth of powerful political and social groups meant that political officials had insufficient support for taking strong actions unfavorable to the chaebol; chaebol reform languished.

The chaebol also faced a form of moral hazard induced by their too-big-to-fail quality. Here, too, the government failed to counterbalance these incentives as it had in the previous era, in part because of the chaebol's influence after democratization and in part because allowing the chaebol to fail would indeed put the entire economy at risk. The chaebol's incentives, many fostered by the government, led them to increase investments and debt, making them significantly more vulnerable to financial problems and subject to larger bailout costs once the crisis hit. In short, political policy choices made the crisis far worse than it otherwise would have been.

The theory of double balance also explains the success of the post-crisis reforms. The immediate political consequence of the 1997 crisis was the opening of the political system, which allowed an opposition party to take power for the first time since the transition to democracy in 1987. As we have emphasized, the increasing power of the chaebol had gradually reduced the economic and political openness of the pre-crisis system. Since it would have been difficult for a conservative government to impose regulatory controls as stringent as those Kim Dae Jung imposed on the chaebol sector, we can argue that a widening of political access during the crisis period was a precondition for the expansion of economic access after the crisis.

The 1997 financial crisis had some positive effects, though how positive is still hard to assess. The swift government reaction to the financial crisis curbed the chaebol's influence. The reforms dramatically changed the rules, diminishing incentives for excessive borrowing, increasing transparency and monitoring, and removing the cross-shareholdings and mutual guarantees that increased the conglomerates' overall risk. These changes also reduced the chaebol's hold on politics so that the government could enforce the rules. And all of these changes have been backed by an active public seeking to prevent future crises that could directly harm their interests. As good times return, however, public attentiveness inevitably lapses. How well the new structures and incentives work over the long term remains to be seen.

CHAPTER 8

The Politics of Economic Policy under Roh Moo Hyun, 2003–2008

The post-crisis reform process initiated by President Kim Dae Jung continued after he left office in 2003. The priority of reforms, however, shifted after 2003. While President Kim pursued the reform of the Korean corporate and banking sectors with strong determination, his focus on economic reform neglected reform of Korean politics, something many people had expected him to carry out, in light of his dissident background. The task of political reform fell instead to his successor, President Roh Moo Hyun. From the perspective of Korea's transition to open access, President Roh's reforms are significant because they represent a continuation of the rebalancing process that began in the aftermath of the economic crisis. Roh's political reforms and post-crisis economic reforms are related, as the former strengthened the political base for forces in favor of the latter.

Roh Moo Hyun took office in 2003 after winning as the ruling party candidate in an upset victory in 2002 over the heavily favored Lee Hoi-chang, the candidate of the opposition Grand National Party. The 2002 election was more than a personal victory for Roh, however. From our perspective on the balance of political and economic openness, the 2002 election was important for two reasons. First, the election significantly increased the openness of the Korean political system. The 2002 election saw new policy views and issues emerging in Korean electoral politics, making Korean elections more competitive and the party system more fragmented. After the 2002 election new political actors and groups entered Korean politics, strengthening the civil society as well, and making both society and politics more pluralistic. Early indications are that both of these effects are significant. As Table 2.1 in Chapter 2 shows, Freedom House raised Korea's rating for political rights to its highest possible score in 2004—the first time it had revised Korea's score since 1987. And a new politically active generation—the so-called 386 generation—emerged as a significant political force in Korean politics.

Second, the 2002 election is important because these new political actors supported and led the economic and political reforms of President Roh, further expanding economic and political access. Strongly based on left-wing ideologies, Roh's economic and political reforms aimed at diffusing the political and economic power that he viewed as concentrated in the hands of a few establishment groups, such as the chaebol, elite universities, and media elites.

In the first section of this chapter we discuss the rise of the 386 generation. We then turn to President Roh's political agenda and sketch the impact of this agenda on economic policymaking. In addition, we will review the new institutional arrangements under Roh and discuss their implications for policy outcomes.

The 2002 Election and the Rise of the 386 Generation

The election of Roh Moo Hyun represented a significant break in domestic politics. In South Korean politics, the years from 1987 to 2002 are called the years of the three Kims (Presidents Kim Young Sam, Kim Dae Jung, and Kim Jong Pil), as a testimony to their dominance of party politics during that period.

Korea's early democracy, dominated by the three Kims, is associated with a distinctive system of voting behavior, party organizations, and campaign finance. The defining characteristic of the politics of the three Kims is regionalism. All three presidents had strong support from their regional bases. Due to the salience of the regional cleavage, the three Kims did not have to pay much attention to policy competition. Since their political fortunes depended on maintaining regional support, they concentrated on maintaining their regional networks through political contributions and patronage. The political parties of the three

Kims were, therefore, highly personal, and some said they were nothing more than entourage parties (Steinberg and Shin 2006).

The 2002 presidential election was significant not only because the last of the three Kims left politics but also because the Kims' style of politics went out with them. Changes in 2002 were so significant that political scientists began to claim that a new system of politics had emerged, calling it the 2002 system (Kim 2006).

The main actors in the new 2002 system of politics pitted generations against each other, not regions. In particular, the 386 generation emerged as the dominant political group under the new system.[1] In 2002, the 386-generation voters were those in their 30s. Together with voters in their 20s, they broke with older voters and threw their support behind Roh Moo Hyun. The generation gap, which became salient in 2002 for the first time, has been the main political line of cleavage ever since (Lee 2004).

Roh Moo Hyun's victory at once elevated the 386 generation to the pivotal voting bloc of the 2002 election and propelled many of its leaders into mainstream politics. During the 2002 campaign, 386-generation politicians were key campaign advisors to Roh Moo Hyun, and they followed him to the Blue House after his victory. The second infusion of 386-generation politicians into positions of power took place in 2004, when at least 58 of them won seats in the National Assembly, representing nearly 20 percent of the total seats (*Hankook Ilbo*, 24 November 2004).

The rise of the 386 generation also meant a shift in the ruling ideology. More than other generations, the 386ers have strong policy preferences, which reflect a number of forces. The leaders of the 386 generation, the 386 politicians, can be best described as progressive (or social democratic) nationalists. Nationalism and socialism were the two leading influences on the student movement of the 1980s, when most of the 386 politicians started their political careers. They struggled for democracy against an authoritarian regime that was pro-American, anti–North Korean, and conservative, so this generation was naturally attracted to

---

1. The name "386" is shorthand for demographics of this group. The 3 stands for their age—they were then mostly in their 30s. The 8 is for the 1980s, the decade when they entered college. The 6 is for the 1960s, when most of them were born.

the opposite views: they were anti-American, pro–North Korea, and progressive.

By the time they propelled Roh Moo Hyun to the presidency, of course, the 386ers' political beliefs had changed. Between nationalism and socialism, the latter had weakened considerably. No major 386 politician openly advocated socialism or even European-style social democracy. But they remained strongly nationalist, that is, anti-American and pro–North Korean. A survey of newly elected Uri Party legislators in 2004 showed that all of them supported a policy of engagement with North Korea (as opposed to one of coercive pressure), and 50 percent of them indicated that China (rather than the United States) was Korea's most important diplomatic partner (*Dong-A Ilbo*, 16 April 2004).[2]

Moreover, most in the 386 generation, especially ordinary voters, display postmodern tendencies; that is, they are highly individualistic and postmaterialistic. They reject traditional authoritarian culture not only in politics but also in everyday life, favoring an equal and horizontal organizational culture. They are also postmaterialistic in that they participate in politics for the sake of participation and self-fulfillment, not just for political competition.

The 386ers have pioneered a new style of politics. They are media savvy and fully immersed in the information age. The young voters' favorite media for politics are the Internet and mobile communication devices, not traditional newspapers and television. They also organize differently. Instead of traditional political organizations based on money and regional ties, they prefer open-access parties with strong democratic governance.

The 2002 system of politics, then, introduced a completely new type of politics. It differed from the old system in all aspects, including leadership structure, policy preferences, values, and style. Before discussing the impact of the 2002 system on economic policymaking, it is important to understand the role of its first president, Roh Moo Hyun.

---

2. The nationalism of the 386 generation is not limited to its leaders. Ordinary 386-generation voters are also strongly nationalistic: 36 percent say that they do not like the United States, while 72 percent say that they do not dislike North Korea (Song 2003). Interestingly, the same survey reports that the voters in their 20s, the so-called post-386 generation, are more anti-American and pro–North Korean than the 386-generation voters.

Roh Moo Hyun and His Agendas

Even though Roh Moo Hyun received overwhelming support from 386-generation voters in the 2002 election and his 386-generation advisors influenced his political beliefs, it is still important to recognize that President Roh himself was not a 386-generation politician. A strong-willed individual, Roh Moo Hyun was determined to leave his own imprint on South Korean politics.

The first difference between Roh Moo Hyun and the 386-generation leadership is seen in their policy preferences and values. Although President Roh was sympathetic to the political values of the 386 generation, he was not as unconditionally committed to them, and where he was strongly committed, his beliefs did not quite coincide with those of the 386ers. President Roh's political beliefs were closer to antiestablishment populism than to the 386-generation types of nationalism and progressivism. The difference between Roh and the 386ers may be natural. Unlike his 386-generation advisors, Roh Moo Hyun did not go to an elite university. In fact, before he entered politics in 1988 he had been a complete outsider in Korean society, a relatively obscure lawyer in Busan. In contrast, the 386ers had always been in the mainstream in terms of their education and careers, even though they had been in the political opposition until 2002.

As an antiestablishment politician, Roh Moo Hyun's basic perspective on Korean society is that it is closed and concentrated, with economic and political powers concentrated in the hands of a few elite groups. He believed that Korea would not become an advanced capitalist democracy unless it weakened the concentrations of power in all areas of society. Roh supporters singled out five representative centers of elite power in Korea: Samsung Electronics (chaebol), *Chosun Ilbo* (conservative media), Seoul National University (elite educational system), Gangnam (the wealthiest district of Seoul), and the Supreme Court (conservative judicial elites). By endeavoring to dilute those existing centers of power, Roh sought to remake the elite structure of South Korean society (Steinberg 2006).

Antiregionalism was an equally important agenda for Roh Moo Hyun. Roh's vision for Korea was to make it a more equal, open-access society. According to the president, Korean party politics was excessively divisive; in that environment, it was impossible for political parties to cooperate and work toward the common good. Among the causes of the divisive nature of Korean politics, the president blamed regionalism. He believed that regionalism as the basis for political divisions created incentives for political confrontation; voters tended to reward politicians for taking a hard-line position against their regional opponents.

To appreciate the president's will to fight regionalism, a bit of personal background is informative. Former president Kim Young Sam first recruited Roh to politics by nominating him to run for the National Assembly in 1988. But he refused to join his patron when Kim merged his party with the two conservative parties in 1990. In the following ten years, Roh ran several times but failed to get elected as a member of the nonregional party. Frustrated by this failure, Roh compromised his principles and joined Kim Dae Jung's Cholla-based New Millennium Democratic Party (NMDP) in 1998. After winning the presidential election in 2002 as the NMDP candidate, he quickly left the NMDP and founded a new party, the Uri Party, in the name of antiregionalism. Thus, building a nonregional, progressive political force was an agenda that spanned his entire political career. President Roh proposed using proportional representation (PR), or multiple electoral-district systems, to increase political competition at the regional level; PR, or multiple districts, would allow nonregional parties to win some seats in strongly regionalistic areas.

While the 386ers helped create and define the 2002 system, their differences with President Roh meant that they were not able to dominate the policy agendas of the first government of the 2002 system. For Roh Moo Hyun, the goals of fighting the elite establishment and regionalism were more important. For example, Roh was less willing to rely on regionalism to win an election against a conservative party than were 386-generation leaders. The same was true for economic policy. Roh was more likely than 386-generation leaders to support balanced development over labor welfare if the two goals conflicted with each other.

The Impact of New Political Views on Economic Policy

The five principles of the Roh Moo Hyun government were nationalism, socialism, postmodernism, antiestablishment populism, and antiregionalism. To understand the character and development of economic policy under the Roh Moo Hyun government, one must first understand the ideological competition within the ruling bloc. After examining how each of the five principles influenced Roh's economic policy, we will discuss the complementarities and inconsistencies that existed among them.

Antiestablishment populism was probably the strongest force of change under the Roh Moo Hyun government. All five sectors of establishment power—the chaebol, Gangnam, the antigovernment press, elite universities, and the judicial system—were subject to extensive reform efforts. Among these reform programs, at least three were directly related to economic policy, namely, chaebol reform, real estate market regulations, and media market reform (Table 8.1).

Chaebol reform, which began in the aftermath of the 1997 economic crisis, was continued in the Roh Moo Hyun government. The basic principles of corporate reform were the same, "five plus three": to

Table 8.1. Ideologies and Economic Policy under the Roh Moo Hyun Government

Actors	Dominant principle	Impact on economic policy
Roh Moo Hyun	Antiestablishment	Targeting centers of power — Seoul, through balanced regional development — Chaebol, through regulations — Gangnam, through real estate market regulations — Conservative newspapers, through media market regulations Global capital as ally — Hard line against big labor — Friendly toward foreign capital — U.S.-Korea Free Trade Agreement
	Antiregionalism	No clear impact
386-generation activists	Nationalism	Economic support for North Korea Northeast Asian economic hub
	Socialism	Broad distribution-oriented, anti-polarization policies — Tax reforms and increases — Social welfare spending
	Postmodernism	Support for cultural industry

the first five principles that the Kim Dae Jung government adopted in 1998—enhancing transparency in accounting and management, resolving mutual payment guarantees among chaebol members, improving firms' financial structure, streamlining business activities, and strengthening managers' accountability—it added three others in 1999—improving management structure of secondary financial institutions, limiting chaebol equity investments, and preventing irregular inheritance and gift giving.

The Roh government's policy differed in its emphasis on promoting fair trade and restraining chaebol expansion through restrictions on equity investment in subsidiary companies. The shift in priority largely reflects the success of post-crisis corporate restructuring and reform—by 2000, the chaebol had regained their financial health, and some had rapidly become dominant companies not only in Korea but also in international markets. The Roh government continued to put pressure on the chaebol through such draconian measures as equity-holding restrictions, revealing the depth of its concern about the chaebol's actual or potential economic power.

Indeed, the relationship between the chaebol and the government finally became an arm's-length one under Roh Moo Hyun. President Roh vowed to sever cozy business-government relations, and he refused to break his promise by accepting political contributions from the chaebol. The Roh government was also relatively free of corruption scandals involving the president's inner circle. Even the reformist Kim Dae Jung government had been dogged by corruption investigations, especially toward the end of President Kim's term.

The real estate market represents another area where the Roh government battled the establishment. Home prices rose so rapidly that many feared a housing-market bubble, a risky development that got the government's attention. But government reactions to the housing boom were unusually emotional and political. First, it singled out one area, Gangnam, as the target of its antimarket campaign, even though real estate prices had risen throughout the country. But the special attention given to Gangnam actually backfired, as it helped attract more investment funds to the area. Second, the government put all of its political capital behind stopping the soaring apartment prices in Gangnam. When the prices kept rising there, the government lost credibility for its entire economic policy, not just its real estate policy.

The Roh government also turned its attention to the newspaper market. The three conservative newspapers, *Chosun Ilbo*, *Dong-A Ilbo*, and *JoongAng Ilbo*, had dominated the market. To introduce more competition, the government passed a newspaper law in 2005 that placed caps on the market shares of leading newspapers and provided subsidies to small papers.

The most ambitious effort to decentralize power, however, was made through "balanced national development projects," including the Roh government's failed attempt to move the capital from Seoul. The economic gap between Seoul and the rest of the country had been growing, and the Roh Moo Hyun government tried to level provincial inequalities through new, large-scale regional development projects. The Presidential Committee on Balanced National Development, established in April 2003, spearheaded various government programs, such as transferring of public institutions to local areas, building innovation-cluster cities, and developing regional industries.

The antiestablishment programs were consolidated under the banner of an antipolarization campaign. In 2005, the Roh Moo Hyun government adopted the rhetoric of economic polarization in response to signs of increasing economic inequality. After the economic crisis of 1997, Korean markets became more open and competitive—and market winners and losers became more conspicuous. During this period, several companies that had competitive advantages blossomed to become global leaders, while most of the second-tier chaebol and small- and medium-size companies languished in the face of increasing domestic and foreign competition. A widely recognized gap opened between the large companies and SMEs. Also, a thriving export sector was pitted against a sluggish domestic sector in another example of economic polarization. Other areas that exhibited economic inequality were education (the rich had unequal access to private tutoring), the labor market (with a growing wage gap between regular and temporary workers), and balanced development (the growing gap between Seoul and the rest of the country).

The politics of populism in Korea is not entirely class based.[3] Roh supporters did not see privilege and power in Korea exclusively in financial

---

3. One reason for the weak sense of economic class among Korean voters may be the relative economic equality in Korean society. It has been argued that the essence of the Korean model of development was growth with equity, not growth alone.

terms. Status and education are as important as wealth, if not more so. In other words, the sense of inequality in Korean society is not always based on economic inequality. In fact, many rich Koreans feel alienated and deprived of opportunity. The common perception now is that opportunities for social advancement are reserved only for residents of Gangnam, the wealthy neighborhood in Seoul, thus prompting even wealthy citizens in other areas to call for more opportunity. This obsession with the Gangnam neighborhood is ultimately tied to access to elite universities: Gangnam high schools send a disproportionate number of students to the top universities. Thus education and school reforms are much more important for achieving a sense of social equality in Korea than the redistribution of income.

Notably, Roh's populism was not classic socialism with respect to labor, foreign capital, and the U.S.-Korea Free Trade Agreement. First, Roh Moo Hyun was not an unconditional supporter of labor. The president considered large-enterprise labor unions as an antireform force, since their privileged position is maintained through the hiring of temporary workers and the squeezing of small subcontractors. His consistent emphasis on the role of public education and the education of service-sector workers shows that he sought equality of opportunity, not necessarily equality of results.

Second, the Roh Moo Hyun government pursued policies favorable to foreign capital. This is especially true in the banking sector, where the Roh government approved the sales of four commercial banks to foreign investors.[4]

Third, to the surprise of many of his supporters President Roh entered into formal negotiations with the United States for a free-trade agreement (FTA) in February 2006. The U.S.-Korea FTA would open traditionally domestically oriented service industries, in addition to such politically sensitive sectors as agriculture, to international competition. More important, it would fundamentally change the nature of the Korean economy to the extent that it would accelerate the convergence of economic institutions between Korea and the United States. It is difficult to characterize a government as leftist when it embraces the U.S.-

---

4. Korea Exchange Bank was sold to Lone Star Funds in 2003, Choheung Bank went to Shinhan Bank in 2003, Hanmi Bank was acquired by Citibank in 2004, and Cheil was purchased by Standard Chartered in 2005.

style market economy as well as the wholesale opening of domestic markets.

The influence of antiregionalism on economic policy is not clearly observable. It is possible that President Roh tied his regional development policy to his political strategy. For example, giving more (or less) support to regions where he was politically weak (or strong) would have weakened the regional polarization in party support. But evidence for such direct effects is lacking. If Roh's strong opposition to political regionalism had any impact on economic policy, it would have worked through party politics. That is, President Roh would have been reluctant to support policies favored by strongly regionalist political forces, such as the Chung Dong-young faction of the ruling Uri Party.

The ideology of the 386ers shaped the economic policy of the Roh Moo Hyun government as well, especially their nationalism on external economic relations. Because 386-generation politicians consider North Korea as a partner for peace and economic prosperity, they support a policy of economic engagement toward the North that calls for large amounts of economic assistance. Roh Moo Hyun's ambitious plan to make Korea a Northeast Asian economic hub should also be understood in the context of 386-generation ideology.[5]

In addition, the 386-generation advisors and politicians were instrumental in moving the Roh government's policy toward economic equality and distribution, especially after 2005. In 2005, the Roh government adopted the rhetoric of economic polarization as the main theme of its economic policy and proposed more conventional leftist solutions, such as tax increases and more social-welfare spending.

Postmodern aspects of economic policy can also be found in the Roh Moo Hyun government's support for popular culture industries. As discussed earlier, the Roh government gave generous funding to nonmainstream media, including online newspapers. Large amounts of government funding went into the Korean movie industry, which had been producing popular movies with strong political messages.

---

5. The concept of a Northeast Asian economic hub is consistent with the engagement policy toward the North, because the economic integration of North Korea is necessary for the full development of the Northeast Asian regional economy. This plan is also consistent with the 386ers' anti-American sentiment, since it moves the center of Korean economic activity toward the Northeast Asian region and away from the United States.

Performing arts and literature also felt the growing influence of the government.

New Institutional Arrangements under Roh Moo Hyun

The Roh Moo Hyun government sought radical changes not only in the substance of policies but also in the processes by which policies were made. Among the changes that the Roh government introduced, two principles of policymaking, participation and transparency, stand out.

What does it mean to increase the mechanisms of participation in policymaking? To the Roh government, increased participation meant the recruiting of new elites to policymaking positions and increasing their input in policymaking. The new policy elites were 386ers and policy experts with backgrounds outside of the mainstream (e.g., NGO activists, or academics at nonelite universities).

Strict rules on bureaucratic appointments limited the number of new elites who could join the government. To bypass this barrier, the Roh government appointed a large number of new policymakers to newly created noncareer positions. The Blue House underwent an extensive reorganization at the beginning of the Roh government and, subsequently, was home to a large number of political appointees.

The main organization in the Roh Moo Hyun Blue House that handled economic policy was the Office of National Policy. That office consisted of three senior officials: the advisor to the president for economic policy, the secretary to the president for policy coordination, and the senior secretary to the president for economic policy. Among these three, the only career bureaucrat was the senior secretary for economic policy; the other two were nonbureaucratic positions. Before the Roh Moo Hyun government, the senior secretary had been in sole charge of economic policy at the Blue House (Figure 8.1). The fact that Roh made this position part of a larger (politically appointed) group in which the senior secretary shared responsibility with the two new appointees shows the extent to which the Roh government desired to check and balance economic bureaucrats with new policy elites.

Whether or not the Roh government succeeded in its Blue House experiment is unclear. Although no hard data exist, the general impression is that bureaucrats regained their influence within the Blue House, especially in economic policy. Further research is necessary to confirm

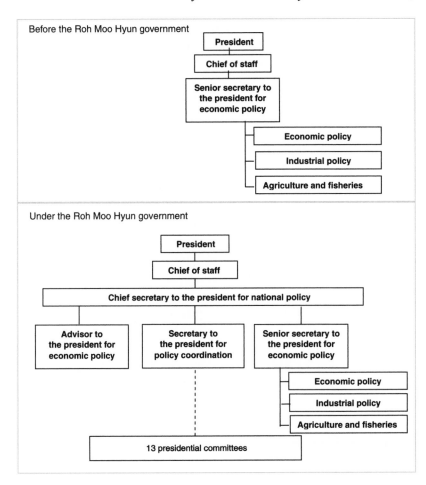

Figure 8.1. Reorganization of Economic Policy Offices at the Blue House

this. Knowing, for example, how many senior positions were held by nonbureaucrat experts in the Office of National Policy, and whether their numbers increased or decreased over time, would give us important clues.[6]

---

6. *Dong-A Ilbo* reported on 2 December 2007 that more than 100 former student activists (386ers) held senior positions in the Blue House as of the end of November 2006.

Presidential commissions were another mechanism for recruiting new elites into the policymaking process.[7] After 2003, President Roh created seven new advisory commissions and tasked them to plan and coordinate on major presidential policy initiatives, such as balanced national development. These presidential commissions were organizationally linked to the Blue House, as the main responsibility of the secretary for policy coordination in the Office of National Policy was to coordinate the activities of the thirteen presidential policy commissions.[8] The drive to recruit new members to policymaking positions also extended to ministries. Ministers were allowed to appoint their own policy advisors, and the number of ministerial policy advisors ranged from one to three in each ministry. According to the Central Personnel Commission, almost half (46.4 percent) of the 84 ministerial advisors who served in the Roh Moo Hyun government until September 2006 came from the ruling party and the Blue House staff. Only 15.5 percent were career bureaucrats.[9]

President Roh also emphasized the principle of transparency in policymaking (Table 8.2). To increase transparency, President Roh often made decisions in large, expanded meetings instead of in closed meetings attended only by close advisors. For example, attendance at regular Blue House staff meetings was expanded to include all secretaries, not just senior secretaries as in previous administrations. The meetings were telecast as well, to the entire staff of the Blue House. President Roh liked to engage and have direct debate with the public. Several "town hall meetings" were organized to discuss important issues. Early in his administration, President Roh made a public stir when he appeared on TV and debated issues with bureaucrats opposed to his policy.

The Roh government undertook efforts to make policy-relevant data and reports available to the public. And at the same time, it expanded and strengthened the communications apparatus at the Blue House and

---

7. "Presidential commissions" here refers to 13 national policy agenda committees, which are a subgroup of presidential commissions. The total number of presidential commissions as of November 2006 was 25.

8. By design, commission members were drawn from both inside and outside of the government. Many new policy elites were recruited to serve as commission members. In some commissions, such as the Presidential Commission on Sustainable Development, NGO members comprised a majority of the nongovernment members.

9. *Dong-A Daily* [English-language edition], 22 September 2006.

Table 8.2. Participation and Transparency in Economic Policymaking

	Mechanisms	*New actors*
Participation	Political appointees in the Blue House	386-generation activists
	Presidential commissions	New policy elites
	Policy advisors to ministers	New policy elites
	Party-administration coordination	Ruling party politicians
Transparency	Open, expanded policy deliberations	N/A
	Greater access to information	
	Direct dialogue with the people	

in the administration in order to explain its policies directly to the people.

One aspect of policymaking that analysts have emphasized as crucial to policy stability and consistency is the length of ministerial tenure. Unlike long-lived authoritarian regimes in which ministers often enjoy relatively lengthy tenures, democratic governments tend to make frequent ministerial changes. The average tenure of cabinet ministers was 22.3 months under the Park Chung Hee regime, but it fell to 10.7 months under Kim Dae Jung. This downward trend was reversed by the Roh Moo Hyun government, when it rose to 12.1 months (Table 8.3). But the average tenure of economic ministers did not change much, which suggests that President Roh may have been less consistent in economic policy than in other areas, such as security or social welfare.

The Impact of the 2002 System on Policy Outcomes

The 2002 system of politics brought in new policy elites, new ideologies, and new policy mechanisms. But the debate over their impact on actual policy choices and economic performance continued to the end of Roh's presidency. Reflecting the plunging popularity of the Roh Moo Hyun government toward the end of Roh's term, popular judgments were fairly negative. Critics pointed to several factors in explaining the "failure" of President Roh's economic policy, including overemphasis on distributive policy preferences, amateurism of the 386-generation advisors, and the president's leadership style. We have already discussed the first two factors, so we now turn briefly to the third, President Roh's style.

Table 8.3. Average Tenure of Cabinet Ministers (months)

Ministerial portfolios	Presidential administration					
	Park Chung Hee	Chun Doo Hwan	Roh Tae Woo	Kim Young Sam	Kim Dae Jung	Roh Moo Hyun
Foreign Affairs and Security	25.66	21.33	17.00	14.07	11.36	14.67
Information and Science	21.48	15.66	15.71	13.55	13.17	10.00
Education and Culture	20.65	16.83	12.93	18.30	10.00	9.50
Economy	20.58	18.61	13.33	10.00	10.69	10.75
Social Welfare	23.86	24.42	11.21	10.36	10.95	16.00
Law, Order, and Human Resources	23.48	13.94	10.43	9.57	8.91	12.75
Average tenure	22.25	17.78	13.02	11.63	10.65	12.14

Source: Data from Lee and Kim 2006.

President Roh shared many of the weaknesses of his 386-generation advisors, particularly a lack of administrative experience and overconfidence in his moral and ideological legitimacy. More damaging, however, was the narrowness of his political interests. Even after winning the presidency Roh thought of himself as largely a partisan politician in that he refused to compromise his political principles, although compromising may have been necessary for governing more effectively. Grassroots partisan politics remained his passion.

More research is needed to identify important empirical patterns of policymaking under the Roh Moo Hyun government and to offer political-economy explanations for them. One important avenue for investigating the dynamics of policymaking in the Roh Moo Hyun government may be in the relationship between Roh Moo Hyun and his 386-generation advisors. We have argued that we need to understand the political beliefs of both Roh Moo Hyun and his 386-generational allies to fully understand the origins of Roh's economic policy. One may counter that Roh Moo Hyun and the 386ers were not very different.

After all, the 386ers themselves have moderated over time. They support a market economy, made easier by the fall of socialism. They also rely on market-economy logic in criticizing Korea's old economic system. They seek a stronger market economy in which economic management is transparent and accountable.

Nevertheless, we treat Roh Moo Hyun and the 386ers separately for analytical purposes. Roh never had the full support of the radical left in Korea, such as the Democratic Labor Party and anti-American activists. But over time President Roh lost the support of some of his core advisors. The trigger for an open split in the pro-Roh camp was the U.S.-Korea FTA. Most of Roh's original advisors supported him because of his economic reform agenda. They had thought that Roh shared their economic vision of a European-type social democracy. Although early signs of betrayal appeared when Roh Moo Hyun adopted the pro-growth slogan "Toward the $20,000 per capita income" and turned against labor in some of the first labor strikes, they continued to support him in the belief that those were isolated cases of compromise. For many of his advisors, however, the FTA was the last straw. The agreement, a symbol of neoliberal economic reform, violated every principle that they believed in.[10]

From the perspective of competition among policy perspectives, then, Roh's policies seem to have prevailed over those of the 386 generation. President Roh showed a strong determination to break down the traditional elite structure of the Korean economy, but he stopped far short of building a domestic economy in the image of Western European social democracy, sought by many of his 386-generation advisors.[11] The same is true for Korea's economic relations. President Roh initially supported many of his young advisors' ideas on North Korea and the Northeast Asian regional economy. But subsequent developments indicate that

---

10. Many analysts call Roh's reforms "neoliberal" (Lim and Jang 2006).

11. We can also see Roh's goal of the diffusion of power in the controversy over history. The Japanese occupation, the Korean War, and the struggle for democracy have left deep scars on Korean society. Victims of political repression during those periods have demanded redress and compensation. In accommodating those demands through legislation and "truth-finding," Roh Moo Hyun was successful in discrediting the traditional elites of Korean society, including the conservative political parties and media.

they did not receive his sustained attention and support. The Northeast Asian regional hub project, which began with big fanfare, was largely forgotten. By 2006, it became apparent that the U.S.-Korea FTA, not the Northeast Asian regional hub, was going to be Roh's legacy in international economic policy. True, President Roh's support for assisting North Korea was steadier. But even there President Roh was much more measured in extending support to North Korea than his 386-generation supporters desired.

Conclusions

In attempting to define the nature of the political system in which the Roh Moo Hyun government operated, we have explained how it differed from the political system of the previous regimes of the three Kims. The new 2002 system of politics differed from the old system in three crucial respects. First, the 386 generation became a pivotal voting bloc, pulling mass politics away from its previous regional basis. Second, former student activists dominated the political leadership of the 386 generation. Third, younger voters and their leaders favored and created new forms of political communication and open, fluid, democratic political organizations.

Under the 2002 system of politics, new policy elites, led by the 386ers, emerged and made inroads in the policymaking process through political appointments, presidential commissions, and other participatory mechanisms. The new policymakers were strongly principled, and clear evidence suggests that their principles largely shaped the policy agenda of the Roh Moo Hyun government. But whether they succeeded in realizing their goals and whether the policymaking system as a whole improved are different matters. Although much more research is necessary, the electoral defeat of Roh's party in the 2007 presidential election indicates that voters became skeptical on both questions.

The 386 generation as a distinctive voting bloc will remain influential, even if it may not capture the government again as it did in 2002. The 386ers' views have created a new electoral dimension that has made the Korean party system more pluralistic, as new parties have emerged and existing parties become more democratic to accommodate young, liberal voters.

After seeing their role diminished following the conservative Grand National Party's victory in the 2007 presidential election, the 386-generation politicians returned to the forefront of Korean politics by winning three governorships in the local elections of May 2010. Since 2007, 386-generation leaders have also shown their continuing commitment to Roh's political and economic reforms, indicating the strength of Roh's legacy in the liberal political establishment.

The impact of the 2002 system on Korea's civil society will also last. Although weakened after the 2007 election, Korean society remains much more vibrant and pluralistic than it was before 1997. One telling episode testifying to its influence occurred after President Roh left office in early 2008. When the new president, Lee Myung Bak, decided to open Korean markets to American beef imports in May 2008, civil groups organized massive street protests in Seoul—the so-called candlelight demonstrations. The anti-American-beef demonstrations continued throughout the summer and ended only after the Lee government promised to revise its market-opening agreement with the United States.

The political progressives in Korea won two consecutive presidential elections, in 1997 and 2002, taking advantage of voter discontent with the conservative party that had held power before the 1997 economic crisis. Presidents Kim Dae Jung and Roh Moo Hyun, as the progressive candidates, had the mandate to reform the pre-crisis system. They carried out the economic and political reforms necessary to overcome the crisis and to reduce the likelihood of future crises. The 1997 economic crisis also produced new political forces that rebalanced the system toward greater economic openness. Theoretically, the reforms under the Kim and Roh presidencies represent the culmination of institutional rebalancing that began in 1997. Whether the rebalancing is complete, however, is still difficult to tell.

The period of active post-crisis rebalancing came to an end in 2008, after the conservative Grand National Party won the 2007 presidential election. The new government of President Lee Myung Bak pursued policies more friendly toward the chaebol than those under his two predecessors and reversed some of their economic reforms, such as restrictions on chaebol investments. But whether Lee was able to reverse Korea's long-term transition to open access, or even intended to, is a different story. By the time Lee came to power in 2008, the political support for economic and political openness was deeply entrenched among South Korean voters. Partly in reaction to this voter sentiment, President Lee began in 2010 to toughen his rhetoric against the chaebol and to reintroduce some of the chaebol regulations that he had lifted before, indicating that efforts to reform the chaebol and promote more economic openness would continue.

CHAPTER 9

Conclusions and a Look Ahead

In this book, we propose a new approach to understanding the political economy of South Korea's transition from an undeveloped to a developed country, from a natural state to an open-access order. Our approach rests on a new view of economic and political development based on the conceptual framework of North, Wallis, and Weingast (2009), or NWW. Three ideas from the NWW framework are central to our discussion.

First, the concept of social order allows us to see that societies organize themselves in very different ways. For our purposes, the NWW framework differentiates between limited-access orders and open-access orders. Limited-access orders use rent creation and limits on access to control the political economy and the problem of violence. These rents and controls, however, also place limits on the economy and hinder long-term growth, especially in a world dominated by open-access orders. Open-access orders, in contrast, use the rule of law to create open access to impersonal institutions and opportunities, generating competition and resulting in Schumpeterian creative destruction.

Second, the idea of double balance suggests that, over the long term, societies must be balanced in their openness. Those societies with limited access in the economy also tend to have limited access in the polity; similarly, those with open access in one tend to have open access in the other. Societies that lack balance face incentives to move toward balance. For example, a regime that uses limited access in the economy to generate rents will have trouble maintaining itself in the presence of open access in the polity, which tends to disperse these rents.

Third, this perspective redefines the problem of economic development as the transition from a limited-access order or natural state to an open-access order. Central to this perspective is the idea that a society initiating the transition must achieve the doorstep conditions: rule of law, perpetual institutions (including perpetual organizations), and consolidated control over the military. Attaining these conditions is the pivotal step in the political development necessary to create conditions favorable to economic development.[1] The doorstep conditions are necessary, as well, for maintaining a thriving market economy and a rich democracy supported by a strong civil society. Also critical to this perspective is the idea of incentives. The transition occurs when members of the dominant coalition have incentives to open access incrementally; to extend benefits to a wide group of citizens based on citizenship, rather than based on personal connections and membership in the coalition; and to create elements of impersonality, perpetuity, and the rule of law for elites.

Explaining the Three Turning Points

The ideas of the doorstep conditions and incentives help us explain South Korea's path toward development. To demonstrate this, we have organized our discussion around three turning points in South Korean history: the initial creation of the developmental state, under President Park Chung Hee in the 1960s and 1970s, out of the previous, unstable natural state; democratization in 1987; and the financial crisis of 1997 and subsequent reform. Korean development since the 1960s can be characterized as periods of smooth progress punctuated by crises, or turning points. To explain the recurrent instability in the Korean political economy, we turn to the idea of double balance, arguing that a political economy is stable only when political and economic openness are balanced.

Over the long term, according to double balance, societies must be balanced in the level of openness in both the economy and the polity. If one of these two systems is considerably more open than the other, the society will lack balance. In addition, various forces press for a return to

---

1. Cox, North, and Weingast (2012) explore this approach to political development in greater detail.

balance. For example, too much political openness relative to economic openness in a natural state can lead organized interests to press for relaxing the economic rents and privileges that support the natural state. The political organizations advocating dismantling and dispersing rents may succeed, thus leading to increased economic openness, or the regime and its constituents may react by curtailing organized groups, and thus diminishing political openness, so as to preserve their rents and privileges. In the opposite form of imbalance, too much economic openness relative to political openness fosters economic growth in the short and medium term, but as firms grow more complex they seek more complex support from the government, in turn requiring greater credible commitments from and constraints on government. And citizens who get richer typically press for greater freedom, protections against arbitrary political action, and, often, democracy. (Citizens seek democracy for a variety of reasons, including the ability to influence more directly the various trade-offs made by the regime—e.g., between higher wages and greater investment—and choices about public goods and tax levels.) Both forms of imbalance can lead to greater political openness to match the degree of economic openness, or to a reaction that limits economic openness as a means of preserving benefit flows provided by the status quo. Although some societies may be out of balance at some time during their transition, over the long term double balance holds. Development requires open access in both the economy and the polity.

The principal question about South Korea's post-1960 development involves its transition from a limited-access order to an open-access order: How did Korea initiate this transition when so many developing countries, qua limited access orders, have failed to do so? Outside of Europe and the Anglo-American countries (Australia, Canada, New Zealand, and the United States), this transition is a rare event: out of upwards of 170 countries, only a few have either made substantial progress (South Korea and Taiwan) or completed the transition (Japan) and become developed, open-access states during the post–World War II era.

In answering the question of how Korea was able to do this, we emphasize Korea's security dilemma; but, following NWW, we note that a security threat alone is not a sufficient reason for a country to enter the transition. A large number of countries have faced similar security dilemmas and yet failed to initiate the transition. South Korea began the postwar era (after World War II and the Korean War) as a typical natural state under President Syngman Rhee. The Rhee regime survived for nearly a decade, in part through unusually high levels of aid from the United States. But this natural state apparently was unsustainable, for the Rhee regime collapsed.

SOUTH KOREA ENTERS THE TRANSITION

The first of the three turning points was General Park's coup in 1961. Park built a new political coalition around a new vision for South Korea and instituted a set of policies and institutions to promote it. The security problem and uncertainty about the American commitment led the coalition to trade off short-term natural-state rents for long-term gains in security. In a series of steps, the new coalition created a developmental state, incrementally opening access. Technocrats implemented a number of critical policies, such as export-led growth and the building of infrastructure, both in rural Korea and for the nation's new industries.

The role of the Korean meritocracy proved central to development, as Amsden (1989), Johnson (1982), and Wade (1990) emphasize. But our perspective provides a different view of the mechanisms underlying the meritocracy. In contrast to previous scholars, we argue that the bureaucracy was not politically independent of the regime. Instead, technocrats had an important influence on policymaking and implementation because they produced results sought by the regime. Because the meritocratic bureaucracy produced results, the regime had an incentive to foster an impersonal bureaucracy that would work according to objective rules and prevent the typical natural-state political meddling and reliance on personal connections.

A broad principle underlay Park's coalition: the sacrifice of short-term rents to improve South Korea's ability to defend itself, especially without relying on the United States. Pursuing the goal of independent national security required Korea to build a growing economy and become competitive in international markets. Accomplishing those goals required, in turn, the ability to make impersonal policies.

Security necessitated not only a large, professional, and efficient army but also widespread support among the citizenry. A central feature of this era, in part responding to the communist threat, was the sharing of the fruits of economic development (Campos and Root 1996). Economic gains were spread far more widely than in a typical natural state, including open access to jobs in both the private and public sectors, and high wage growth. The regime also provided a variety of public goods for citizens, including education, rural development, and infrastructure.

Under Park, South Korea began the transition. In building the economy, the government and bureaucracy pursued a policy of export-led growth, relying on objective, impersonal indicators from the world market to help generate a larger economy and profits from the international market. The government allocated various forms of rents, subsidies, and tax credits to firms that succeeded on the international market. Although this process involved state allocation of rents, it differed from more common developing-country rent-allocation, in that rents were not distributed on a personalistic basis to favored constituents or clients. Instead, rents helped serve the larger development and security goals of the ruling coalition. Sharing the benefits of growth also involved increasing levels of access among the population to job opportunities and markets, to various public goods (infrastructure, education, security), and to a share of the overall gains from long-term economic growth. The opening of access benefitted both the bureaucracy and the economy, because both could draw from a much wider talent pool than in a limited-access society.

DEMOCRATIZATION

The second turning point was Korea's democratization in 1987—a peaceful transformation of the authoritarian regime into a democratic one. Open economic access under the previous authoritarian regime had allowed some growth in aspects of the civil society, including unions, a middle class that favored democracy and greater public goods, and dissident groups among students and the church. The opposition had also gained representation, particularly in the National Assembly. In the 1985 National Assembly elections the New Korea Democracy Party took so many seats that it became a factor in the government, forcing the authoritarian regime under President Chun Doo Hwan to consider the opposition's interests. In addition, the attitude of the United States had changed, from supporting Chun's military coups in 1979 and 1980 to openly supporting the movement toward democracy.

All these factors, combined with the credible threat of the opposition to disrupt society, forced Chun to negotiate with opposition groups calling for democratic presidential elections. Indeed, when Chun temporarily suspended negotiations, it led to the largest demonstrations thus far in Korea's history. The lack of support for a new authoritarian government forced Chun to accommodate the opposition's demands for a constitutional revision to return to presidential elections. The result was the June 29 Declaration and the government's sudden move to democracy.

FINANCIAL CRISIS

The third turning point involved the financial crisis of 1997 and the wide range of economic and political reforms that followed in its wake. Several political factors greatly exacerbated the economic crisis. South Korea had begun its democracy with a clear lack of double balance. Years of economic openness and policy benefits had created large and powerful economic organizations, the chaebol, while the lack of political openness had resulted in a stunted civil society. Too few civil or political organizations existed that could provide support for political officials who opposed the chaebol. While the previous authoritarian regime had had the power to control moral hazard incentives affecting the chaebol's behavior, including excessive risk taking, a major change under democratization was that the new democratic regime did not have the power to control chaebol moral hazard. Democratic elections gave the business conglomerates a new source of political power: political officials needed campaign funds, and they received large amounts of money from chaebol donors. Among other things, campaign funds created a new dependence among political officials, who now found they could not control or sanction the chaebol as the previous authoritarian regime had, because they could not afford to lose their financial support.

In addition to blocking reform efforts, the chaebol used their leverage to seek a range of benefits, such as the relaxing of regulatory constraints, notably regulations on borrowing. Because the government no longer had the ability to force the restructuring of insolvent firms, the chaebol kept borrowing. This borrowing financed the huge investment boom of the mid-1990s, but it also created significant moral hazard: the chaebol had become too big to fail (TBTF). Because the chaebol had become such a large part of the economy, the government would have to bail them out if they failed, externalizing the costs of their risky behavior.

Given their TBTF incentives, the chaebol increased their investments and created much greater risk exposure. Had good economic times continued, those investments would have produced large profits. But the investments also made the chaebol much more vulnerable to a financial crisis—and with them, the entire Korean economy. When the crisis occurred in 1997, it was made far worse by the government's relationship with the chaebol in the decade between democratization and the crisis: in particular, by the government's inability to pursue reforms or to discipline the chaebol, for example, and its promotional economic policies, such as credit expansion, which had been sought by the chaebol.

In response to the 1997 financial crisis and the failure of so many firms, the government implemented a wide range of economic and then political reforms. In principle, the much-diminished influence of the chaebol, combined with great changes in regulations, mean that the chaebol will now have greater difficulty taking risks that could be socialized to the entire economy. But will these regulations be enforced, and will they be enough?

Are the political forces that proved insufficient to counterbalance the chaebol during the first ten years of democracy sufficient to succeed now? A major open question is whether South Korea's new reforms have managed to create a stable double balance. In particular, are the reforms and the growth of the civil society sufficient to counter the chaebol? Have the TBTF incentives been eliminated? In many ways, it remains too early to tell.

On the negative side, the chaebol remain powerful and concentrated. Although new regulations have increased transparency and market and political supervision, it is difficult to evaluate whether these have eliminated the TBTF incentives or whether South Korea could, once again, be caught in a major financial crisis that forces huge bailouts.

On the positive side, however, are the positive dynamics of the Korean political economy. Although South Korea has faced several crises since 1960, it has managed to respond to these events without falling into disorder or falling back into a natural state with low growth. This contrasts with what commonly happens in natural states, such as those in Latin America or Africa, where crises lead to disorder or to backward moves away from the transition, including coups, economic crises to which the government cannot adequately respond, the collapse of democracy and liberal reform, and even civil wars and other forms of violence. Although the 1997 crisis in Korea required a huge injection of public funds into the economy, the country retained fiscal discipline. Similarly, the new demand for greater social services following democratization was financed by raising taxes and lowering expenditures elsewhere, rather than by amassing unsustainable debt.

In sum, South Korea has taken big strides toward becoming an open-access order. In comparison with most developing countries, it has become rich. Korea has made progress on all the doorstep conditions and for decades has included a wide range of the population in the growth process. It has also provided a wide range of impersonal public goods. Its political and economic institutions are highly durable, if not yet obviously perpetual. However, as we have noted, the question remains: Has South Korea achieved double balance?

Reflections: Does South Korea Provide a Useful Model?

South Korea has made substantial progress in the transition from a natural state in the 1950s to an open-access order. An important question is whether South Korea can serve as a model for other countries in their struggles with economic development. The answer is not obvious. On the one hand, creating a technocracy that can deliver policies and benefits on an impersonal basis was clearly central to South Korea's success (Amsden 1989, Wade 1990). The incremental transformation from personal to impersonal allocations of rents and privileges is a possible template for other countries seeking to make the transition.

On the other hand, very few developing countries have made significant progress on the transition, suggesting that this is a sufficiently great hurdle and that policy advice alone is inadequate to help them (Easterly 2006). We have emphasized the importance of incremental incentives to open access, and the substantial security threat of the mid-twentieth century was a significant incentive for the dominant coalition in Korea to sacrifice short-term (natural state) rents for long-term economic gains. This situation is relatively rare, however. Indeed, as Bates (2001) suggests, in many parts of the world the Cold War principals, European powers, or international organizations (such as the UN) have policed borders in ways that have reduced external security threats.[2] As a result, most natural states do not have sufficient security incentives to forgo short-term rents and open access incrementally. Although natural states evolve—they are not static—their evolution is not always positive; the vast number of natural states remain such over long periods.

Other countries can, therefore, attempt to imitate the sequence of policies used by South Korea in its transition, such as impersonal export-led growth, reliance on education, open access to labor markets, and so on. But without the immediate pressure of the security dilemma, it is unclear whether most other developing countries would have sufficient incentive to pursue them in the same way, to trade off short-term rent creation today for long-term economic and security gains. The NWW framework suggests that the threat of violence in natural states is sufficiently strong that they allocate rents in proportion to power. Deviation from this basic principle risks violence in turn. Taken as a whole, this logic suggests that few natural states have incentives to give up present rents for future economic gains. The central difficulty for a typical natural state is sustaining the impersonal method of allocating rents based on performance, rather than using more overtly political criteria.

The developments following the initial transition in the 1960s also question the universality of the Korean model. Both the transition to democracy in 1987 and the breakout of the 1997 financial crisis show that the path that Korea took toward an open-access order was not predetermined but was subject to unanticipated events. The June 29 Declaration initiating democracy in 1987, for example, came as a complete shock to the Korean people, and the decision of the Chun regime easily could have gone the other way. In retrospect, the 1997 financial crisis—especially the conditions that the International Monetary Fund imposed on Korea for its loans—were not predetermined outcomes; the United States and Japan could have extended currency-swap lines to the South Korean central bank before Seoul was forced to seek IMF assistance, or the IMF could have imposed much less demanding conditions on Korea. Importantly, the IMF has made similar agreements with a large

---

2. A large literature supports this idea, most notably Tilly (1992), which focuses on the role of war in the development of Western Europe over the past millennium.

number of developing countries, but few of those countries have managed to attain the reforms' goals.

Despite these reservations, we suggest that South Korea holds some
lessons for other developing countries.[3] First, Korea has followed an
economic-growth-first path. The transition to an open-access order,
which is the most important step in political and economic development,
began under the growth-oriented Park regime. Seen this way, the subsequent developments can be viewed largely as a process of post-takeoff
adjustment, that is, of the politics catching up with the level of economic
openness that was first initiated.[4]

Second, critical to South Korea's transition were the incremental incentives to open access and to transform the system of personal allocation of resources to an impersonal one. The incremental incentives to
create this transformation are the general lesson of South Korea's development path; the specific focus on export-led growth resulted from
Korea's specific context. The aid community may well use its resources
to help foster this process of incremental incentives in some developing
countries.

Third, the post-transition process has been stable. The Korean economy quickly recovered from its periodic shocks, especially the 1987 crisis
during negotiations over democratization and the 1997 financial crisis.
One reason for this is that a strong social consensus on the importance
of catching up has taken root since Korea's high growth period under
the Park regime; economic success has been the most important standard of success for every administration since. Another reason is that
Korean politics was relatively competitive by the time of democratization.
Regional rivalries, generational change, and the tradition of dissent have
kept Korean politics competitive, resulting in two changes of government during the twenty-year period of democracy.

Fourth, another interesting—and open—question is whether South
Korea is headed toward an open-access order that differs in some fundamental way from those in the developed West. NWW did not theorize

---

3. North et al. (2012) pursue these themes.

4. As we have emphasized throughout, it is premature to declare that South Korea's
transition to open access is complete. We must wait for further progress on economic
openness in Korea, especially the subjection of the chaebol to market discipline and the
rule of law, before we can pronounce the final word on the success of South Korea's
growth-first strategy.

about whether open-access orders, like natural states, may occur in different forms. Certainly the path of development in South Korea, and East Asia more generally (including China and Taiwan), differs from that of the West. Open-access countries in the West tended to move incrementally toward greater access in both economics and politics; the transition typically took longer, over many steps, especially for the first movers. France began its transition, for example, in the seventeenth century but did not complete it until the end of the nineteenth century. Further, steps in the West's transition were incremental. Britain's extension of inclusion occurred over centuries, not immediately, with full democratization for all adults at one time.

The final lesson is the main thesis of our book, the importance of balanced development over the long term. Openness in politics and economics must go hand in hand. When the openness of one area falls behind the other area, the contradictions it creates in the economy give rise to correcting or equilibrating forces. The three major turning points in the Korean political economy all involved lack of balance. They are therefore' testimony to the force of double balance.

References

Acemoglu, Daron, and James A. Robinson. 2006a. "Economic Backwardness in Political Perspective." *American Political Science Review* 100 (1): 115–31.

———. 2006b. *Economic Origins of Dictatorship and Democracy*. New York: Cambridge University Press.

Alesina, Alberto, and Dani Rodrik. 1994. "Distributive Politics and Economic Growth." *Quarterly Journal of Economics* 109 (2): 465–490.

Amsden, Alice H. 1989. *Asia's Next Giant: South Korea and Late Industrialization*. New York: Oxford University Press.

Ang, Yuen Yuen. 2012. "Dual Fiscal Incentives: Informal Compensation and the Paradoxical Economic Behavior of China's Public Agents." Paper presented at the China Social Science Workshop, Stanford University, February 2012.

Bark, Dong-suh. 2001. "The Administrative Process in Korea." In Soong Hoom Kil and Chung-in Moon, eds., *Understanding Korean Politics: An Introduction*. Albany: State University of New York Press.

Barro, Robert. 1998. *Determinants of Economic Growth*. Cambridge, MA: MIT Press.

Barzel, Yoram. 2001. *A Theory of the State*. New York: Cambridge University Press.

Bates, Robert H. 1981. *Markets and States in Tropical Africa*. Berkeley: University of California Press.

———. 1983. "The Nature and Origin of Agricultural Policies in Africa." In Robert H. Bates, *Essays in the Political Economy of Rural Africa*. Cambridge: Cambridge University Press.

———. 2001. *Prosperity and Violence*. New York: W. W. Norton.

Bates, Robert H., Avner Greif, and Smita Singh. 2002. "Organizing Violence." *Journal of Conflict Resolution* 46 (5): 599–628.

Baumol, William, Robert Litan, and Carl Schramm. 2007. *Good Capitalism and Bad Capitalism.* New Haven: Yale University Press.

Besley, Timothy. 2006. *Principled Agents? The Political Economy of Good Government.* Oxford: Oxford University Press.

Brady, David, and Jongryn Mo. 1992. "Electoral Systems and Institutional Choice." *Comparative Political Studies* 24, 405–429.

Breton, Albert, and Ronald Wintrobe. 1986. "The Bureaucracy of Murder Revisited." *Journal of Political Economy* 94 (5): 905–926.

Brumbaugh, R. Dan. 1988. *Thrifts under Siege: Restoring Order to American Banking.* Cambridge, MA: Ballinger Publishing.

Bueno de Mesquita, Bruce, Alastair Smith, Randolph M. Siverson, and James D. Morrow. 2001. *The Logic of Political Survival.* Cambridge, MA: MIT Press.

Campos, José Edgardo, and Hilton L. Root. 1996. *The Key to the Asian Miracle: Making Shared Growth Credible.* Washington, DC: Brookings Institution.

Cha, Dongse. 1998. *The Road to the Great Transformation of the Korean Economy.* Seoul: 21st Century Books (in Korean).

Chafuen, Alejandro, and Eugenio Guzman. 2000. "Economic Freedom and Corruption." In Gerald P. O'Driscoll, Kim R. Holms, and Melanie Kirkpatrick, eds., *2000 Index of Economic Freedom.* Washington, DC: Heritage Foundation.

Chang, Ha-Joon. 1999. "The Hazard of Moral Hazard: Untangling the Asian Crisis." Paper presented at the American Economic Association annual meeting, New York (January).

———. 2003. *Kicking Away the Ladder: Developing Strategy in Historical Perspective.* London: Anthem Press.

Chang, Oh-Hyun. 1992. "The Role of Non-Market Institutions in Korean Economic Development." Working paper, Finance and Private Sector Development, Policy Research Department, World Bank, Washington, DC.

Cho, Yoon Je. 1996. "Government Intervention, Rent Distribution, and Economic Development in Korea." In Masahiko Aoki, Hyung-Ki Kim, and Masahiro Okuno-Fujiwara, eds., *The Role of Government in East Asian Economic Development.* Oxford: Clarendon Press.

———. 1998. "Financial Crisis of Korea: Causes and Challenges." Working Paper 98–05, Graduate School of International Studies, Sogang University.

Cho, Yoon Je, and Joon-Kyung Kim. 1995. "Credit Policies and Industrialization of Korea." World Bank Discussion Paper 286, Washington, DC: World Bank.

Cole, David, and Youngchul Park. 1979. *Financial Development in Korea, 1945–1979.* Cambridge, MA: Council on East Asian Studies, Harvard University.

Cotton, James. 1989. "From Authoritarianism to Democracy in South Korea." *Political Studies* 37, 244–259.

Cox, Gary W. 2012. "Was the Glorious Revolution a Constitutional Watershed?" *Journal of Economic History* 72 (03): 567–600.

Cox, Gary W., Douglass C. North, and Barry R. Weingast. 2012. "A Theory of Political Development." Working Paper, Hoover Institution, Stanford University.

Cumings, Bruce. 2005. *Korea's Place in the Sun: A Modern History*. Updated ed. New York: W. W. Norton.

Diamond, Larry, and Doh Chull Shin. 2000. *Institutional Reform and Democratic Consolidation in Korea*. Stanford, CA: Hoover Institution Press.

Diaz-Cayeros, Alberto. 2012. "Entrenched Insiders: Limited Access Order in Mexico." In Douglass C. North, John Joseph Wallis, Steven B. Webb, and Barry R. Weingast, eds., *In the Shadow of Violence: The Problem of Development for Limited Access Order Societies*. Cambridge: Cambridge University Press.

Dornbusch, Rudigar, and Sebastian Edwards, eds. 1991. *The Macroeconomics of Populism in Latin America*. Chicago: University of Chicago Press.

Easterly, William. 2003. *The Elusive Quest for Growth*. Cambridge, MA: MIT Press.

———. 2006. *The White Man's Burden: Why the West's Efforts to Aid the Rest Have Done So Much Ill and So Little Good*. New York: Penguin.

Eckert, Carter. 1990. *Korea Old and New: A History*. Seoul: Ilchokak Publishers.

Evans, Pater. 1995. *Embedded Autonomy: States and Industrial Transformation*. Princeton: Princeton University Press.

Fowler, James. 1999. "The United States and South Korean Democratization." *Political Science Quarterly* 114, 265–288.

Fukuyama, Francis. 2011. *The Origins of Political Order: From Pre-Human Times to the French Revolution*. London: Profile Books.

Gleysteen, William H. 1999. *Massive Engagement, Marginal Influence: Carter and Korea in Crisis*. Washington, DC: Brookings Institution.

Goldstein, Morris. 1998. *The Asian Financial Crisis: Causes, Cures, and Systemic Implications*, Policy Analyses in International Economics 55. Washington, DC: Institute for International Economics.

Gong, Byeong-Ho. 1993. *The Risk and the Fall of Korean Enterprises*. Seoul: Maekyung Daily Press (in Korean).

Greif, Avner. 2006. *Institutions and the Path to the Modern Economy: Lessons from Medieval Trade*. Cambridge: Cambridge University Press.

Grossman, Gene M., and Elhanan Helpman. 2001. *Special Interest Politics*. Cambridge, MA: MIT Press.

Haber, Stephen, Herbert Klein, Noel Maurer, and Kevin Middlebrook. 2007. "The Second Mexican Revolution: Economic, Political and Social Change since 1980." Unpublished manuscript, Hoover Institution, Stanford University.

Haggard, Stephan. 1990. *Pathways from the Periphery: The Politics of Growth in the Newly Industrializing Countries*. Ithaca: Cornell University Press.

Haggard, Stephan, Richard N. Cooper, and Susan Collins. 1994. "Understanding Korea's Macroeconomic Policy." In Stephan Haggard et al., *Macroeconomic Policy and Adjustment in Korea, 1970–1990*. Cambridge, MA: Harvard University Press.

Haggard, Stephan, Richard N. Cooper, Susan Collins, Choongsoo Kim, and Sung-Tae Ro. 1994. *Macroeconomic Policy and Adjustment in Korea, 1970–1990*. Cambridge, MA: Harvard University Press.

Haggard, Stephan, David Kang, and Chung-in Moon. 1997. "Japanese Colonialism and Korean Development: A Critique." *World Development* 25 (6): 867–881.

Haggard, Stephan, and Robert Kaufman. 1995. *The Political Economy of Democratic Transition*. Princeton: Princeton University Press.

Haggard, Stephan, Byung-Kook Kim, and Chung-in Moon. 1991. "The Transition to Export-Led Growth in South Korea: 1954–1966." *Journal of Asian Studies* 50 (4): 850–873.

Haggard, Stephan, Wonhyuk Lim, and Euysung Kim, eds. 2003. *Economic Crisis and Corporate Restructuring in Korea*. Cambridge: Cambridge University Press.

Haggard, Stephan, and Jongryn Mo. 2000. "The Political Economy of the Korean Financial Crisis." *Review of International Political Economy* 7 (Summer): 197–218.

Haggard, Stephan, and Chung-in Moon. 1990. "Institutions and Economic Policy: Theory and a Korean Case Study." *World Politics* 42, 210–237.

———. 1993. "The State, Politics, and Economic Development in Postwar South Korea." In Hagen Koo, ed., *State and Society in Contemporary Korea*. Ithaca: Cornell University Press.

Hahm, Chaibong. 1999. "The Confucian Tradition and Economic Reform." In Jongryn Mo and Chung-in Moon, eds. *Democracy and the Korean Economy*. Stanford, CA: Hoover Institution Press.

———. 2008. "South Korea's Miraculous Democracy." *Journal of Democracy* 19, 128–142.

Hahm, Joon-Ho, and Wonhyuk Lim. 2006. "Turning a Crisis into an Opportunity: The Political Economy of Korea's Financial Sector Reform." In Jongryn Mo and Daniel Okimoto, eds., *From Crisis to Opportunity: Financial Globalization and East Asian Capitalism*. Stanford, CA: Asia-Pacific Research Center, Stanford University.

Hall, Peter, and David Soskice, eds. 2001. *Varieties of Capitalism*. Oxford: Oxford University Press.

Han, Sung-Joo. 1974. *The Failure of Democracy in South Korea*. Berkeley: University of California Press.

———. 2000. "The Shifting Korean Ideological Divide: From the Korean War to the Pyongyang Summit." *Pacific Forum Online* (July 11).

Hellman, Thomas, Kevin Murdock, and Joseph Stiglitz. 1996. "Financial Restraint: Toward a New Paradigm." In Masahiko Aoki, Hyung-Ki Kim, and Masahiro Okuno-Fujiwara, eds., *The Role of Government in East Asian Economic Development*. Oxford: Clarendon Press.

Henderson, Gregory. 1968. *Korea: The Politics of the Vortex*. Cambridge, MA: Harvard University Press.

Hibbs, Douglas. 1976. "Industrial Conflict in Advanced Industrial Societies." *American Political Science Review* 70, 1033–1058.

Higley, John, and Richard Gunther. 1992. *Elites and Democratic Consolidation in Latin America and Southern Europe*. Cambridge: Cambridge University Press.

Huntington, Samuel. 1968. *Political Order in Changing Societies*. New Haven: Yale University Press.

———. 1987. "The Goals of Development." In Myron Weiner and Samuel Huntington, eds., *Understanding Political Development*. Boston: Little, Brown.

Hutchcroft, Paul D. 2011. "Reflections on a Reverse Image: South Korea under Park Chung Hee and the Philippines under Ferdinand Marcos." In Byung-Kook Kim and Ezra Vogel, eds., *The Park Chung Hee Era*. Cambridge, MA: Harvard University Press.

Im, Hyug Baeg. 1987. "The Rise of Bureaucratic Authoritarianism in South Korea." *World Politics* 39, 231–257.

Jang, Hasung. 2000. "An Analysis of Effects of Corporate Restructuring Following the Economic Crisis." Working paper presented at the Korea Development Institute symposium "Three Years after the IMF: The Results, Reflections and Future Choices" and the Korea Finance Academy, Special Symposium (December).

Jesse, Neal G., Uk Heo, and Karl DeRouen, Jr. 2002. "A Nested Game Approach to Political and Economic Liberalization in Democratizing States: The Case of South Korea." *International Studies Quarterly* 46, 401–422.

Johnson, Chalmers A. 1982. *MITI and the Japanese Miracle*. Stanford, CA: Stanford University Press.

———. 1989. "South Korean Democratization: The Role of Economic Development." *Pacific Review* 2, 1–10.

Jones, Leroy P., and Il Sakong. 1980. *Government, Business, and Entrepreneurship in Economic Development: The Korean Case.* Cambridge, MA: Harvard University Press.

Kane, Edward J. 1989. *The S&L Mess: How Did It Happen?* Washington, DC: Urban Institute Press.

Kang, David C. 2002. *Crony Capitalism: Corruption and Development in South Korea and the Philippines.* Cambridge: Cambridge University Press.

Karl, Terry. 1990. "Dilemmas of Democratization in Latin America." *Comparative Politics* 23, 1–21.

Kihl, Young Whan. 2005. *Transforming Korean Politics: Democracy, Reform, and Culture.* Armonk, NY: M. E. Sharpe.

Kim, Byung-Kook. 2011. "The Leviathan: Economic Bureaucracy under Park Chung Hee." In Byung-Kook Kim and Ezra Vogel, eds., *The Park Chung Hee Era.* Cambridge, MA: Harvard University Press.

Kim, Eu Mee. 1997. *Big Business, Strong State: Collusion and Conflict in South Korean Development, 1960–1990.* Albany: State University of New York Press.

Kim, Hyung-A. 2004. *Korea's Development under Park Chung Hee: Rapid Industrialization, 1961–79.* London: RoutledgeCurzon.

Kim, Jun Il, and Jongryn Mo. 1999. "Democratization and Macroeconomic Policy." In Jongryn Mo and Chung-in Moon, eds., *Democracy and the Korean Economy.* Stanford, CA: Hoover Institution Press.

Kim, Se-Jin. 1971. *The Politics of Military Revolution in Korea.* Chapel Hill: University of North Carolina Press.

Kim, Se Joong. 2004. "Trends and Consequences of Civil-Military Relations in the 1950s." In Chung-in Moon and Sangyoung Rhyu, eds., *A Reexamination of Korean History in the 1950s.* Seoul: Yonsei University Press (in Korean).

Kim, Sunhyuk. 1997. "State and Civil Society in South Korea's Democratic Consolidation." *Asian Survey* 37, 1135–1144.

———. 2000. *The Politics of Democratization in Korea: The Role of Civil Society.* Pittsburgh, PA: University of Pittsburgh Press.

Kim, Yongho. 2006. "Political Change after the 2002 Presidential Election." *Korean Political Science Review* 5 (1) (in Korean).

Kohli, Atul. 1994. "Where Do High-Growth Political Economics Come From? The Japanese Lineage of Korea's Developmental State." *World Development* 22 (9): 1269–1293.

Koo, Hagen. 1991. "Middle Classes, Democratization and Class Formation." *Theory and Society* 20, 485–509.

———, ed. 1993. *State and Society in Contemporary Korea.* Ithaca: Cornell University Press.

Kornai, Janos. 1992. *The Socialist System: The Political Economy of Communism.* Princeton: Princeton University Press.

Kuran, Timor. 2004. *Islam and Mammon: The Economic Predicaments of Islamism.* Princeton: Princeton University Press.

Kwack, Sung Yeung. 1994. *The Korean Economy at a Crossroad: Development Prospects, Liberalization, and South-North Economic Integration.* Westport, CT: Praeger Publishers.

Lazear, Edward, and Sherwin Rosen. 1981. "Tournaments." *Journal of Political Economy* 89: 841–864.

Lee, Hongkyu, and Byungkook Kim. 2006. "Government Capabilities in an Age of State Competition." In Hoon Jaung and Byungkook Kim, eds., *A Democracy That Can Save the Economy.* Seoul: East Asia Institute (in Korean).

Lee, Hong Yung. 2004. "South Korea in 2003: A Question of Leadership?" *Asian Survey* 44 (1): 130–138.

Lee, Sook-Jong. 2004. "The Transformation of South Korean Politics: Implications for U.S.-Korea Relations." Paper, Center for Northeast Asian Policy Studies, Brooking Institution, Washington, DC.

Lee, Sook-Jong, and Taejoon Han. 2006. "The Demise of 'Korea, Inc.': Paradigm Shift in Korea's Developmental State." *Journal of Contemporary Asia* 36 (3): 305–324.

Lee, Su-Hoon. 1993. "Transitional Politics of Korea, 1987–1992: Activation of Civil Society." *Pacific Affairs,* 66, 351–367.

Levi, Margaret. 1988. *Of Rule and Revenue.* Berkeley: University of California Press.

Lie, John, and Myoungkyu Park. 2006. "South Korea in 2005: Economic Dynamism, Generational Conflicts, and Social Transformations." *Asian Survey* 46 (1): 56–62.

Lim, Hyun-Chin, and Jin-Ho Jang. 2006. "Neo-Liberalism in Post-Crisis South Korea: Social Conditions and Outcomes." *Journal of Contemporary Asia* 36 (4): 442–463.

Lim, Wonhyuk, and Randall Morck. 2010. "The Long Shadow of 'Big-Push' Partnership: Government and Business Groups in Korea's Economic Development." Unpublished manuscript, Korea Development Institute.

Lindert, Peter H. 2004. *Growing Public: Social Spending and Economic Growth since the Eighteenth Century.* Cambridge: Cambridge University Press.

Linz, Juan. 1978. *Crisis, Breakdown and Reequilibration.* Baltimore: Johns Hopkins University Press.

Lipset, Seymour Martin. 1959. *Political Man.* Baltimore: Johns Hopkins University Press.

————. 1963. *Political Man: The Social Bases of Politics*. Garden City, NY: Anchor Books.

Magaloni, Beatriz. 2006. *Voting for Autocracy: Hegemonic Party Survival and Its Demise in Mexico*. New York: Cambridge University Press.

Magaloni, Beatriz, and Ruth Kricheli. 2010. "Political Order and One-Party Rule." *Annual Review of Political Science* 12, 123–143.

Manion, Melanie. 1996. "Corruption by Design: Bribery in Chinese Enterprise Licensing." *Journal of Law, Economics, and Organization* 12, 167–195.

McCubbins, Mathew D., Roger G. Noll, and Barry R. Weingast. 1987. "Administrative Procedures as Instruments of Political Control." *Journal of Law, Economics, and Organization* 3 (Fall): 243–277.

————. 1989. "Structure and Process, Politics and Policy: Administrative Arrangements and the Political Control of Agencies." *Virginia Law Review* 75 (March): 431–482.

McIntyre, Andrew. 2001. *Business and Government in Industrializing Asia*. Ithaca: Cornell University Press.

Mittal, Sonia, and Barry R. Weingast. 2013. "Self-Enforcing Constitutions: With an Application to Democratic Stability in America's First Century." *Journal of Law, Economics, and Organization* (forthcoming).

Mo, Jongryn. 1996. "Political Learning and Democratic Consolidation: Korean Industrial Revolutions, 1987–1992." *Comparative Political Studies* 29, 290–311.

————. 1999. "Democratization, Labor Policy, and Economic Performance." In Jongryn Mo and Chung-in Moon, eds. *Democracy and the Korean Economy*. Stanford, CA: Hoover Institution Press.

————. 2001. "Political Culture and Legislative Gridlock: The Politics of Economic Reform in Pre-Crisis Korea." *Comparative Political Studies* 34, 467–492.

————. 2005. "The Microfoundations of the Developmental State." *Global Economic Review* 34 (1).

————. 2009a. "How Does Democracy Reduce Money Politics? Competition versus the Rule of Law." In David Brady and Jongryn Mo, eds., *The Rule of Law in South Korea*. Stanford, CA: Hoover Institution Press.

————. 2009b. "The Korean Economic System Ten Years after the Crisis." In John Ravenhill, T. J. Pempel, and Andrew McIntyre, eds., *Crisis as Catalyst: Asia's Dynamic Political Economy*. Ithaca: Cornell University Press.

Mo, Jongryn, and Chung-in Moon, eds. 1999. *Democracy and the Korean Economy*. Stanford, CA: Hoover Institution Press.

————. 2003. "Business-Government Relations under Kim Dae-jung." In Stephen Haggard, Wonhyuk Lim, and Euysung Kim, eds., *Economic Crisis and Corporate Restructuring in Korea*. Cambridge: Cambridge University Press.

Montinola, Gabriella. 2012. "The Philippines as a Limited Access Order." In Douglass C. North, John Joseph Wallis, Stephen Webb, and Barry R. Weingast, eds., *In the Shadow of Violence: The Problem of Development for Limited Access Order Societies*. Cambridge: Cambridge University Press.

Montinola, Gabriella, Yingyi Qian, and Barry R. Weingast. 1995. "Federalism, Chinese Style: The Political Basis for Economic Success in China." *World Politics* 48 (October): 50–81.

Moon, Chung-in, and Rashemi Prasad. 1994. "Beyond the Developmental State: Networks, Politics, and Institutions." *Governance* 7, 360–386.

Myers, Ramon H., and Mark R. Peattie. 1984. *The Japanese Colonial Empire, 1895–1945*. Princeton: Princeton University Press.

Myerson, Roger B. 2008. "The Autocrat's Credibility Problem and Foundations of the Constitutional State." *American Political Science Review* 102 (1): 125–139.

Nam, Duck Woo. 1994. "Korea's Economic Takeoff in Retrospect." In Sung Yeung Kwack, ed. *The Korean Economy at a Crossroad: Development Prospects, Liberalization, and South-North Economic Integration*. Westport, CT: Praeger Publishers.

Nellis, Nahalel A. 1996. "Bureaucratic Efficiency in South Korea in the Park Administration." Unpublished senior thesis, Stanford University.

North, Douglass C. 1981. *Structure and Change in Economic History*. Cambridge: Cambridge University Press.

———. 1990. *Institutions, Institutional Change and Economic Performance*. New York: Cambridge University Press.

North, Douglass C., John Joseph Wallis, Stephen Webb, and Barry R. Weingast, eds. 2012. *In the Shadow of Violence: The Problem of Development for Limited Access Order Societies*. Cambridge: Cambridge University Press.

North, Douglass C., John Joseph Wallis, and Barry R. Weingast (NWW). 2009. *Violence and Social Orders: A Conceptual Framework for Interpreting Recorded Human History*. Cambridge: Cambridge University Press.

North, Douglass C., and Barry R. Weingast. 1989. "Constitutions and Commitment: The Evolution of Institutions Governing Public Choice in 17th Century England." *Journal of Economic History* 49 (December): 803–832.

O'Donnell, Guillermo, Phillipe Schmitter, and Lawrence Whitehead, eds. 1986. *Transitions from Authoritarian Rule*. Baltimore: Johns Hopkins University Press.

Olson, Mancur. 1993. "Dictatorship, Democracy, and Development." *American Political Science Review* 87 (3): 567–575.

Parikh, Sunita A., and Barry R. Weingast. 2003. "Partisan Politics and the Structure and Stability of Federalism, Indian Style." Working paper, Center for Research on Economic Development and Policy Reform, Stanford University.

Parker, Geoffrey. 1988. *The Military Revolution: Military Innovation and the Rise of the West 1500–1800.* Cambridge: Cambridge University Press.

Pastreich, Emanuel. 2005. "The Balancer: Roh Moo-hyun's Vision of Korean Politics and the Future of Northeast Asia." *Japan Focus,* August; http://japanfocus.org/products/details/2041.

Persson, Torsten, and Guido Tabellini. 2000. *Political Economics: Explaining Economic Policy.* Cambridge, MA: MIT Press.

Powell, Robert. 1999. *In the Shadow of Power.* Princeton: Princeton University Press.

Przeworski, Adam. 1991. *Democracy and the Market.* Cambridge: Cambridge University Press.

Przeworski, Adam, Michael E. Alvarez, José Antonia Cheibub, and Fernando Limongi. 2000. *Democracy and Development: Political Institutions and Well-Being in the World, 1950–1990.* New York: Cambridge University Press.

Przeworski, Adam, and Fernando Limongi. 1997. "Modernization: Theories and Facts." *World Politics* 49, 155–183.

Putnam, Robert. 2000. *Bowling Alone: The Collapse and Revival of American Community.* New York: Simon & Schuster.

Rajan, Raghuram G., and Luigi Zingales. 2003. *Saving Capitalism from the Capitalists: Unleashing the Power of Financial Markets to Create Wealth and Spread Opportunity.* New York: Crown Business.

Rhee, Yung Whee, Bruce Ross-Larson, and Garry Pursell. 1984. *Korea's Competitive Edge: Managing the Entry into World Markets.* Baltimore: Johns Hopkins University Press.

Rodrik, Dani. 1995. "Getting Interventions Right: How South Korea and Taiwan Grew Rich." *Economic Policy* 20, 55–97.

———. 1999. "Where Did All the Growth Go? External Shocks, Social Conflict and Growth Collapses." *Journal of Economic Growth* 4 (December): 385–412.

Rodrik, Dani, A. Subramanian, and F. Trebbi. 2004. "Institutions Rule: The Primacy of Institutions over Geography and Integration in Economic Development." *Journal of Economic Growth* 9 (2).

Roland, Gerard. 2000. *Transition and Economics: Politics, Markets, and Firms.* Cambridge, MA: MIT Press.

Root, Hilton. 1996. *Small Countries, Big Lessons.* Oxford: Oxford University Press.

Rueschemeyer, Deietrich, Evelyne Huber Stephens, and John D. Stephens. 1992. *Capitalist Development and Democracy.* Chicago: University of Chicago Press.

Rustow, Dankwart. 1970. "Transitions to Democracy: Toward a Dynamic Model." *Comparative Politics* 2 (3).

Scheve, Kenneth, and David Stasavage. 2010. "The Conscription of Wealth: Mass Warfare and the Demand for Progressive Taxation." *International Organization* 65 (4): 529–561.

Schultz, Kenneth A., and Barry R. Weingast. 2003. "The Democratic Advantage: The Institutional Sources of State Power in International Competition." *International Organization* 57, 3–42.

Shin, Doh Chull. 1995. "Political Parties and Democratization in South Korea." *Democratization* 2, 20–55.

Shin, Kwangshik. 2003. "Competition Law and Policy." In Stephan Haggard, Wonhyuk Lim, and Euysung Kim, eds. *Economic Crisis and Corporate Restructuring in Korea.* Cambridge: Cambridge University Press.

Song, Byung-Nak. 1990. *The Rise of the Korean Economy.* Oxford: Oxford University Press.

Song, Ho-geun. 2003. *What Is Happening in Korea? The Esthetics of Generational Conflict and Harmony.* Seoul: Samsung Economic Research Institute (in Korean).

Spiller, Pablo T., and Mariano Tommasi. 2007. *The Institutional Foundations of Public Policy in Argentina.* Cambridge: Cambridge University Press.

Stein, Ernesto, et al. 2005. *The Politics of Policies: Economic and Social Progress in Latin America, 2006 Report.* Washington, DC: Inter-American Development Bank; Cambridge, MA: David Rockefeller Center for Latin America Studies, Harvard University.

Steinberg, David I. 2006. "The New Political Paradigm in South Korea: Social Change and the Elite Structure." *New Paradigms for Transpacific Collaboration, U.S.-Korea Academic Studies* 16, 81–103.

Steinberg, David I., and Myung Shin. 2006. "Tensions in South Korean Political Parties in Transition: From Entourage to Ideology?" *Asian Survey* 46 (4): 517–537.

Stiglitz, Joseph E., and M. Uy. 1996. "Financial Markets, Public Policy, and the East Asian Miracle." *World Bank Research Observer* 11 (2): 249–276.

Thirsk, Joan. 1957. *English Peasant Farming: The Agrarian History of Lincolnshire from Tudor to Recent Times.* London: Routledge & Kegan Paul.

Tilly, Charles. 1992. *Coercion, Capital, and European States: AD 990–1992.* Rev. ed. Cambridge, MA: Blackwell.

Tocqueville, Alexis de. 2000 [1835]. *Democracy in America.* Chicago: University of Chicago Press.

Vogel, Ezra F. 1991. *The Four Little Dragons: The Spread of Industrialization in East Asia*. Cambridge, MA: Harvard University Press.

Wade, Robert. 1990. *Governing the Market: Economic Theory and the Role of the Government in East Asian Industrialization*. Princeton: Princeton University Press.

Weber, Max. *The Theory of Social and Economic Organization*. New York: Free Press, 1947.

Weingast, Barry R. 1997. "The Political Foundations of Democracy and the Rule of Law." *American Political Science Review* 91: 245–263.

———. 2009. "Second-Generation Fiscal Federalism: The Implications of Fiscal Incentives." *Journal of Urban Economics* 65 (May): 279–293.

———. 2010. "Why Developing Countries Prove So Resistant to the Rule of Law." In James J. Heckman, Robert L. Nelson, and Lee Cabatingan, eds., *Global Perspectives on the Rule of Law*. New York: Routledge.

Wildasin, David. 1997. "Externalities and Bailouts: Hard and Soft Budget Constraints in Intergovernmental Fiscal Relations." Unpublished typescript, Vanderbilt University.

Woo, Jung-en. 1991. *Race to the Swift: State and Finance in Korean Industrialization*. New York: Columbia University Press.

World Bank. 1993. *The East Asian Miracle*. Oxford: Oxford University Press.

———. 1998. *East Asia: The Road to Recovery*. Washington, DC: World Bank.

You, Jong-Sung. 2012. "A Transition from a Limited Access Order to an Open Access Order: The Case of South Korea." In Douglass C. North, John Joseph Wallis, Stephen Webb, and Barry R. Weingast, eds., *In the Shadow of Violence: The Problem of Development for Limited Access Order Societies*. Cambridge: Cambridge University Press.

Index

Harvard East Asian Monographs
(*out-of-print)

Harvard East Asian Monographs

138. Heinz Morioka and Miyoko Sasaki, *Rakugo: The Popular Narrative Art of Japan*

139. Joshua A. Fogel, *Nakae Ushikichi in China: The Mourning of Spirit*

140. Alexander Barton Woodside, *Vietnam and the Chinese Model: A Comparative Study of Vietnamese and Chinese Government in the First Half of the Nineteenth Century*

*141. George Elison, *Deus Destroyed: The Image of Christianity in Early Modern Japan*

142. William D. Wray, ed., *Managing Industrial Enterprise: Cases from Japan's Prewar Experience*

*143. T'ung-tsu Ch'ü, *Local Government in China Under the Ching*

144. Marie Anchordoguy, *Computers, Inc.: Japan's Challenge to IBM*

145. Barbara Molony, *Technology and Investment: The Prewar Japanese Chemical Industry*

146. Mary Elizabeth Berry, *Hideyoshi*

147. Laura E. Hein, *Fueling Growth: The Energy Revolution and Economic Policy in Postwar Japan*

148. Wen-hsin Yeh, *The Alienated Academy: Culture and Politics in Republican China, 1919–1937*

149. Dru C. Gladney, *Muslim Chinese: Ethnic Nationalism in the People's Republic*

150. Merle Goldman and Paul A. Cohen, eds., *Ideas Across Cultures: Essays on Chinese Thought in Honor of Benjamin L. Schwartz*

151. James M. Polachek, *The Inner Opium War*

152. Gail Lee Bernstein, *Japanese Marxist: A Portrait of Kawakami Hajime, 1879–1946*

*153. Lloyd E. Eastman, *The Abortive Revolution: China Under Nationalist Rule, 1927–1937*

154. Mark Mason, *American Multinationals and Japan: The Political Economy of Japanese Capital Controls, 1899–1980*

155. Richard J. Smith, John K. Fairbank, and Katherine F. Bruner, *Robert Hart and China's Early Modernization: His Journals, 1863–1866*

156. George J. Tanabe, Jr., *Myōe the Dreamkeeper: Fantasy and Knowledge in Kamakura Buddhism*

157. William Wayne Farris, *Heavenly Warriors: The Evolution of Japan's Military, 500–1300*

158. Yu-ming Shaw, *An American Missionary in China: John Leighton Stuart and Chinese-American Relations*

159. James B. Palais, *Politics and Policy in Traditional Korea*

*160. Douglas Reynolds, *China, 1898–1912: The Xinzheng Revolution and Japan*

161. Roger R. Thompson, *China's Local Councils in the Age of Constitutional Reform, 1898–1911*

162. William Johnston, *The Modern Epidemic: History of Tuberculosis in Japan*

163. Constantine Nomikos Vaporis, *Breaking Barriers: Travel and the State in Early Modern Japan*

164. Irmela Hijiya-Kirschnereit, *Rituals of Self-Revelation: Shishōsetsu as Literary Genre and Socio-Cultural Phenomenon*

165. James C. Baxter, *The Meiji Unification Through the Lens of Ishikawa Prefecture*

166. Thomas R. H. Havens, *Architects of Affluence: The Tsutsumi Family and the Seibu-Saison Enterprises in Twentieth-Century Japan*

Harvard East Asian Monographs